UNDERSTANDING
BRITISH AND EUROPEAN
POLITICAL ISSUES

Aquinas College LRC

949808

MANCHESTER
UNIVERSITY PRESS

UNDERSTANDING POLITICS

Series editor **DUNCAN WATTS**

Following the review of the national curriculum for
16–19 year olds, UK examining boards have
introduced new specifications for first use in 2001
and 2002. A level courses will henceforth be divided
into A/S level for the first year of sixth form studies,
and the more difficult A2 level thereafter. The
Understanding Politics series comprehensively
covers the politics syllabuses of all the major
examination boards, featuring a dedicated A/S level
textbook and three books aimed at A2 students. The
books are written in an accessible, user-friendly and
jargon-free manner and will be essential to students
sitting these examinations.

Already published

Understanding political ideas and movements
Kevin Harrison and Tony Boyd

**Understanding American government
and politics**
Duncan Watts

Understanding
British
and European
political issues

A guide for A2 politics students

NEIL McNAUGHTON

Manchester University Press

Manchester and New York

distributed exclusively in the USA by Palgrave

Copyright © Neil McNaughton 2003

The right of Neil McNaughton to be identified as the author of this work has been asserted by him in accordance with the Copyright, Design and Patents Act 1988.

Published by Manchester University Press
Oxford Road, Manchester M13 9NR, UK
and Room 400, 175 Fifth Avenue, New York, NY 10010, USA
www.manchesteruniversitypress.co.uk

Distributed exclusively in the USA by
Palgrave, 175 Fifth Avenue, New York,
NY 10010, USA

Distribued exclusively in Canada by
UBC Press, University of British Columbia, 2029 West Mall,
Vancouver, BC, Canada V6T 1Z2

British Library Cataloguing-in-Publication Data
A catalogue record for this book is available from the British Library

Library of Congress Cataloging-in-Publication Data applied for

ISBN 0 7190 6245 4   *paperback*

First published 2003

11   10   09   08   07   06   05   04   03   10 9 8 7 6 5 4 3 2 1

£8·6

COUTTS   AG031183
ACC Nº   949808
INTER LOAN
CLASS Nº   320.942 MAC
DATE   9.10.03

Typeset by Northern Phototypesetting Co. Ltd, Bolton
Printed in Great Britain
by Bell & Bain Ltd, Glasgow

Contents

List of tables		*page* vii
Introduction		ix
List of abbreviations		xi

1	The economy	1
2	The Welfare State	32
3	Health	38
4	Education	52
5	Social security	66
6	Law and order	78
7	Issues concerning women	97
8	Racial issues and the multicultural society	106
9	The environment	120
10	Northern Ireland	129
11	Constitutional reform	151
12	Devolution	171
13	The development of European integration	191
14	Institutions of the European Union	211
15	European Union issues	234
16	Britain and European Union	249

Additional reading and research		265
Index		267

Tables

1.1 Decline in manufacturing industry in the UK   *page* 3

1.2 Workforce employed in distribution, hotels, catering, finance
     and other services (%)   4

3.1 Britain's ageing population: proportion of the UK population
     aged 65 and above, as % of the total   51

3.2 Increases in health provision: employment of NHS staff (000s)   51

4.1 Education: conflict and consensus   65

6.1 Crimes reported in the British Crime Survey (millions)   81

6.2 Total drugs seizures, 1981–99   81

6.3 Offences per 10,000 people, by age range   82

8.1 Britain's ethnic mix, 2001   118

10.1 Northern Ireland Assembly election, 1998   140

12.1 Allocation of seats in the Scottish Parliament after 1999   179

12.2 Seats in the Welsh Assembly after 1999   182

12.3 Northern Ireland election result, 1999   188

13.1 EU members' voting strengths before 2004 enlargement   200

14.1 National and party representation in the European Parliament   221

15.1 Stages of EU enlargement, 1957–95   239

Introduction

This book has been produced to serve a number of needs. Most importantly, there is always a need to bring students and teachers of politics up to date with the great political issues of the day. By their nature, such issues are constantly changing in character, the political agenda is moving on and critical events can change the political landscape. This book, therefore, seeks to review the state of political issues early in the twenty-first century, when New Labour is in its second term of office.

As part of the updating process it became necessary to choose *which* political issues are important. Clearly it would be an enormous volume which sought to cover every conceivable issue. Choices have, therefore, to be made. In this case the rationale has been to include the main issues which appear in current **Advanced Level Politics syllabuses**. In the case of Edexcel, which offers a specific political issues option in its A2 specification, all the specified issues have been included. In addition there are some chapters dealing with the process of constitutional and political change which are issues in themselves. Thus we have included material on constitutional reform (incorporating the recent development of human rights in Britain), and devolution.

With **Citizenship** now a part of the National Curriculum for key stages three and four, the book will make a useful companion to those teachers who wish to enrich their teaching of the subject with a fuller understanding of political issues and the European Union.

The book also covers the kind of issues which will be of interest to more **general readers**. The student of politics needs to have a grasp of how substantive issues are developing, even if they are not specific parts of his or her field of study. He or she may also need a **general introduction** to the British political landscape. Politics is, after all, important, because of what its processes achieve, or fail to achieve. There may also be some who come to politics simply out of interest and who need to be able to take a detached and informed view of how such issues have developed. This book will be of value and interest to them.

A substantial section of the book deals with the **European Union** and Britain's relationship to it. Again there is more than one reason for this. Current A level syllabuses all require students to have a thorough knowledge of various aspects of the European Union. There are four elements to this section: an understanding of how the European project developed and the conceptual ideas which have underpinned it; a description of the institutions of the EU, how they are organised, what their functions are and what issues have emerged concerning their operation and powers; a review of the main issue facing the EU currently; and finally an account of how Britain's involvement with the EU has developed and what problems have resulted from this process.

A second reason for having a substantial section on Europe is simply that it is now extremely important to British politics. Most issues now have a European dimension. Furthermore, a wide variety of decisions are now made in EU institutions, with British political bodies playing a marginal role. Finally, it must be emphasised that Britain's relationship to the EU is in itself a political issue which has fundamentally changed the party system.

The general approach taken on each topic is to examine the following aspects:

1 a description of the background information, sometimes stretching back to World War II, sometimes returning only to the period when the issue became central in British politics;
2 analysis of how the issue has developed, its main features, including landmark events and periods of change;
3 a further analysis of the nature of the issue today, including an examination of how parties and other political groups have approached it;
4 where appropriate, a certain amount of speculation concerning the immediate future of the issue, identifying those aspects which require solutions.

Where necessary, summary boxes, lists of main events, statistical tables and definitions have been included to guide readers and help students learn factual material in an organised way.

Clearly, political issues are, by their nature, constantly evolving and fresh events alter their nature. However, this book is designed to give a framework of knowledge and conceptual understanding into which such changes can be incorporated. Thus, for example, if there are significant developments in social security, police powers or the political system of the EU, the changes can be reviewed and understood in the light of the principles explained in the book.

There is, therefore, something for everybody who needs an analysis and review of modern British political issues, whether they be teachers, students or general readers.

List of abbreviations

British and other

AMS	Additional Member System
AV	Alternative Vote
BMA	British Medical Association
CCT	compulsory competitive tendering
CCTV	closed circuit television
CHI	Commission for Health Improvement
CJA	Criminal Justice Act
CPAG	Child Poverty Action Group
CRE	Commission for Racial Equality
CSE	Certificate of Secondary Education
DEFRA	Department for the Environment, Food and Rural Affairs
DUP	Democratic Unionist Party
ERA	Education Reform Act
ERM	Exchange Rate Mechanism
GDP	Gross Domestic Product
GFA	Good Friday Agreement
GLA	Greater London Authority (or Assembly)
GLC	Greater London Council
GM	Genetically Modified
HMIP	Her Majesty's Inspectorate of Pollution
HRA	Human Rights Act
ILEA	Inner London Education Authority
IMF	International Monetary Fund
INLA	Irish National Liberation Army
IRA	Irish Republican Army
LMS	Local Management of Schools
MPC	Monetary Policy Committee
NC	National Curriculum
NHS	National Health Service
NICE	National Institute for Clinical Excellence
NRA	National Rivers Authority
OECD	Organisation for Economic Co-operation and Devolopment
OFSTED	Office for Standards in Education
PACE	Police and Criminal Evidence Act

PC	Plaid Cymru
PR	Proportional Representation
RCN	Royal College of Nursing
RCS	Royal College of Surgeons
RSPB	Royal Society for the Protection of Birds
RUC	Royal Ulster Constabulary
SDLP	Social Democratic Labour Party
SDP	Social Democrat Party
SNP	Scottish National Party
SPA	Special Health Authorities
STV	Single Transferable Vote
UDA	Ulster Defence Association
UUP	Ulster Unionist Party
UVF	Ulster Volunteer Force
VAT	Value Added Tax

European Union

CAP	Common Agricultural Policy
CESDP	Common European Security and Defence Policy
CFP	Common Fisheries Policy
CFSP	Common Foreign and Security Policy
COREPER	Council of Permanent Representatives
EC	European Community or European Commission
ECB	European Central Bank
ECHR	European Convention (or Court) of Human Rights
ECJ	European Court of Justice
ECSC	European Coal and Steel Community
EEC	European Economic Community ('Common Market')
EFTA	European Free Trade Association
EMC	European Military Committee
EMS	European Military Staff (or European Monetary System)
EMU	European Monetary Union
EP	European Parliament
ESC	Economic and Social Committee
MEP	Member of the European Parliament
NATO	North Atlantic Treaty Organisation
OSCE	Organisation for Security and Co-operation in Europe
PSC	Political and Security Committee
QMV	qualified majority voting
SEA	Single European Act
WEU	Western European Union

The economy

1

➤ The post-war background to economic policy making in Britain

➤ The nature of the post-war economic consensus

➤ The economic 'revolution' which took place under Margaret Thatcher after 1979

➤ The movement away from Thatcherite policies in the 1990s

➤ The policies of the Labour government after 1997

POST-WAR OVERVIEW

The end of Empire

At the end of World War II it became clear that the best days of the British empire were over. For a number of reasons, policy makers had to face up to the fact that British economic prosperity could no longer rely upon the advantages of controlling a wide range of colonies.

The lesson of two world wars for Britain was that the maintenance of a far-flung empire was no longer feasible in both economic and military terms. The onset of the Cold War in the late 1940s polarised the world into two great power blocs and Britain could certainly not stand alone in this new world order. She had to shelter under the nuclear umbrella provided by the United States. Defending an empire in the face of Soviet and, later, Chinese power, was not going to be possible. At the same time a Labour government had been elected in 1945. On the whole the party was ideologically opposed to imperialism. Although the pragmatic elements in the Labour party recognised the economic benefits of clinging on to the colonies, the political will to remain as a great imperial power was weakening.

India was granted independence in 1947. There was a moratorium on the independence movement for ten years or so (corresponding to the return of the Conservatives to power), but the dismantling of the empire resumed at the end of the 1950s. The disaster of Britain's failed attempt to maintain its dominance of the Middle East in the 1956 Suez crisis and the advent of Harold Macmillan as a realistic, pragmatic prime minister in 1957 provided a spur to this process. During the late 1950s, 1960s and early 1970s most of the empire in Africa, South-East Asia and the Caribbean was granted independence.

Put simply, the empire had underpinned British prosperity for over a hundred years by providing both a source of cheap raw materials and ready markets for her own manufactured goods. Although preferential trade agreements were made with the former colonies to protect Britain's privileged economic position, things would never be the same again. When Britain joined the European Community at the beginning of 1973, it had to give up these special trade agreements, and so the benefits of empire were finally lost.

What this meant for the British economy was essentially twofold. First, the country would now have to pay the full price for its raw materials in world markets (except for the temporary trade agreements referred to above). Secondly, Britain would have to compete on even ground with all the other industrial powers for markets for its manufactured goods. There was an economic dividend arising from the loss of empire in that defence expenditure could be cut back drastically, but the net effect on Britain was detrimental. The problem was exacerbated by the post-war recovery of the western European economies and the 'economic miracle' which Japan was enjoying.

The management of economic decline

As a result partly of its imperial status, and partly the sophisticated industrial infrastructure built up over two hundred years, Britain retained its position as a leading economic power into the 1950s. Thereafter, however, the story has been one of relative economic decline, when British performance is measured against its main competitors.

This is not to say that this was the fault of successive British governments. To some extent the relative decline can be seen as inevitable. What it has meant, however, is that governments have had to deal with this reality and to try to reduce the effects of the process. The repercussions of decline were considerable. Among them were the problem of maintaining public services, maintaining capital investment when the profitability of British industry was declining, the difficulty of staying competitive in a world where competition was intensifying and, perhaps most seriously, of dealing with poverty which inevitably resulted from the decline of traditional industries in several specific regions.

From the 1950s until the 1990s economic management in Britain can be viewed very much in this vein. For two generations the country was forced to adjust to its new, lower, economic status. Governments could not realistically hope to reverse British fortunes. All they could do was to ameliorate the effects of relative decline. So, for example, the Labour governments of Harold Wilson in 1964–70 attempted to modernise British industry, but this largely failed in the face of a number of economic crises. The development of the Concorde aircraft at that time was a typical example. British science and engineering was capable of producing the world's first supersonic airliner, but it never reached full-scale commercial production. The same happened to an infant computer industry which was easily overcome by American and Japanese competition.

Membership of the European Community (later European Union) provided one possible long term answer to this process. However, it was not until the 1990s that the benefits of European integration began to show real progress.

European integration

When Britain became a member of the European Community in January 1973, there were genuine fears that the inherent weaknesses which by then existed in the economy would bring special problems. Faced by membership of a free market, with more intense competition for overseas customers, it was felt by many that Britain would suffer. Among the problems of the economy were lack of capital investment, low levels of labour productivity, unsettled industrial relations and poor management. Britain seemed to lag behind its European partners in all these areas. Worse still, the British market was now thrown wide open to European exporters.

The new economic structure

While Britain was moving from being a world imperial power to a European player, the nature of its economy was also changing. The old, traditional industries steadily declined and were replaced by new, service-based or 'tertiary' activities. The manufacturing infrastructure, which had been the basis of British prosperity, began to disappear. Staple industries such as textiles, iron and steel, shipbuilding and coal mining all suffered gradual decline. In increasingly free global markets, British heavy industry could not compete with the rest of Europe, Japan, parts of the Third World and the new 'Asian tiger' economies such as Korea, Taiwan and Malaysia. The diminishing importance of these industries can be seen in table 1.1.

Table 1.1   Decline in manufacturing industry in the UK

Year	% of male workforce	% of female workforce
1981	32	17
1991	25	12
2001	22	8

Source: Office for National Statistics.

The most serious effects of this process were experienced in the 1970s and 1980s. The economy failed to adjust to the new realities and economic decline worsened. Towards the end of the 1980s, however, progress began to be made. Partly as a result of the reforms of the Thatcher era, which are described below, and partly fuelled by the strength of the higher education system (a legacy of the growth of this sector in the 1960s), Britain was ready for the emergence of new industries. Such sectors as finance, leisure and entertainment, technology, computer software, communications and electronics were growing in Britain as quickly as anywhere else in the world. In these fields Britain could and did compete successfully with Far Eastern powers, the USA and Germany. This shift in the 'balance' of British industry is shown clearly in table 1.2.

Table 1.2   Table shows the percentage of the workforce employed in distribution, hotels, catering, finance and other services

Year	Men	Women
1981	45	73
1991	44	83
2001	59	86

Source: Office for National Statistics.

This is not to say that manufacturing disappeared completely. In the 1990s Britain became an attractive subject for inward investment. Foreign companies, particularly from the Far East, set up factories all over the country, producing cars, electrical equipment, telecommunications equipment and computer technology. The decline of trade union power, resulting in more settled industrial relations, relatively low wage levels and large government grants and subsidies helped to attract such multinational corporations as Toyota, Nissan, Honda, General Motors, Siemens and Motorola to Britain.

The net result, by the 1990s, was that the British economy had drastically changed its structure. There was still a large manufacturing sector, but it was now largely foreign owned. The service and technology sectors, on the other hand, were growing fast and were largely home grown.

Globalisation

The governments of the 1990s were forced to face up to a new challenge beyond that of European integration. This was the reality that all markets – in products, commodities, labour and finance – were becoming increasingly global.

The effects of globalisation are yet to be fully revealed, but some certainties have already emerged. In order to survive in world markets it has become clear that Britain will have to develop a number of economic qualities. Among them are a well educated, trained and flexible workforce, management which is geared to world-wide competition, a willingness to respond to intense competition, higher levels of capital investment, leadership in the field of information technology and full involvement with international institutions such as the European Union, World Trade Organisation, World Bank, International Monetary Fund, G7 and the Organisation for Economic Co-operation and Development (OECD).

The management of economic success

As we have seen above, much of the story of post-war economic policy making has been concerned with relative decline. During the 1990s, however, when Britain emerged from the world recession in better shape than Japan, the Far East and her European partners, a new set of circumstances became apparent.

Many of the inherent and seemingly incurable problems of the British economy began to respond to treatment. As we have already seen, industrial relations had improved during the 1980s. In addition, labour productivity began to rise and Britain became known for low, rather than excessively high, wage costs. The new 'tertiary', service and technology industries were finding a leading place in world markets. Above all, however, the recurring problem of inflation receded in the second half of the 1990s. The record of British economic management had reached an all time low in 1992 when the country was unceremoniously dumped out of the European Exchange Rate Mechanism – the ERM – (of which more below). This event, known as 'Black Wednesday', was the culmination of several years of indecisive attempts to adjust to the new European and global realities. Since 1992, more responsible governments under John Major and Tony Blair have understood that it was necessary to conquer the British economy's natural tendency to rapid inflation in order to compete successfully.

From the mid-1990s onwards, therefore, Britain has enjoyed a number of years of almost unprecedented low inflation, low interest rates and low unemployment. Economic growth was consistently healthy and there were rises in investment in public services. Relative prosperity was, however, to present as many problems for government as economic decline.

The principal dilemma faced by politicians in this period has been how to distribute the new-found wealth. Those in the centre and to the left of the political spectrum wished to see rises in expenditure of public services such as education, social security, housing, public transport and health. They have also demanded reductions in tax levels for the poorer sections of the community. In this way the inequalities in standards of living may be reduced. On the right of politics, however, economic growth is seen as an opportunity to reduce taxation for all. This, they suggest, will increase incentives, reward initiative and so safeguard future growth. This political tendency is not concerned with inequalities in wealth within the population. For them higher disposable incomes can take the pressure off state-run public services and the private sector can expand to compensate.

Not surprisingly, politicians in all the main parties have tended to gravitate towards the centre of this conflict, suggesting that both of these objectives can be achieved at the same time as long as some compromises are accepted. This new 'consensus' will be the subject of further discussion below.

THE KEYNESIAN CONSENSUS

The economic beliefs of Keynes and the Keynesians

The economist John Maynard Keynes (1883–1946) was a prominent British academic and political figure in the 1920s and 1930s. His economic beliefs, however, did not gain full acceptance in the political arena until after World War II. In fact, it is likely that his policies would have been implemented earlier had the war not intervened. Ironically, Keynes died before he could see the practical fruits of his work.

What became known as 'Keynesian economics' has many technical aspects beyond the scope of this book. There are, however, a number of principles which are relatively easy to understand. But before studying them we need to examine briefly what had gone before.

So-called 'classical economics' had flourished for about a century, from the 1830s to the 1930s. This tradition believed that the economy would inevitably suffer from 'periodic cycles', moving regularly from boom periods, when there was rapid economic growth, to periods of slow-down or slumps in which growth was slow or even ceased altogether. Governments, the classical economists argued, should not interfere with these natural processes. Indeed, excessive interference would be detrimental. Rather, the periods of slump would correct themselves. The process would be that, as there was little economic activity, wages and prices would stop rising and might actually fall. The falling prices would encourage consumers to buy more and companies to invest more in capital. The lower wages would mean that more labour would be employed. The effect of these changes would be to kick start the economy into renewed growth and the recessions would come to a natural end. The role of government was to do nothing except to ensure that the currency remained stable by controlling the amount of money in circulation.

These beliefs held up until the Great Depression of the 1930s. In that period the theory ceased to work. The economic recession would not end even though governments obeyed the golden rule that they should not attempt to interfere. Keynes' theories, however, provided an explanation for the new phenomenon.

He suggested that, in the modern economy, there is no reason why economic activity should pick up spontaneously as the classical economists suggested. In short, recessions like this one could recur and grow worse. Keynes offered a new set of policy options. Governments *should* intervene, he argued. They should take positive steps to boost the level of aggregate demand in the economy. Aggregate demand consists largely of consumer spending, government expenditure and capital investment by companies. By ensuring that consumers, companies and government all spent more money in the economy, the recession could be ended, as industry expanded to meet the higher level of demand. At the same time, by careful adjustments, many of the recessions could be avoided in the first place.

How could this be done? In direct opposition to classical economic beliefs, Keynes argued that, by lowering the level of taxation, and by increasing government spending, the overall level of aggregate demand would rise. Even if the policy led to government debt, it could still be justified by the positive economic results. Future generations would be able to pay off the debts out of the increased prosperity which his policies would bring. His ideas became known as **demand management**, underpinned by active **fiscal policy**. The classical economists were sceptical, but by the 1940s Keynes' policies had won the day.

The consensus in action

For the sake of neatness we can say that the keynesian consensus lasted from 1950 (when many of the immediate economic effects of the war had begun to recede) until about 1979, when Margaret Thatcher was first elected prime minister. So we are dealing with a period of about thirty years.

Economic policy making is a complex business, with many variables being manipulated by government. However, the great age of the consensus can be reduced to a few basic principles, as follows:

- The main way to try to manipulate economic activity was to control the level of demand.
- Demand was best controlled through levels of taxation (especially income tax) and government expenditure.
- When economic activity slowed down it was normal for government to reduce taxation levels and raise government expenditure (typically on social security and pensions or on building projects). This usually resulted in a growth in government debt, financed out of borrowing from banks or the general public in national savings schemes.

- When economic activity was growing fast and there was a danger of inflation arising or too many imports being attracted in, the opposite measures were used, i.e. higher taxation and reduced public spending.

Both the Conservative and Labour parties based economic policy making on these principles, with only minor variations.

Competition between the parties was not, therefore based on *principles*, but on how *effectively* they could manage the economy on keynesian lines. Elections were fought less on how best to run the economy than on other issues such as competence, foreign policy, industrial relations policy, the running of public services and which party was best for the business community. There was also some disagreement over how taxation was to be *distributed* among the population. Clearly Labour tended to favour higher levels of tax on high income groups, while the Conservatives opposed high taxes on business profits or on property. Labour also adopted, after 1965, a policy of direct legal controls over excessive rises in prices, wages and business profits. The Conservatives were less enthusiastic, but even they followed the Labour lead on this issue under Edward Heath in 1971–74.

So there was inter-party competition between the parties in this period. There was not a consensus on *all* issues. But the fundamental ideas of keynesian theory were shared by the al the main parties.

THE END OF CONSENSUS AND THE RETURN OF NEO-CLASSICAL ECONOMICS

The first cracks: Edward Heath

Faced by the prospect of a third successive defeat at the 1970 general election, the Conservative leadership took a decision to engage in a complete re-think of the basis of economic policy. In 1969, at the Selsdon Park Hotel in Surrey, this group produced a blueprint for radical change. Or, rather, they proposed a reversion to classical economic ideas as described above. With another crisis apparently looming, the Conservatives won the election and Edward Heath found himself in power with a commitment to the new policies.

He immediately announced that controls on price and wage rises were to be removed. There was to be no aid for failing industries and the government was to disengage itself from strict economic management. In other words there was a return to the pre-keynesian theories. The consensus seemed to be at an end.

By the end of 1971, however, the new policy was in tatters. Inflation was rising alarmingly, as was the level of imports. British industry began to suffer from the effects of rising wages and prices and several large companies were threatening to go out of business. When Rolls-Royce went bust, the writing was on the wall. Heath did what he said he would never do and stepped in to save Rolls-Royce with government money. He also imposed a six-month freeze on wage rises, to be replaced later by strict controls. His Chancellor, Anthony Barber, was forced to raise taxation in order to control aggregate spending and price inflation. The dramatic change of policy was known as Heath's 'U-turn' and the brief pause in the economic consensus was over. Keynesian policy was back.

Nevertheless, the experience left a deep impression on some Conservatives, not least two of its leading figures. One was Keith Joseph, one of the party's leading intellectuals. The other was the education minister, Margaret Thatcher. The seeds had been sown for what was to happen after 1979.

Margaret Thatcher and monetarism

It is normal for economic commentators to take 1979 as a watershed year in British history and this is certainly logical as it saw the election of perhaps the most radical prime minister of the twentieth century. Nevertheless that year did *not* mark a dramatic change in the nature of economic policy making. There were two main reasons for this.

Firstly, and perhaps most importantly, the country was entering a deep and enduring recession. Both inflation and unemployment were rising alarmingly (which defied keynesian logic) meaning that radical measures were not feasible. Secondly, Mrs Thatcher herself was far from politically secure in her first three years in office. A number of senior members of the Conservative party were firmly opposed to a departure from traditional policies. These were the so-called 'wets' and they included such key figures as Lord Carrington, Francis Pym and Peter Walker. However, her victory in the Falklands conflict in 1982 gave her the political confidence to remove her opponents from the cabinet.

So the real watershed came in 1982–83 as the economic climate began to improve and the prime minister was more able to dominate the political scene. By then, however, the seeds had been sown and it is important to identify those seeds. The main element was the theory of monetarism. This represented the basis for what was to come.

Monetarism has two main elements. The best known is the principle that the most effective way to control the economy is to ensure that the money supply (i.e. quantity) does not rise faster than the growth in economic activity. This practice of responsible financial management is designed to ensure high inflation is avoided and that industry can operate within a stable economic environment. At the same time monetarism, as a philosophy, implies that governments should not interfere with the rest of the economy. In this sense it is a *liberal* theory as it proposes minimum state activity.

So it was at the beginning of the Thatcher era that the government largely withdrew from active economic management. Unemployment rose unchecked, but it did have a positive aspect. Wage increases moderated as workers faced intense competition for scarce jobs. The influence of the trade unions also began to wane. The level of strikes fell (a normal situation in times of unemployment) and industrial activity started to pick up. In other words unemployment became a price worth paying for economic recovery, though the inhabitants of the dole queues would not agree!

But it was not until 1982–83 that the next phase of the Thatcher revolution was to begin. We may describe this period as the supply-side stage. Indeed supply-side economics has dominated policy making ever since.

Supply-side economics

Keynesian economics was characterised by the need for governments to control the level of aggregate demand, notably through the manipulation of levels of tax and public expenditure. Supply-side economics returns to the classical principle that such control is counter-productive and that there is a natural process whereby such problems as inflation, or high interest rates will correct themselves automatically. However, this process depends on the ability of the economy to adjust to these mechanisms. In particular the 'supply side' (i.e. production and distribution of goods and services) needs to be both flexible and dynamic.

Margaret Thatcher and her advisers were of the opinion that the long-term problem of the British economy was that the supply side was neither dynamic nor flexible. She therefore saw the role of her governments to correct these faults. The main objectives of policy were the following:

1 To make labour markets more flexible. That implied that wages could freely rise or fall according to market conditions, workers would be able to adapt quickly to new technologies and growing industries and there would be real incentives to work and improve output.
2 To create more incentives for entrepreneurs. By making it an attractive proposition to set up new businesses or to expand existing ones, it is assumed that the economy can expand quickly.
3 Free competition is seen as a means by which businesses will be forced to become efficient.
4 Regulation by the state should be minimised. Too much control over such factors as wages, prices, profits and production systems is believed to stifle business expansion. The most dramatic form of regulation occurs in nation-alised industries, so they became a major target of reform.

Most economic policy from the 1980s onwards was, therefore, directed at achieving these ends. As we have seen above, most of the practical measures could not be implemented until after the 1983 general election when the Conservative party was returned to office with a huge parliamentary majority.

TAXATION

One decision had already been made four years before the 1983 landslide. This was the reduction in the level of income tax, effected in 1979. The basic rate fell from 33 per cent to 30 per cent and the higher rates of tax from 83 per cent to 60 per cent. By 1988 there were only two rates of income tax: 25 per cent and 40 per cent. These were almost the lowest rates in western Europe. The reductions in tax revenue which resulted were replaced by an increase in VAT from 8 per cent to 15 per cent and later by increasing revenue from North Sea oil and the privatisation programme.

The purpose of this change was to create greater incentives by allowing entre-preneurs and their employees to retain a much higher proportion of their incomes. The idea that business activity is crucial to wealth creation and must be encouraged through generously low rates of tax on incomes and profits has remained central to economic policy making by both Conservative and Labour administrations. Indeed, as we shall see, Labour governments after 1997 have continued the process of reducing the basic rate of income and corporation tax for just this reason.

There was also a general reduction in other forms of direct taxes such as inher-itance and capital gains tax. But Conservative governments after 1979 failed to achieve their greatest ambition which was to seriously reduce the *overall* level of taxes. Indirect taxes, such as duties on petrol, alcohol and tobacco continued to rise as taxes on income were falling.

Tax incentives were only the first element in the change in policy direction. More radical measures were soon to follow. The key developments were as follows.

PRIVATISATION

The process of transferring industries from public ownership and state control to private ownership (i.e. from nationalised industries into public limited companies owned by shareholders) was seen in the 1980s to incorporate four main advantages.

Firstly, it was expected that they would become far more dynamic as their managers pursued higher profits to satisfy the shareholders and to further their own careers. These incentives had been lacking when the industries had been state run. Secondly, it presented an opportunity for a wider range of the population to own shares, including the workers in the privatised industries themselves, and so give them a vested interest in their economic success. Thirdly, the sale of these industries would bring in much needed revenue to the government who could use it either to pay off some accumulated national debt or to finance higher public spending without having to raise taxes. By 1990 the sales of publicly owned assets had yielded nearly £20 billion.

Above all, however, this *disengagement* of the state was very much at the heart of what has become known as 'Thatcherism'. Classical economics assumed that state interference was nearly always negative and Margaret Thatcher always considered herself to be a modern heir to the that classical tradition. So her ideas can be described as 'neo-classical economics'.

The most celebrated privatisation was also the first – that of British Telecom in 1984. It was greeted with loud opposition from the Labour party, but the public's imagination was caught by the prospect of owning shares in this huge, growing industry, and by the promise of cheaper phone calls as fresh investment was to pour into the new private enterprise. When the new shares began to be traded freely on the stock exchange and their price rose sharply, the public were hooked and ready for more. The high point of national excitement was reached when the gas supply industry was put up for sale. A massive advertising campaign was launched to encourage the public to take up the share issue and once again there was a successful flotation with thousands of new shareholders being created and quick profits realised on the rising share price. 'Privatisation fever' was beginning to set in and the government was riding the crest of this wave of enthusiasm. More was to follow. Electricity generation and supply, water, coal, steel, British Airways, British Petroleum and Rolls-Royce Engines were among the principal examples. Under John Major possibly the most significant – and most controversial – of all the privatisations took place when the railways were sold off in 1996.

As we shall see below, privatisation was not only a policy of the 1980s. It is a process which continued into the twenty-first century. The Labour party was converted to privatisation by the time it came to office in 1997, thus abandoning one of its most cherished principles – the public, democratic control of the commanding heights of the economy.

COMPETITION AND LIBERALISATION

The nationalised industries, apart from being state controlled, were also mostly monopolies. Serious competition was forbidden by law in such industries as coal, steel, electricity, telephones, gas and water supply. After privatisation, therefore, there remained the problem of how to ensure that the industries remained competitive when they did not have to contend with normal market forces. Two kinds of response were introduced.

The first was simply to introduce competition: to allow other private firms to compete. This is what occurred with British Airways, municipal public transport, and steel and coal. In other industries, however, competition was not feasible at first. These are the 'natural monopolies' where there would be major disruption if more than one firm were operating in the same market. Utility industries such as telephones, gas, water and electricity are clear examples. They required a second type of solution. This was to introduce regulatory bodies which would force them to operate as if they were in a competitive market. This spawned a whole raft of new quangos such as OFTEL (office of telecommunications), OFWAT (Water), and OFGAS (gas supply) which would protect consumers from monopoly power. In due course, genuine competition was introduced in these utilities, but in the 1980s they suffered much criticism for their monopoly status, despite the growth of regulatory bodies.

In the existing private sector steps were also taken to create competition. Most importantly, financial services were de-regulated in 1986, allowing greater competition in the stock market and among banks and building societies. This had several effects. Firstly, it reduced banking costs generally. Secondly it made finance more easily available for consumers, house purchasers and business in general. Thirdly, it reinforced London's position as the leading financial centre in Europe. The professions were also forced to engage in real competition so that dentists, opticians and even lawyers were allowed to advertise themselves and adjust their charges to attract more business. In general, too, the laws on competition were stiffened and the Office of Fair Trading was given wide powers to ensure that consumers were given a fair deal.

There were also partial privatisations in the 1980s which were usually described as *liberalisation*. The main example was the introduction of *compulsory competitive tendering* (CCT). The scheme forced many state run services to compete with private companies to retain their contracts. This mainly applied to local government activities such as refuse collection, building maintenance, parks and gardens care and road repairs. CCT was also applied to some central government departments with parts of the health and prison service. Indeed some prisons have since been privatised altogether.

The effects of CCT were twofold. It promoted efficiency and competitiveness, but also had the effect of reducing wage levels in many sectors of the economy. Private companies, when bidding for contracts from the state, tended to offer lower wages than the state, so that high paid workers were often replaced by people on lower pay levels. During the 1980s and 1990s increasing numbers of services were subjected to CCT until the incoming Labour party abandoned the scheme after 1997.

LABOUR MARKETS

Supply side economics demands that wage levels are free to rise and fall according to employment conditions. When there is high unemployment, wages (at least in real terms) should fall and vice versa. The same applies to regional variations in economic activity. Wages should be significantly lower in depressed regions than in successful ones so that employers should be attracted to invest where they can reduce their labour costs.

In the 1980s Conservative governments under Margaret Thatcher saw high wage costs as perhaps the most difficult problem to overcome. Their perception of the problem was that organised labour, mainly in the form of trade unions, was simply too powerful. They therefore aimed to alter the balance of economic power between employers and employees.

The first solution was very much of Mrs Thatcher's own creation. She made it clear to workers' leaders that she believed that excessive wage demands simply led to unemployment. This was particularly true in economically depressed areas such as the north east, Merseyside and the Clyde valley in Scotland. Unlike previous governments, however, she asserted that her government would not take measures to combat unemployment. This was to be the price which workers would have to pay for demanding high wages – they would run the danger of losing their jobs. By 1986 unemployment had reached 3.4 million, the highest level since the 1930s. The medicine was severe, but she believed it would cure the disease of high wage costs. Certainly, in the mid-1980s the number of strikes began to fall and wage demands were moderating.

Secondly her government abolished most of the wages councils after 1986. These councils, made up of union and employers' representatives, operated in a variety of industries. One of their tasks was to set minimum wage levels in the industry. The effect was to protect the interests of the workers, but also to prevent wages falling below a certain level when there was a labour surplus. This led to persistent unemployment in some sectors and regions. By getting rid of them, the government struck a blow for more flexible labour markets.

Thirdly, levels of social security benefits, notably for the unemployed were steadily reduced in real terms. Over-generous social security was seen as a disincentive for people to seek work. In other words they meant that workers were unwilling to work for low wages as they would be better off relying on social security. This method of using a 'stick' to beat people into work was certainly effective. However, as we shall see below, it was to become one of the main issues of contention between the Conservative and Labour parties in the 1990s.

But these three policies did not compete with Margaret Thatcher's principal assault on organised labour. It was her struggle against the unions which was to set the tone for both economic and industrial relations policy for twenty years.

Margaret Thatcher and the unions

There can be little doubt that the outcome of the conflict which occurred between the trade unions and the governments of the 1980s dramatically altered the economic and social landscape of the country. It was also to set the scene for the transformation which was to take place in the Labour party after 1987. There were two strands to Thatcher's attack on the unions. One was a generalised confrontation with their leadership and the other was a programme of legislation designed to curb their power.

Confrontations

Mrs Thatcher was fond of lecturing union leaders and the workers whom they represented about the realities of supply-side economics which are described above. She also looked for opportunities to set the forces of the state against those of organised labour. Many conflicts occurred, but two are worthy of note as perfect illustrations of how and why she was so determined to win victory in what she saw as the frontline of economic reform.

The first concerned a series of disputes which broke out in the printing industry. Two newspaper owners – Eddie Shah and Rupert Murdoch – wished to break the power of the unions in their industry. Unions held a stranglehold in the printing industry, enforcing closed shops whereby only union members were allowed to work, and preventing the introduction of labour-saving technology. In both cases Thatcher made it clear that she backed the employers and was prepared to introduce legislation to reduce union power. Ultimately, and partly as a result of political backing, Murdoch and Shah prevailed. The printing conflict demonstrated two of the problems of union power as perceived by the supply side theorists. One was that powerful trade unions tend to lead to over-manning as, not unnaturally, they wish to see as much employment for their members as possible. The other was resistance to technological progress. Unions can be conservative bodies, suspicious of changes in working practices and unwilling to welcome more efficient equipment if it leads to job losses. So the printing employers' victory led to rapid advances in technology as well as – as the unions had feared – severe redundancies in the industry.

The second battle was more dramatic. This was the great miners' strike of 1984–85. A programme of pit closures had been instigated and, as expected, the miners' union chose a national strike as their way of expressing opposition. Led by the marxist Arthur Scargill, the miners, all members of the National Union of Mineworkers, blockaded the pits, preventing non-unionised labour from replacing them. The police were mobilised to keep the pits open and the courts were in almost continuous session prosecuting miners who were accused of breaking laws restricting picketing and mass demonstrations. Throughout the winter, police, encouraged by the strong backing of the prime minister, battled with enraged miners and their leaders. Public opinion polarised on the issue. It became a symbol of a wider conflict between the free market policies of the government and the fear that the interests of the workers was being sacrificed for the sake of economic dogma.

It is part of Conservative party folklore today that Mrs Thatcher won a resounding victory. The miners were forced back to work and the pit closure programme continued. This, together with her stand against the Argentine invasion of the Falkland Islands two years earlier, earned her the title 'Iron Lady'.

LEGISLATION

The legal reforms which were effected during the 1980s, and into the 1990s under John Major, completely altered the balance of power in the industrial relations field. They also changed the nature of trade unionism for ever. Before considering the consequences, the legislation should be reviewed:

- *1980 Employment Act.* Forced unions to hold secret, democratic ballots in order to take industrial action (mainly strikes). It also introduced secret ballots for union leadership elections. Before this Act union leaders were able to force even reluctant members to take industrial action and leaders were not democratically elected.
- *1982 Employment Act.* This made it more difficult for unions to enforce closed shops, i.e. they could no longer force workers to join unions in order to be given employment.
- *1984 Trade Union Act.* The main piece of legislation. Before this Act unions could not be sued for compensation if industrial action led to losses by affected businesses. The legal immunity of unions has always been one of

their most cherished privileges. The loss of this immunity was the most serious blow to their power. After the Act it was possible for firms to sue unions if a strike or other industrial action was called without a democratic, secret ballot. The Act also enabled union members to opt out of allowing some of their union dues to be paid to the Labour party, thus weakening Labour party–Union links.

- *1986 Wages Act*. Reduced the ability of Wages Councils to set minimum wages in some industries.
- *1988 Employment Act*. Union members refusing to take industrial action could no longer be disciplined. Closed shops were further undermined and most of them disappeared. Union funds could effectively no longer be used for political purposes.
- *1990 Employment Act*. Further losses of legal immunities for unions. It also made it virtually impossible for unions to take industrial action for political reasons: i.e. industrial action was legal only if it was directly concerned with the wages and conditions of members.
- *1993 Trade Union Reform and Employment Rights Act*. This finally abolished wages councils and gave workers rights to join or not join a union of their own choice.

There were a number of consequences of this onslaught on union powers and immunities:

1 Union membership began to fall. To some extent this was caused by the decline in traditional industries where membership had always been high. However, the outlawing of closed shops, the greater freedom of workers to join or not to join a union and their reduced influence also resulted in a leakage of members.
2 Labour markets did indeed become more flexible. Over-manning was reduced in many industries, productivity of workers rose and in some industries wages actually began to fall, thus reducing costs. In other words, the legislation had exactly the effects which supply side economists had expected.
3 The number of strikes and other forms of industrial action fell dramatically. This was partly the result of higher unemployment, but mostly resulted from tighter legal controls and loss of immunity.
4 The reduction in membership cut off a major source of funding for the Labour party. This forced them to search for corporate funding, which may have begun to influence policy making.
5 It forced the Labour party to re-evaluate its long-standing and close relationship with the trade unions.

The Thatcher / Major economic reforms summarised

- Laissez-faire policy towards industry and unemployment, allowing the free market to make its own adjustments.
- Concentration on controlling inflation as the main priority.
- Privatisation of many major industries such as telecommunications, gas, electricity generation and supply, railways, steel, car industry, water.
- Less reliance on fiscal policy, more on monetary controls – interest rates, money supply and sterling exchange rates.
- Reduction in trade union power to make labour markets more flexible.
- Reductions in direct taxes on personal and corporate incomes, replaced by higher indirect taxes.
- Reductions in welfare benefits to reduce the 'dependency culture' and force people into work.
- Stricter controls on monopoly power to promote competition.
- Forcing industries and professions, such as banks, building societies and other financial institutions, legal profession, opticians, dentists, some postal services, public transport, to open themselves up to competition.

LABOUR'S REACTION TO THE END OF CONSENSUS

The reaction of the Labour party to the economic reforms of the 1980s and early 1990s was to dominate the course of politics in Britain in the final twenty years of the twentieth century. For convenience we can divide Labour's reaction into two parts: 1979–87 and 1987–97.

1979–87: trauma

Labour's election defeat in 1979 had partly been caused by the so-called 'winter of discontent' of 1978–79 when a wave of public service industry strikes hit Britain over wage controls. Nevertheless, the left wing of the party was convinced that the reason for the loss was that the party was not socialist enough in its economic outlook. Led by such senior figures as Michael Foot (leader from 1980 to 1983), Tony Benn and Barbara Castle, the Labour left forced the party to adopt a number of proposals which were to shift it markedly away from the Conservative government, which was moving to the right.

The Labour left wished not only to reverse the reforms made by the Thatcher administrations, but to adopt some socialist policies which had not been implemented by previous Labour governments. Among the proposals were the following:

- the privatised industries to be re-nationalised and new candidates for nationalisation to be considered;
- restoration of a steeply progressive direct tax system so that there would be a re-distribution of real income from rich to poor;
- large increases in expenditure on welfare, including generous social security increases;
- the introduction of a national minimum wage;
- the restoration of the powers and immunities of trade unions;
- curbs on company profits and shareholders' dividends;
- the re-introduction of keynesian economic demand management.

These economic policies were added to a range of other radical proposals in defence, foreign policy, law and order and social policy. Together they mark the period in British political history when political opinion was at its most polarised. Consensus politics seemed a distant memory in the mid-1980s.

The verdict of the electorate on the left-wing policies of the Labour party was a resounding rejection. The Conservatives won landslide victories in the 1983 and 1987 elections. To make matters worse for Labour, the economy began to improve markedly after 1986 and a mini-boom (especially in house prices) ensured that their reactionary policies would find little favour. The party was at its lowest ebb since before World War II.

The right wingers in Labour fought a rearguard action against the lurch to the left. Indeed many leading members formed the breakaway Social Democratic Party (SDP) which fought the two general elections of the 1980s, winning many votes but relatively few seats in parliament. Such leading Labour figures as David Owen, Roy Jenkins, Shirley Williams and Bill Rodgers left the party, never to return.

But some moderates stayed in the party, notably the new leader, Neil Kinnock (who had replaced Michael Foot in 1983). Kinnock, who had considered himself a left winger until he became leader, realised after 1987, that the British people had no stomach for socialism. However many criticisms there were of the policies of the Thatcher governments, the electorate did not want a return to the pre-1979 economic system.

Backed by younger supporters for reform such as John Smith, Gordon Brown and Tony Blair, Kinnock began the long road to changing the Labour party for good.

1987–97: reform

Neil Kinnock, his successor John Smith (leader 1992–94) and Tony Blair (leader after 1994) instituted a process of reform which was to culminate in

1996–97 with the emergence of what became known as 'New Labour'. Kinnock's ideas can be summarised as follows:

- Free market capitalism was working. It was therefore unacceptable to the people that excessive state interference or public ownership of industry should threaten economic success.
- Though some union power could be restored, there could be no return to the days when unions were able to hold up economic progress in the pursuit of their own interests.
- Re-nationalisation of most industries was not feasible. Apart from being too expensive, most of the privatised industries seemed to be relatively successful. Privatisation was popular on the whole and it worked.
- High income and corporate taxation was indeed a disincentive to economic dynamism. The levels of before 1979 could therefore not be restored.
- The growing inequalities which were resulting from the operation of free markets could be tolerated provided there was a robust social security and welfare system to protect the less well off. The interests of workers could be protected by a minimum wage system and appropriate legislation to protect workers' rights.
- The state should continue to offer high levels of expenditure on pensions, social security, health and education and general taxation levels would reflect this. However, any increased tax burden would largely rely on indirect taxation (i.e. VAT, duties etc.).

The reforms represented both a pragmatic attitude to economic management, and a compromise with those Thatcherite policies which had proved to be successful.

The changes in Labour's economic stance came too late to win them the 1992 general election, even though there had been nearly three years of deep recession. But the die was cast. Kinnock gave way to John Smith and then to Tony Blair following Smith's early death in 1994. Blair set about turning party reform into full-scale transformation. Hence the development of the idea of 'New Labour'. He denied that his policies were merely pragmatism or compromise. Coined by Anthony Giddens, a prominent Labour supporter from the London School of Economics, the term 'third way' expressed the idea that economic (and other) policies of New Labour were neither socialism nor Thatcherite neo-liberal. They were claimed to be a fresh start.

NEW LABOUR AND THIRD WAY ECONOMICS

Prelude: Britain and the ERM

The development of Labour's economic policy in 1996–97 can be better understood in the light of Britain's experience with economic recession in the early

1990s, and particularly of her ejection from the European Exchange Rate Mechanism (ERM) in 1992.

In some ways the final piece in the Conservative party's jigsaw of supply side economics was the manipulation of Britain's foreign exchange rate. The argument went like this: Britain had been fundamentally uncompetitive for decades. This was borne out by the periodic balance-of-payments crises which had been suffered (notably, 1964, 1966–67, 1975–76). The country had been cushioned from the effects of being less efficient than her main trade competitors by a steadily falling value in the exchange rate of sterling. The effects of the falling international value of the pound is to make British exports artificially cheaper. This has enabled Britain to trade with the rest of the world successfully despite her lack of efficiency and therefore competitiveness. The price to be paid is that low sterling values also means high import prices. As Britain heavily depends on imports (about one-third of total consumption), rising import prices has also created nagging inflation.

Margaret Thatcher, and particularly her Chancellor of the Exchequer, Nigel Lawson (1983–89) were of the view that, if Britain were no longer protected by the low value of sterling, the British economy would be *forced* to be more competitive. She would have to compete on equal terms and, as a benefit, import inflation would be controlled.

Lawson's plan was to 'shadow' the deutschmark. This meant keeping the value of sterling 'pegged' to the value of the German currency, then considered to be Europe's strongest and most stable. The way this was done was to raise interest rates when the value of sterling was to go up, and reduce them we wanted it to fall. In other words the basics of the British economy were forced to 'copy' what was happening in Germany.

Lawson was removed as Chancellor in 1989 and replaced by John Major. Major persuaded Thatcher to join the European Exchange Rate Mechanism. This tied the British currency to *all* the leading West European currencies, not just the deutschmark. This was an even more severe discipline for the economy. When recession struck Europe, however, in 1990 it was clear that the value of sterling was too high in the ERM and that the economy could not survive under these circumstances. After disastrous delay, now the responsibility of the new Chancellor, Norman Lamont, Britain was forced out of the ERM in September 1992 (an event known as Black Wednesday). The value of sterling fell dramatically in the months which followed, relieving the pressure, but causing mounting inflation.

Britain's ejection from the ERM was a huge humiliation and an indictment of Conservative economic policy. It is ironic that the effects were beneficial in the medium term. The inflation subsided, exports picked up because of the low value of sterling and economic growth improved. But these events were to be to the advantage of New Labour rather than John Major's Conservative government.

Labour, especially Gordon Brown, learned some lessons from the ERM disaster. Most importantly, it was seen that attempts simply to force the economy to be more competitive would not work on their own. Positive steps would have to be taken to improve efficiency. Secondly, and in the longer term, attempts by politicians to control the economy as a whole were usually compromised by political considerations. Thirdly, Brown also understood that inflation was not an acceptable price to be paid for other economic policies. These three lessons were to make a significant impact on New Labour's economics of the third way.

Fundamentals of the third way

When Labour took power in 1997, its first Chancellor, Gordon Brown, was very clear as to what economic principles to adopt. They were as follows:

1 Supply-side economics is, in general, effective. However, it is not enough to assume that the production side of the economy will grow satisfactorily if left to its own devices by government. There have to be positive steps of a *micro-economic* nature to underpin the effects of free market economics. Micro-economic policy includes measures designed to give a direct boost to different sections of the economy (such as the labour force, individual industries, regional economies etc.), rather than attempting to control the economy as a whole, which is described as *macro-economic* policy. The precise nature of these micro-economic policies is described below.

2 The social security system should play a positive role in encouraging the unemployed to find work. It is not sufficient simply to set benefits at such a low level that people prefer to work than to be on benefit. Rather, the social security system should provide *incentives* for people to enter the world of work. In other words, benefits should be a carrot rather than a stick.

3 On the whole politicians should not interfere with the workings of the macro economy, either with monetarist or keynesian policies. They are usually reluctant to take decisions which might be good for the economy, but bad for the fortunes of the government, and are always tempted to take popular measures which might damage the economy. Thus they like to reduce interest rates and tax levels but raise public spending before elections, but have to reverse these measures if inflation begins to rise too quickly. Macro-economic policy, therefore, should be taken out of the hands of politicians and given to independent, non-political bodies. As this is done by two of the world's most successful economies – those of Germany and the USA – the evidence in favour of the principle is compelling.

4 The operation of free markets may be beneficial on the whole, but problems arise if there is not genuine competition in the these markets. It is the role

of government, therefore, to ensure that there is genuinely free competition to ensure the best interests of consumers are served and that British industry remains competitive with the rest of the world.

5 The long-term success of the economy is dependent on eliminating the wild fluctuations in economic growth, unemployment and inflation from Britain had suffered for forty years or more. What Gordon Brown called the 'boom and bust' economy had to be replaced by long-term stability.

These policies were in part an extension of past Conservative policies, but also, in some regards, a departure from them. The details below indicate where the continuities and the divergences lie.

Continuities

- Free market capitalism is the best way to create wealth and economic growth.

- Measures to stimulate the supply side of the economy are more effective on the whole than management of the demand side.

- Inflation is the most serious problem for the economy. It causes unemployment, lack of competitiveness and reduces business and consumer confidence. Economic policy should concentrate, therefore, on inflation control.

- Excessively high levels of tax on incomes and company profits are a disincentive to economic enterprise and so should be avoided.

Divergences

- Conservatives are less enthusiastic about interfering with the economy on the micro-economic level.

- Conservatives oppose excessive measures to promote competition. They oppose regulation of industry and business in principle.

- Conservatives are wary of the idea of a national minimum wage. They reluctantly accepted it after 1997, but would set it at a very low level as they believe it may cause unemployment if set too high.

- There is a fear among Conservatives that the Bank of England is too limited in its function of setting interest rates to control inflation. They believe it should have a wider role in controlling economic factors, including foreign exchange rates of sterling.

- The Conservatives remain more determined than Labour to reduce the overall burden of taxation, even if this may mean reductions in spending on public services in the short run.

- Where public services are seen to be failing, Conservatives generally favour outright privatisation, whereas New Labour prefers the solution of creating a partnership between public and private sectors, in other words only *partial* privatisation.

● The greatest divergence between Labour and Conservative attitudes to economic policy concerns the European Union. This is examined in more detail below, but it revolves mainly around opposition to the adoption of a single European currency and a fear that economic policy making is falling increasingly into the hands of distant, undemocratic bureaucrats and bankers.

A new consensus?

At first sight it may appear that there are a significant number of differences between Conservative and Labour attitudes to economic policy. Closer examination, however, reveals that, if we consider *basic principles*, there is a large measure of agreement. Distinctions are largely confined to detail and emphasis. For example, there is now agreement that the Bank of England's Monetary Policy Committee should set interest rates independently, but Conservative want to widen its role. Similarly, the national minimum wage is now accepted on all sides, but the parties will disagree on the level at which it should be set.

The Liberal Democrats have introduced some fundamental dissent since 1997. They place much less importance on the level of taxation, believing that governments should not fear rises in direct taxation if this is necessary to maintain a good level of public services. The Liberal Democrats are also much less enthusiastic about the involvement of the private sector in services such as education, health and public transport than either Labour or the Conservatives.

But the general picture does suggest a new economic consensus, at least in the domestic sphere, which is as solid as the old keynesian certainties of the 1950s, 1960s and 1970s. It is in the European dimension where genuine divisions exist and consensus remains a distant prospect, at least until the controversy over British participation in the single European currency is resolved.

ECONOMIC POLICIES SINCE 1997

We can now examine the main developments which have occurred since 1997 in more detail. The most important decisions were taken at the beginning of Labour's administration and have proved to be the most radical changes which have occurred since the end of the keynesian consensus.

Macro-economics: monetary and fiscal policy

Monetary policy

Gordon Brown made two immediate decisions which were to dominate policy for years to come. The first, and most important, was to grant operational independence to the Bank of England and to establish a Monetary Policy Committee (MPC) which was to set base interest rates.

The committee has nine independent members, none of them politicians, who meet every month to set the base interest rate of the Bank of England, thus effectively determining mortgage and other main rates on loans and savings. The committee was to publish details of its deliberations and even the internal voting is revealed. It has only one task which is to set interest rates to keep the inflation rate within a maximum set by the government. This is based on the assumption that raising interest rates will curb inflation by reducing borrowing and therefore spending. Conversely, if inflation is falling, indicating a slow-down in the economy, spending can be stimulated by reducing the interest rate.

Initially the ceiling rate was a stiff 2.5 per cent and was still in place in 2002. Should the rate rise above this, or fall below a floor of 1.5 per cent the committee must write an open letter of explanation and, of course, put the matter right as soon as possible. There can be no political interference and no considerations, other than inflation, can be taken into account.

At first sight this might seem a minor detail of policy. In fact it has been viewed as one of the most important economic decisions to be taken since World War II. Its significance can be summarised as follows:
- It provides a stable economic platform, free from interference by politicians. This inspires confidence among consumers, the business community and financial markets.
- If politicians do try to over-expand the economy dangerously through keynesian fiscal management they will simply be thwarted by the Monetary Policy Committee which will raise interest rates to keep inflation down.
- It demonstrated the government's determination to behave in an economically responsible manner.
- It put a key element of economic policy into the hands of neutral experts who would not be influenced by short-term political considerations.

The immediate reaction among Conservatives was to oppose the introduction of the MPC. Very quickly, however, they came to see the sense of it and finance spokesman, Michael Portillo, soon accepted it. However, as we saw above, the Conservatives remain concerned that the MPC has too narrow a role, and should take factors other than inflation into consideration. Opposition was futile, in any case, when the operation of the committee proved successful, with inflation remaining within target throughout New Labour's first term.

Fiscal policy

Gordon Brown had gone halfway towards removing macro-economic policy making from political hands with the introduction of the MPC. But this was not enough for him. He also wished to see an end to governments' tendency to run up huge borrowing during recessions (by reducing taxes and raising public expenditure). He wanted a straitjacket placed around fiscal policy. He was influenced heavily by the fact that he had inherited a huge burden of public debt from the previous government. His response was the so-called 'golden rule'.

The golden rule, whose official name is the 'Code for Fiscal Stability', states that a government should not borrow money for the purpose of simply spending more than it is raising in taxes (i.e. for current account debt). Rather, there can be borrowing only to finance investment, that is, projects which will have lasting benefit such as roads, schools or hospitals. What this effectively means is that a government cannot simply spend and borrow its way out of a recession without breaking the rule.

To demonstrate his determination, Brown risked unpopularity by tightening public spending for the first three years of the new government's term. Public spending as a proportion of national income (i.e. the economy's total output) fell from 41.2 per cent in 1996 to 38.9 per cent in 1999. At a time when the government as a whole was promising improvements in public services, he was actually reducing public expenditure from £343 billion to £340 billion! As a result, the government finances moved from a deficit (i.e. government borrowing) of 3.6 per cent of national income in 1997 to a surplus (i.e. repayment of government debt) of 2 per cent of national income in 2000 – an improvement over three years of £40 billion.

This responsible attitude to government budgeting was underpinned by a cautious stance on taxes. Brown also refused to court political popularity by reducing the tax burden. But the Labour government's policy on taxation as a whole proved to be less coherent than its stance on macro-economics.

Taxation

The overall effects of tax policy after 1997 were largely neutral. There was a small rise in the burden of taxation from about 36 per cent of national income in 1997 to 38 per cent in 2000. However, most of this was caused by 'fiscal drag' rather than policy changes. Fiscal drag refers to a natural process whereby, as prosperity rises, which it did fairly rapidly between 1997 and

2001, the *proportion* of National Income taken in tax is bound to rise as individuals and companies move into higher tax brackets. Increased spending by consumers also raises more in VAT and various duties.

Having said that, Gordon Brown did make some important decisions. These added up to a sizeable shift in the emphasis on taxes away from income tax towards indirect taxes and other subtle or 'hidden' tax changes. A new income tax bracket was introduced at 10 per cent instead of 20 per cent for many of the low paid. Several million were also taken out of taxation at the bottom end of the earnings scale. Tax credits (i.e. benefits paid through the tax system) were made available for poorer families and there were reductions in the tax burdens on businesses, especially small ones.

To pay for these reductions the government increased a wide range of other taxes which became known by the Opposition as 'stealth taxes'. This was because most payers were not fully aware that there had been an increase. A typical example was the loss of tax relief on many private pension schemes. Tobacco and petrol duties also rose sharply and the married couples' tax allowance was abolished.

The general direction of Gordon Brown's tax policies has been mildly socialist. There has been a reduction in the burden of taxation on the low paid and working families with children, including lone parents, have all done well. However, he has resisted the temptation to raise the top rate of income tax above 40 per cent or to introduce greater tax burdens on high levels of business profits. But Brown had plenty of room to relieve tax burdens even more on the low paid after 1999. Instead, he has chosen to pay off chunks of the national debt and raise levels of expenditure on public services.

Micro-economic policy

As we saw above, New Labour moved supply-side economics a stage further than the Conservatives by taking a number of direct, positive measures to improve the efficiency and productivity of British commerce and industry.

As with the Conservatives, the Labour government laid great stress on the effectiveness of competition in promoting efficiency and there has been a sustained drive to introduce market forces into such industries as telecommunications, transport, electricity, retailing and the car industry. At the same time the Office of Fair Trading was given increased powers in 1999 to outlaw uncompetitive practices by large manufacturers who were attempting to exert too much control over retail distribution.

Persistent problems in depressed areas such as the north east, south west and north west were a further concern. Twelve Regional Development Agencies were set up in 1998 to distribute public funds for regeneration of existing industry and to attract new investment into these areas. Although this has not solved long-term unemployment in the regions, it has contributed to a steady reduction in overall unemployment.

But the main thrust of micro economic policy fell on labour markets. Union powers were not, on the whole, restored in spite of intense pressure from the left wing of the party. Although the national minimum wage was introduced it was set at such a low level (£3.80 per hour), that employment was little affected. Thus the downward trend in level of industrial unrest was maintained and wage costs fell to be increasingly in line with the rest of Europe.

In the longer term, Tony Blair continually stressed the need for a more highly trained and educated workforce. His clarion call for 'education, education, education' in 1997 was not just for social reasons. He recognised that a higher-quality labour force would be more able to compete and to handle new technologies. So the drive for higher standards from pre-school to university was as much about economics as it was about education. A Training and Skills Council was also set up to organise more training on an industry-by-industry basis.

In common with his Conservative predecessor, John Major, Blair also saw small businesses as the driving force of economic growth, so they were granted substantial concessions on taxes and employment.

These micro-economic measures represented a continuation of Conservative policies in the 1990s. However, they were now being conducted within a stable macro-economic environment. Progress along these lines had been thwarted in the past by the uneven nature of economic growth, Blair's government hoped that the healthier climate would enable Britain to compete in the long term.

EUROPE AND THE ECONOMY

The impact of the European Union on Britain is considered later in this book. But some mention of Europe must be made here as British involvement has had a growing effect on the conduct of economic policy making, especially since the Single European Act came into force in 1987. This finalised the creation of a single market in Europe. In other words the British economy was thereafter strongly influenced by European events. The main effects on policy can be summarised as follows:
 • British interest rates are affected by the level of European rates which are determined by the European Central Bank. The Monetary Policy Committee of the Bank of England does not have to follow European rates, but recognises that there may be an impact on British inflation.

- The Labour government after 1997 has been committed to creating favourable conditions for entry into the single European currency. These are known as the 'convergence criteria', a set of conditions which will bring Britain's economy into line with that of the rest of the EU. They include low inflation and interest rates, controlled levels of public debt and low unemployment. Britain has moved steadily towards the criteria and had achieved them by the end of 2000. In the event, the government would probably have worked towards similar objectives, single currency or not, but it has been a factor in the background of policy consideration.
- The exchange rate between sterling and the euro has been significant. The weakness of the euro (and therefore the relative strength of sterling) during 2000–1 made British exports to Europe expensive (but imports have also been cheap – a great help with inflation control). The government was able to do little to counteract this trend, but it has made the competitiveness of British industry an even more pressing problem.
- Competition policy must conform to European rules. In fact this has speeded the process as controls in Europe have traditionally been tighter than in Britain. European policy has therefore suited the supply side stance of New Labour.

Labour's 'third way' economic policies since 1997 summarised

- Transferring control over interest rates to the Monetary Policy Committee of the Bank of England.
- Introducing the 'golden rule' establishing fiscal responsibility – no public borrowing other than for investment.
- Making labour markets more flexible at the lower end through low tax bands and welfare benefits for poorer families.
- Raising indirect taxes to fund spending on improved public services, but not direct taxation.
- Encouraging partnerships between public and private sector enterprises to fund investment in public services such as health, education and transport.
- Preparing the British economy to enter the euro-zone in due course.
- Increased spending for regional industrial development.

SUMMARY: SOME THEMES

We can identify several important features of economic policy in the period since the 1960s.

1 The existence of a conflict and consensus on economic policy has ebbed and flowed. There was a strong consensus in the 1950s, 1960s and most of the

1970s. This collapsed in the late 1970s, culminating in an extreme schism in the mid-1980s as the Conservative party moved to a right-wing, neo-liberal position and Labour shifted dramatically to a left-wing, socialist position. During the 1990s the two main parties, supported by the Liberal democrats moved slowly back towards consensus. This was based on the success of New Labour's third way policies. In the early years of the twenty-first century, however, this new consensus was threatened by divisions over the future of Britain's involvement with the European Union.

2 British economic policy making has been characterised by periodic recessions, followed by rather shorter intervals of growing prosperity. Policy has, therefore, usually been dominated by the need to combat the existing recession or avoiding the next one. Recession policies are, ironically, rather easier to develop than the decisions which have to be made when economic growth is healthy. In times of economic slowdown, inflation has been low, interest rates have fallen and the exchange rate of sterling drops, making it easier for industry to export. The problems for policy makers are, therefore, how to deal with unemployment and how to finance the public debt which inevitably mounts up in a recession. It was also normal to reduce taxation at such times to try to boost consumption, so governments were able to make decisions which enjoyed short-term popularity.

3 Governments have conspicuously failed to maintain sustained periods of economic growth, at least until after 1995. Tempted by the availability of increased funds governments have tended to raise public expenditure and reduce taxation dramatically in the good times. However, such measures have typically created rapid inflation and have simply forced a clampdown in the following years. This kind of cycle became known as 'stop–go' policy. This was certainly the experience in the late 1960s, late1970s and late 1980s.

4 Faced by an unusually long period of sustained economic growth between 1995 and 2001 governments have found new problems in prosperity. Various groups, for example demanded tax cuts, from poor families to motorists to businesses. At the same time, calls on the public finances grew from different groups who wanted their fair share of the prosperity. The obvious examples are the health, education, law and order and transport authorities. But other groups want some of the action too. Farmers, small businesses, local author-ities and cultural or sporting bodies have demanded a bigger share. The more cautious chancellors in this period – Ken Clarke and Gordon Brown – have avoided the sins of their predecessors by keeping public expenditure under control and maintaining tax levels, but have paid a high political price for doing so.

5 The growing importance of Europe and the global economy will bring new, longer-term pressures on economic policy makers. Certainly there is bound to

be a loss of flexibility and independence as international forces exert an increasing influence on the British economy.

SAMPLE QUESTIONS

1 To what extent have New Labour's economic policies been different from those of other governments since 1979?

2 What was meant by Gordon Brown's claim to have established 'prudence with a purpose'? How has he sought to achieve it.

3 What have been the differing attitudes towards taxation and welfare demonstrated by Conservative and Labour governments since 1979?

4 Has a new economic consensus emerged since 1992?

The Welfare State

2

➤ Definition of the term 'Welfare State'

➤ What is included as part of the Welfare State

➤ Basic principles of the Welfare State

➤ The future of the Welfare State

This short chapter is designed to introduce the subject of the Welfare State as a complete concept before we discuss some of its individual elements – education, health and social security – in further chapters. The origins and principles of the Welfare State will be discussed and the changing attitude of the parties and their policy makers to it will be traced.

DEFINITION

There is no agreed definition of the term 'welfare state', though we can say that the description became widely used in the early years of the twentieth century. We can also make a clear distinction between a situation where the state provides a wide variety of welfare provision and one where there is a systematic arrangement for providing universal welfare through the state. This distinction can be illustrated by referring to health care provision in Britain.

Before 1946 health care was either privately supplied, in which case individuals simply paid for their own health care, while others were offered a state-subsidised system of health insurance. Those who did not take advantage of the insurance scheme were left without such care unless they could rely on charity and on local authority hospitals. Hospitals and doctors would save lives without reference to ability to pay, but other forms of health care were reserved for the well off or the state insured. Britain was, therefore, a state which provided basic health care for all and a voluntary insurance system, but the system was not universal. After the establishment of the National Health Service in 1946, however, the state guaranteed to provide health care for all, on demand and according to need. At the same time everybody in work was required to contribute through National Insurance payments. The NHS was both universal and compulsorily funded. A small private health sector remained for those whom preferred to pay for care.

We could apply a similar analysis to other services such as housing, education and social security, to illustrate the difference between the Welfare State as such and what had gone before. For our purposes we can identify a number of features which define the Welfare State (see box).

The Welfare State

- Benefits are universal, supplied free according to people's needs. Nobody is excluded.
- Contributions are compulsory, at least by those who are in work.
- The state guarantees to maintain certain minimum standards of welfare services. This is to ensure that state-run services are not significantly inferior to those supplied by the private sector.

WHAT IS INCLUDED

The term welfare is not a precise one so that a Welfare State may contain a variety of different services. In Britain, where the system is broad based, there is a large number of services included in the term. These are:

- The provision of *personal health services*, including medical research. These are centrally organised.
- *Public health provision* such as protection from virulent diseases, mass inoculation, services for the unborn child and young infants, provided by local authorities.
- *Social services* at a local government level. These deal with such issues as protection of children, including orphans, family support, care of the elderly at home and support for single parents.
- *Subsidised housing*, again at local level. Rents were heavily subsidised and local authorities were responsible for housing all residents and maintaining the housing stock.
- *Education* (under the 1944 Education Act) was to provided free for all those between the ages of 5 and 15 (later raised to 16), and for those who reached a good educational standard at 16–18 years. Places on degree courses were available for a small proportion of the most able. Later, post-16 education was made available for all, and the number of university places were greatly expanded.
- A comprehensive system of *social security* was established. There were a wide variety of benefits available to all according to need. These included

maternity benefits for pregnant women and nursing mothers, sickness benefits to compensate those who lost wages through illness, unemployment benefit, housing benefit for the very poor, family income support, again for the poor, child benefits for all families with children up to 16 years, free school lunches and uniform grants, old age pensions, death grants for funeral expenses and widows' benefit. In other words, benefits for all kinds of need which may occur within a family.

BASIC PRINCIPLES

These are more difficult to establish than a clear definition. This is because different political movements in Britain after World War II, while agreeing to the establishment of the Welfare State, presented differing attitudes to welfare. Here we shall examine three political traditions: Liberalism, Conservatism and Democratic Socialism (i.e. Labour).

Liberalism

It was Liberal thinkers from the nineteenth and early twentieth centuries such as T.H. Green, L. Hobhouse and T. Hobson who had proposed the ideas that a civilised, modern state should provide some broad levels of welfare for its people. This tradition (known as 'New Liberalism') provided the philosophical grounding for early state welfare systems at the start of the twentieth century. It was politicians such as Joseph Chamberlain (mayor of Birmingham) and David Lloyd George (prime minister 1916–22) who introduced the first practical measures.

Their view was that individuals could only be truly free if they were provided with opportunities and relief from the worst excesses of deprivation. They believed that people have a moral obligation to contribute to the welfare of others and that this was best achieved through the state.

The synthesis of theory and action came to its height with the rise to prominence of William (later Lord) Beveridge in the 1940s. A civil servant and later Liberal peer, Beveridge produced a report on the future of social policy in Britain in 1942. This was forever after known as the 'Beveridge Report' and represents the origin of today's Welfare State. The Beveridge principles, which are also those of the modern Liberal movement, were as follows:

- A variety of social evils, including poverty, lack of education and unemployment represented limits to the freedom of those who suffered them.
- It follows that the state should intervene in order to reduce these evils and so enhance freedom.

- All are entitled to a minimum standard of living.
- In order to ensure such a standard of living it is necessary that all members of society should contribute to a pool of welfare.
- That all are entitled to draw from this pool according to their need.

Liberals and the Liberal Democrat party itself have supported the principles of the Welfare State ever since Beveridge. They consider it a vital part of a modern, civilised society.

Conservatism

Between the 1950s and the 1970s traditional Conservative thinkers and politicians supported the Welfare State. Being a pragmatic movement, Conservatism has accepted that this kind of welfare has improved the condition of the people and has become a popular device for promoting the common good. Though they may have had suspicions that a compulsory system of welfare inhibits individualism, they have supported it as part of a popular consensus.

When a new brand of Conservatism – the new right – emerged in the 1970s and 1980s, led by Margaret Thatcher, attitudes to welfare changed markedly. The new right feared that a 'dependency culture' had grown up whereby people had become used to depending on the state and this had sapped their sense of individual enterprise. They therefore sought to reduce the role of the Welfare State in a number of ways, replacing it with private-sector provisions.

The first target was subsidised housing. Council properties were offered for sale, at a discount, to their tenants. By the end of the 1980s many thousands of former council tenants had become home owners. Most of the rest of the subsidised housing system was transferred to voluntary housing associations which are outside the control of the state. The social security system also came under attack. Various benefits, such as unemployment support, child benefits and the old age pension were steadily eroded. These benefits were seen as a deterrent to work and to private insurance schemes or pension schemes.

Though education and health systems remained largely intact, new right Conservatives made no secret of their preference for private services and people were encouraged to take out private health insurance and to send their children to private schools. Private pensions, health and education all received generous tax reliefs in a period when the public services were in decline. Nevertheless the Conservative party could not bring itself to dismantle the Welfare State and its principles survived the onslaught which took place between 1979 and 1997.

Labour

Although the Welfare State was essentially developed by Liberals, its establishment was seen as the crowning glory of the post-war Labour government. It became a symbol of the British form of socialism and was staunchly defended. That is not to say that Labour governments always treated the Welfare State kindly. It was Labour which introduced and often increased charges for prescriptions, dental care and eye checks. The principle that welfare benefits should be free at the point of demand was thus eroded almost immediately by the party which had introduced it.

Although the Labour party, while in opposition, defended the Welfare State against Conservative reforms in the 1980s, it failed to maintain the real value of pensions while in office and did not increase the proportion of National Income spent on either health care or education.

The advent of New Labour in the 1990s under John Smith and Tony Blair changed the party's attitude to the Welfare State. Their new interest in individualism led them to suggest that it was indeed up to individuals to make provision for their own welfare if they could afford to. A number of key measures have been taken by Labour which have gone some way to eroding welfare provision. The most striking act was to introduce tuition fees for university students. At the same time a system of 'stakeholder pensions' was introduced – a private pension scheme sponsored by the state, but left to individuals to make their own provisions. It was clear from this that there is an intention to erode or remove the state pension from future generations.

Labour's loss of enthusiasm for the Welfare State should not, however, be exaggerated. Its principles are still intact and there were substantial increases in pensions, child benefit and family benefits in the early part of the twenty-first century. Similarly large increases in expenditure on the National Health Service and on schools followed, demonstrating that a strong faith in public sector welfare provision remained in the Labour party.

THE FUTURE OF THE WELFARE STATE

None of the major parties will admit that there is a possibility of the main aspects of the Welfare State being dismantled; but its prospects do not appear to be rosy. A future Conservative government, especially under its new leader, Iain Duncan Smith, may well decide to replace state health or education provision with private-sector arrangements. They have a sense that the Welfare State is not appropriate for a modern, pluralist society as there is sufficient prosperity for people to be able to make private arrangements. Furthermore, many in the party believe the private sector will provide better, more efficient, services than the state can do.

The Liberal Democrats still support the Welfare State staunchly. However, they are unlikely to form a government in the foreseeable future and their political influence remains weak. The best they can hope for is to influence the devolved governments of Scotland and Wales so that welfare remains under state control.

Uncertainty surrounds the future attitude of the Labour party towards the welfare State. The ordinary members of the party are unlikely to allow the principle to die, but the parliamentary leadership is much less attached to the idea of the Welfare State and may wish to modify, if not abolish it. As we have seen above, pensions and education seem to be most at risk, it may be that private health may make inroads into state welfare provision. Some form of universal social security will always be necessary, but it is very possible that future Labour administrations will continue to chip away at the benefits system.

If any government were to allow individuals to 'opt out' of the system in the future the Beveridge principles will have died, since universal contribution is what defines the Welfare State.

SAMPLE QUESTIONS

1 Assess the extent to which the neo-liberal economic reforms of the 1980s and 1990s resulted in fundamental changes in the UK economy.

2 Assess the view that Gordon Brown is a cautious rather than a radical Chancellor of the Exchequer.

3 How much consensus on economic policy now exists in the British political system?

Health

3

➤ **The basic principles of the National Health Service**

➤ **The origins of modern problems in health policy**

➤ **Review of Conservative policies on health in the 1980s and 1990s**

➤ **Review of Labour policies after 1997**

➤ **Critique of these policies**

➤ **Analysis of the enduring problems in making health policy**

The National Health Service came into existence in 1948 after a prolonged period of negotiation between the reforming Labour government of the day and various sections of the medical profession. It was an idea with great popular support, but which also created great misgivings among health professionals. Very soon, however, it became the centrepiece of British social policy. Its main creator, Nye Bevan, was lionised for his efforts and it became an apparently immovable institution within a few years.

Its principles were relatively simple. It was to be funded from taxation and the National Insurance system, which had also been introduced by Atlee's government. All taxpayers were thus obliged to contribute, but at the same time all citizens were entitled to free consultations and treatments, free at the point of delivery and granted entirely according to need.

Although private medical practice was allowed to continue for those who wished to pay separately, the vast majority of doctors, dentists, opticians, nurses, hospitals and other health specialists were contracted to work for the state. Their salaries would be fixed and not dependent on how many patients they treated. As a compromise, most of these professionals were allowed to undertake a limited amount of private work to top up their earnings.

So the great experiment began – the creation of a health service which was entirely free and totally managed by the state. Funding was passed down through a hierarchy of health authorities which fell under centralised control. Up to the nineteen seventies, all seemed to go well. Economic growth kept pace with the increasing demands for health care. The only challenge to the system – a shortfall in funding as the NHS was unexpectedly popular so that visits to the doctor and demand for drugs rose alarmingly – was met by the introduction of prescription charges in 1950.

These charges for doctors' prescriptions were the only way in which patients were expected to contribute. They were introduced for two reasons. Firstly to help fund the NHS, and, secondly, as a way of deterring too many visits to the doctor for minor ailments. The very young and the old were exempt, as were social security claimants, so the new charges were not seen as an excessive hardship.

THE SYSTEM COMES UNDER STRAIN

The first signs of crisis in the NHS appeared in the second half of the 1970s. To a certain extent this was the result of events which were in no way under British control. Two huge increases in the world price of oil – in 1973–74 and in 1978–79 – created serious reductions in world trade and an economic downturn in the western world. Britain, under Jim Callaghan's Labour government suffered as badly as the rest. As a result, tax revenues were falling and unemployment rose which put pressure on government finances. The National Health Service almost inevitably lost out in these times of economic hardship.

Ironically, the health service was also becoming a victim of its own successes. During the 1960s and 1970s a wide range of new treatments were becoming available. Typical examples were transplants – mainly kidneys and hearts, heart bypass operations, hip replacements, new forms of cancer treatment and cures for ulcers. These developments were both popular and expensive. To add to the problems, Britain's ageing population was placing even more strain on health care. So the NHS was suffering from pressure from two directions – falling levels of expenditure and rising expectations of how much it could deliver. Some of the strain was taken up by growth in the private health sector, but the vast majority of people still expected free health care and could not afford the alternative.

The signs of trouble could be seen in growing waiting lists, longer waiting times, declining general practitioner services and disquiet among the medical professions. The worst problems were to be found in what are known as *acute* services, such as accident and emergency and intensive care.

These were some of the problems which Margaret Thatcher inherited when she took office in 1979. To make matters worse the economic recession deepened. All public services came under scrutiny to see if expenditure cuts could be made. Thatcher was also committed to avoiding large tax increases. This was both a philosophical motion, based on the idea that high taxes are a disincentive to enterprise, and a necessity as the economy needed greater stimulation. It was to take three years before the new government could take stock and decide what to do.

HEALTH UNDER THE CONSERVATIVES, 1979–97

Funding

The most obvious reaction to the growing crisis was to examine the whole basis upon which the NHS was being funded. There were a number of alternatives:

- **Go to the American model**. This would require people to make their own health insurance arrangements. Those who were unable or unwilling to do so would be provided only with emergency services or, for the poor, a very basic set of general services. This would have entailed a number of problems. Health insurance in the USA was, and still is, notoriously expensive. Services for the poor are usually inadequate, creating ghettoes of chronically poor health mainly in the big cities. Children often go without essential optical or dental care and those who have no insurance are sometimes relentlessly pursued for contributions to the cost of emergency care. Above all, however, the US model would have been unacceptable to public opinion.

- **Adopt the French system**. There is a subsidised insurance scheme combined with a national service which does provide a wide range of services free. In other words, it is a hybrid system, part state funded, part privately funded but with incentives to keep the cost of health care down to a minimum. This was clearly an attractive option, but it was rejected, partly because it would have been opposed by health practitioners and partly because the French experience is that services are patchy, with excellent services available where private insurance provides the funding, and poor state run services. Thus, France has a good record of treatment of major problems such as cancer and heart disease, but it primary care services do not match up to those available in the UK.

- Pressure could have been taken off the National Health Service by **encouraging as many people as possible to take up private health insurance**. This could have been done by offering substantial tax incentives to those taking up such schemes. Tax breaks could also have helped the companies providing private health. This promising idea was rejected as it would have been seen as a measure designed purely to help the wealthier middle classes. Working class public opinion would have been disenchanted.

● **Leave NHS funding essentially as it is, but introduce a wider range of charges** to 'top-up' tax revenues. This was an attractive proposition as it could be claimed that the principles of the NHS were not being attacked. Like the other options, however, it was rejected by the Health Minister, Norman Fowler. At a time when the government was seeking to keep tax levels down, more NHS charges would have been seen as a form of hidden taxation.

Fowler decided in 1982 to leave NHS funding as it was. An election was due and the Conservatives were unwilling to fight it with accusations surrounding them that they were attacking the NHS. Despite its problems, public support for the principle of a fully funded state system was unshakable. Instead he decided, with Thatcher's enthusiastic backing, to look for ways of ensuring that the existing funding was used more efficiently and that forms of saving should be found. Attention therefore switched to management. Before leaving the issue of funding, however, it should be emphasised that, in the early years of the twenty-first century, the same options are available and have to be considered in view of the enduring problems of the NHS.

Management of the NHS

When Margaret Thatcher came to power in 1997, she did so with a determination to improve the performance of public services. She saw most state run activities as inefficient, wasteful, poorly managed, overstaffed and lacking in innovation. The Civil Service came in for her closest attention and Lord Rayner was hired from Marks & Spencer to introduce radical reforms. The NHS, being the country's largest employer was another obvious candidate for reform.

Roy Griffiths, managing director of Sainsbury's was engaged to carry out a review of the management structure of the NHS. He reported in 1983. The Griffiths report was highly critical of the way the service was being run. Among his criticisms were:

- The NHS was extremely inefficiently run.
- There was a lack of decisive management.
- Too many spending decisions were made on an *ad hoc* basis and took little account of how to provide value for money and how to deal with the needs of patients on a rational basis.
- He told doctors that they had to play a bigger role in management. In return for the freedom they enjoyed in clinical decision making, they were required to look at the broader management needs of the system.
- He recommended a comprehensive management structure to be put in place in all levels of the NHS. The new managers would be charged with the job of making savings through greater efficiency and of ensuring that expenditure should be focused more effectively on patient care.

- Management was to be conducted by a combination of executives recruited from outside and of doctors who made themselves available for this role.

The management bureaucracy which Griffiths created might have solved most of the NHS's problems, just as the Rayner reforms had transformed the Civil Service. Unfortunately for him and for the government, another funding crisis hit the service in the mid-1980s so it became difficult to establish whether the new system was working. More certainly, the introduction of a professional management hierarchy has been controversial ever since. Doctors, nurses and other health workers have always criticised the interference of managers in their medical decision making. The managers themselves have also been accused of eating up large proportions of NHS funding. Ironically, in other words, the very management system which was designed to save money and improve efficiency, itself became the cause of wastage.

The internal market

By 1987, not long after the Griffiths structure had been introduced, a major funding crisis struck the NHS. As we have seen above this was the result of a squeeze on the service whereby the government was reluctant to raise spending as this would put pressure on taxpayers, while demand for health care was growing alarmingly. More radical measures were needed.

Better prevention of illnesses was the first method which was suggested to take the financial pressure off the NHS. In 1987 general practitioners (GPs) were given budgets for more inoculations against serious disease, for regular check-ups on older patients and on disease early screening systems. But the effects of these schemes would not be felt for some years to come. The crisis was a short-term problem for the government.

The fundamental problem for the NHS, as with many public services, was that it was never likely to be as efficient as private enterprise because it was not subject to the kind of competition which breeds such efficiency. Despite this, Conservative governments of the 1980s tended to judge the performance of public services against the private sector. So the question was: how was it possible to subject a public service to the disciplines of the market without actually privatising it?

A White Paper, published in 1989, entitled 'Working for Patients' seemed to have the answer. This was a complicated set of proposals, but its principle was relatively simple. The NHS was to split into two halves. One half would be known as **purchasers**, and the other half as **providers**. This division would imitate a normal market situation where there are buyers and sellers. As long as the purchasers had a choice of providers, it could be expected that they would look for the best value for money. Any savings made by purchasers could be used as an incentive, so that they would pursue even more savings.

The two halves of the system were: **providers** – NHS trusts, special health authorities, non-fundholding GPs – and **purchasers** – Health authorities, GP fundholders.

The **providers** were of three types:

1 *NHS trusts* were groups of hospitals, clinics and other services run by a non-profit-making trust. They provided treatments at a price which was to be paid by purchasers. The trusts were run by professional managers and other representatives from the local community and from the medical profession. As they were in competition with others, they would have the discipline of the market to contend with. The penalty for not competing successfully would be contraction in size, less funding and even closure. The rewards for doing well and selling their services successfully would be increased funds and the possibilities of expansion.

2 *Special health authorities* are a variety of specialised organisations such as blood services and teaching hospitals. They provide some of the services not available through the trusts.

3 *Non fundholding GPs.* These were family doctors who chose to stay outside the system. They were given separate contracts to deal with patients on the basis of a fixed annual payment and a 'capitation' allowance which depended on how many patients they had on their books. About 60 per cent of their income depended on how many patients they had.

There were two kinds of **purchasers**:

1 *Health authorities* receive their funding from the government. They purchase services from hospitals, clinics etc. to provide health programmes within their districts, including accident and emergency and long-term treatments. In order to maximise the use of their funding they would search for the best deal from providers.

2 *GP fundholders* applied for, and were given annual budgets with which they were to run their surgeries, received a salary and could purchase hospital and other treatment services from providers. Like health authorities they would look for the best value for money. As an incentive their incomes could be increased by using their budgets more effectively. The more patients for whom they could find treatment and the better the financial deal they could get, the more healthy their income.

The system was duly set up by the **NHS and Community Care Act of 1990**, under the control of Health Minister of the day, Kenneth Clarke. The medical profession was uneasy about the changes and it was difficult to persuade doctors to become fundholders and hospitals to form themselves into trusts. Gradually over the next few years, however, the internal market was introduced.

Two other measures were introduced at this time. Firstly, charges were introduced for most eye tests and for dental checks. This effectively meant that eye and dental services were mainly privatised, but that the poor, children and the elderly would have their treatments paid for by the state.

Secondly, a number of community health services were transferred to the responsibility of local authorities. At first sight this may have been nothing more than a transfer of responsibility and funding. However, at the same time that the transfer was taking place, increasing pressure was being placed on local authority finances. This meant that community health services had to be reduced.

The most notorious example was the so-called **care in the community** scheme. This policy closed down many of the mental hospitals which were dealing with patients who had long-term, low-level mental health problems. They were transferred into community hostels or even into private accommodation. This much cheaper solution saved money and, it was claimed, provided better conditions for the mentally ill. However, many mental health interest groups did not agree and many residents complained that they were being plagued by homeless vagrants, often with drug problems.

A review of Conservative policies, 1979–97

Nobody could accuse Conservative administrations under Thatcher and Major of not trying to reform the NHS while they were in power. They were, of course, constrained by the fact that a fundamental change in the way in which the NHS is funded was politically unacceptable. It was therefore the case that the performance of the health service was always going to be at the mercy of economic forces. As long as health is funded from general taxation, it will be affected by the broader economic policies of the government.

Some have argues that the system of the internal market was actually a first step to privatisation. In other words, had the Conservatives remained in power after 1997, it is suggested that this would have been the next step. Indeed on the day before the 1997 election, the Labour party produced the slogan *24 Hours to Save the NHS*. It proved to be one of the keys to their election victory. Naturally, the Conservative party has always denied this, but there can be no disguising their frustrations at being unable to find new sources of funding.

To replace extra financial support the Conservatives tried these measures:
1 new management techniques;
2 a new management structure;
3 the internal market;
4 the transfer of some community health services to local authorities.

Yet despite these innovations, health care was seen as a service in crisis. New Labour was elected in 1997 partly in the hope that it could get to grips with the problems. Many of these hopes, however, were soon to be dashed.

NEW LABOUR AND HEALTH

Basic principles

1 The first assertion to make about the experience of Labour governments since 1997 is that it remains committed to the basic principles of the National Health Service. The party leadership could never carry the membership with it if it looked to change the method of funding. Nor could it persuade public opinion to accept it. Opinion polls consistently show that people place the principles of the NHS high on their list of priorities. In spite of the many criticisms which have emerged since the early 1980s, few people wish to replace it with something else.

2 If the NHS is to continue to be funded out of general taxation it will always be the subject of difficult choices which government has to make between competing demands placed on taxpayers' money. Unless its funding could be separated from the general government budget, this will always be true.

3 The Labour government's 1997 commitment to stick to existing Conservative spending plans meant that the NHS would continue to be modestly funded. Any significant improvements to the service were, therefore, inevitably put 'on hold' for the first three years of the new government.

4 The Chancellor of the Exchequer, Gordon Brown, is fundamentally committed to the maintenance and improvement of health care in Britain. This is not merely a preference on his part, it is a part of his basic philosophy. It is therefore inevitable that, as long as Brown remains Chancellor, he will attempt to protect the NHS from fluctuations in the economy.

5 By 2001 all main political parties joined a consensus that the NHS is seriously under-funded and that taxpayers will ultimately have to accept that they must expect to pay for large increases in expenditure.

So, in many ways, New Labour was subject to a similar array of constraints to those experienced by the Conservatives in the 1980s and 1990s.

Early changes

The first task of the Labour government in 1997 was to abolish the internal market. However, they did not dismantle the whole system. There were still to be purchasers and providers. However, the new system was designed to reduce the amount of competition which was taking place. Reducing the competitive system had several aims:

1 It was felt that the internal market created a large amount of paperwork and bureaucracy. This was expensive and time consuming, diverting attention away from patient care.
2 Competition did not necessarily provide the best system of care. For example, the trusts had been expected to provide and compete for business in *all services*. This prevented them from specialising in the types of care at which they were best.
3 The Fundholding GPs were also engaged in a competitive system which did not recognise the general patterns of health care needed in their communities. For example in some areas care of the elderly is a priority, in others it is children, in some localities there is a young, transient population.

Therefore the whole system became more flexible. This is especially true of primary care – mainly the work of GPs. A new kind of organisation is coming into existence, known as **primary care trusts**. These are groups of GPs covering about 200,000 patients each. These trusts will provide primary health care, including minor operations and nursing services. They will also purchase. It is hoped and believed that these large primary care groups will come to understand better the needs of patients and will therefore direct the work of the higher tier of care – hospitals, acute units, accident and emergency etc. more effectively.

The trusts which continue to be the providers of treatments, are required to co-operate rather than compete with one another. They must still earn their funding by selling services to GPs and to health authorities and so are in a kind of 'market' situation, but they are less reliant on their ability to generate large volumes of business.

Funding

As we have seen, large increases in health service funding were not forth-coming in 1997–2000. Whatever his inclinations, Chancellor Brown's determination to control spending and to pay back public debt took precedence.

After 2000, however, he found himself free to spend some of the large amounts of expenditure he had available to him. The British economy was healthy, tax revenues were rising as a result of economic growth and the calls on expenditure from unemployment and social security were falling. Brown was therefore able to announce the beginning of a long-term programme of expenditure increases. In general there is a five-year plan to raise spending on the NHS by at least three times the rate of inflation.

Tony Blair in 2001 made an ambitious pledge to bring health spending, as a proportion of the country's total income, up to typical European standards. Economic forecasters immediately cast doubt on this commitment. Long-term underspending has taken its toll. It is also unlikely that Britain will be able to compete with systems like the French, which is topped up by extensive charging and private insurance schemes. Using the example of Scandinavian countries, where the state does fully fund the health service, British taxes would have to rise alarmingly. The taxpayers of countries like Sweden and Norway are used to paying for first-class public services with very high income tax rates. Their British counterparts are unlikely to accept such a regime.

Nevertheless, a long-term spending plan is in place and there is a strong commitment to maintain it. Indeed, to deal with the frustrations of waiting for increased spending to 'kick in', as it takes so long to train additional health professionals, the NHs has been allowed to recruit doctors and nurses from abroad.

Blair and Brown have staked the future electoral prospects of their party on improved health services. The future funding of the NHS does, therefore, appear to be 'ring fenced' until 2006.

Further reforms

The Labour party, with the reformer Alan Milburn as Health Secretary, has tried to be as innovative as the Thatcher governments of the 1980s. Apart from the changes to the internal market and the increased funding commitment, they have introduced the following developments:
- The private sector should be used to provide investment in the health service. Private companies will be offered the opportunity to invest in and manage NHS properties in return for management fees. The existing policy of offering some non-medical services to private-sector firms in competition with the NHS will continue and be extended.
- Where there are acute waiting lists for standard treatments, NHS authorities are allowed to use private health sector facilities, paying for them out of their own funds. In some cases they have also been allowed to send patients abroad for treatment.
- Following a number of problems emerging in the care offered by particular hospitals and individual doctors, consultants and surgeons, performance tables for both hospitals and individual doctors are to be introduced. The **Kennedy Report** into events in the heart surgery services at Bristol Royal Infirmary, led to the introduction of performance statistics concerning individual surgeons to be published.
- Hospitals are to be given star ratings so that patients can judge which are high performing and which are failing.

- Where Health Service trusts are seen to be failing, they may be taken over by other bodies including charities and private companies.
- The more successful trusts will be given the opportunity to become more independent from government, allowing them to develop new services and involve the private sector

New institutions

Two particular bodies were set up soon after Labour was elected in 1997 and are expected to make an impact in health care in the long run:

- *The Commission for Health Improvement (CHI).* This is a permanent body which is dedicated to finding ways of improving care for patients. It can investigate the work of hospitals and trusts. Suggesting ways in which they can improve. It also advises the government on any new innovations which might improve health care in general.
- *The National Institute for Clinical Excellence (NICE).* NICE was a response to the problem of expensive new drugs becoming available, but hard-pressed health authorities being unable or unwilling to buy them for their patients. This problem, sometimes known as the *postcode lottery,* meant that treatments were available in some parts of the country but not others. The new regime means that, if NICE decides that a new drug is effective and provides value for money, it should become available to all.

These and a number of other new agencies are designed to try to make rational decisions about health care, rather than allowing health authorities to make decisions on an individual, *ad hoc* basis.

The principles of Labour policies

Amid all the many innovations and initiatives which New Labour has produced since 1997 it is possible to discern a number of principles which inform their policy making. Among them are the following:

- All those involved in the Health Service – doctors, other health workers, hospitals, clinics etc. – are to be more accountable both for the standard of service they give and the way they spend money. Workers in the Health Service must accept that, in return for greater staff recruitment and more expenditure, they must be more responsible for what they do.
- There is no reason why the private sector cannot be used if it does not interfere with two principles: that services are provided free according to need, and that it improves services to the patient.
- The country has to accept that it must spend a significantly higher proportion of its national income and public expenditure on health care.
- Primary health care is critical to performance. GP services must, therefore, be improved and be made more sensitive to needs.

- Health Care is a government priority. If it fails to deliver significant improvements in terms of more treatments, shorter waiting lists and reduced waiting times for treatment, it will have to accept the electoral consequences.

Some criticisms

Despite the political consensus which has developed over health, a number of important criticisms have been levied against Labour's policies. Among them are:

- It waited too long to increase funding significantly.
- Having begun the process of increasing expenditure, it is still not devoting enough funds to make a significant difference.
- Constant reforms, and the drive to make health workers and hospitals more accountable has sapped morale in health professions.
- The government has failed to tackle fundamental problems in the career structure of doctors. Nurses have been given a better structure with the development of senior nurse practitioners and consultants, but doctors have been left behind.
- The government has failed to address problems in management, including excessive bureaucracy, inefficiency and wastefulness.

These are familiar themes. Some can be detected in the 1970s and 1980s. It is clear that problems in the provision of health care are likely to be with us for some time.

CONCLUSION: THE FUNDAMENTAL PROBLEMS

Having reviewed the course of health policy since the 1970s we can now identify the major problems which have dogged *all* governments over the issue. There are, in other words, fundamental elements of health policy which make it an especially difficult aspect of governance. The evidence suggests the following features.

1 As long as health care is paid for out of general taxation it has to compete with other demands on government, such as social security, local government services, defence, transport etc. Health care, of course, is always likely to be a high priority, but it is inevitably a target when public spending is reviewed. Reducing health expenditure levels does not show up immediately in the way that social security benefit cuts, for example, do. Furthermore, if the minister responsible is relatively weak and fails to battle effectively for a fair share of the government's budget, the service will suffer.

2 For the same reason, health expenditure depends on the economic state of the country. In a recession tax revenues fall but social security payments and industrial support payments rise. It is a brave Chancellor or Health Minister who is able to maintain or increase real levels of spending on health in a time of recession.

3 It is almost inevitable that public expectations of what the health service can deliver will continue to rise. Furthermore, this rise in expectations has also tended to outstrip the NHS's ability to deliver. As prosperity increases, health care is one of the benefits which people expect.

4 As new treatments come on line for such illnesses as cancer, heart disease, strokes and arthritis, the calls on health expenditure are bound to increase. Keeping people alive longer is an important objective for the health service, of course, but it does mean that individuals are tending to consume more medical care over their lifetime. Many of the new treatments are also very expensive and so create a need to review priorities. The case of Interferon is a typical example. This drug which can help with nervous diseases such as multiple sclerosis, is exceptionally expensive but can benefit a small number of people a great deal. Health care professionals and politicians find it extremely difficult to decide whether this is a good use of scarce resources. There will always be a temptation to buy cheaper treatments which will bring down waiting lists and so make the newspaper headlines. It is also attractive to develop treatments which will benefit the many rather than the few.

5 Health is a policy area which is inhabited by a large number of powerful and vociferous pressure groups. There are the medical groups such as the British Medical Association (BMA), the Royal College of Nursing (RCN) and the Royal College of Surgeons (RCS), unions representing other health service workers, mainly UNISON and there is a veritable army of interest groups representing sufferers from every major disease and condition. From a democratic, representative point of view this is a very healthy state of affairs. However, for policy makers it presents special problems. Virtually every decision, especially those about the allocation of funds, will please some and anger others. Only by spending more across the board – an unlikely option – can everybody be kept happy.

6 As we have remarked before, the British population is ageing. An increasingly greater proportion of the population is old (see table 3.1). Older people naturally place a heavier burden on medical services. Furthermore, they also contribute less to tax revenues: their incomes fall as they become pensioners. So the dependency ratio is worsening: fewer and fewer people are having to support the health care of more and more. Table 3.2 illustrates the growth in NHS provision.

So it seems that future governments will face the same problems in this field as their predecessors. It may be that the battle to preserve the basic principles of a free service funded out of taxation will eventually be lost and individuals will be forced to make additional contributions in addition to public funding.

Table 3.1 Britain's ageing population: proportion of the UK population aged 65 and above, as % of total

Year	% 65 and above	% 75 and above
1901	10	3
1931	15	4
1961	23	8
1991	31	14
2000	31	14
2011 (estimate)	33	15
2025 (estimate)	41	20

Source: Office of National Statistics.

Table 3.2 Increases in health provision: employment of NHS staff (000s)

Year	Hospital and community staff	GPs	Dentists
1981	601	27	15
1991	639	31	18
2000	676	37	21

Source: Department of Health.

SAMPLE QUESTIONS

1 Why has the provision of health care proved to be a problematic area for policy making since 1979?

2 To what extent have the basic principles of the National Health Service been eroded since 1979?

3 In what ways has the Labour government since 1997 attempted to make health a higher priority?

4 To what extent has there been a consensus on health policy since 1979?

Education

4

➤ The background to education after World War II

➤ The principles of the 1944 Education Act

➤ The change to comprehensive schooling

➤ Analysis of Conservative policy in the 1980s

➤ The importance of the 1988 Education Act

➤ The effects of the National Curriculum, testing and league tables

➤ New Labour policies on education

Until World War II the involvement of the state in British education has been variable and, at times, has even seemed reluctant. Being fundamentally a liberal culture, there has been a fear that state intervention might jeopardise the free and independent nature of much of what went on in education at all levels. Independent schools were, as their name suggested, largely free of external interference, Church schools, meanwhile retained their own form of autonomy. Catholic schools drew authority from their own Church, while the Church of England sought to retain its independence from influence by the secular state. Schools which were secular (i.e. non-religious) were also substantially free from at least *central* state control. Instead they were overseen by local boards and authorities, which were subject to local democracy. At university level, too, institutions fiercely retained their right to set their own educational agendas.

Since 1944, however, the history of education in Britain has been one of increasing centralised state control and interference. This was the result of two factors. Firstly, there was a growing understanding that education could be used as a tool of social and economic policy. There was a growing need to ensure that each new generation should have a wide range of knowledge and skills in an ever more complex economy. At the same time, the social pressures on individuals were becoming more significant as society as a whole was growing more complex. Secondly, the steady decline in religious observance and in the integrity of family life threatened to create a vacuum in the transmission of values and morality from one generation to the next. Education was increasingly viewed as a way of filling this vacuum.

In summary, therefore, we can say that the second half of the twentieth century has seen a whole new set of responsibilities placed on the education system at all levels. These can be described as follows.

- Schools are now seen as a key vehicle for the transmission of morality and cultural values. As family life has begun to break down and Church membership has slipped away, there was a need for schools to take up the reins. Recent initiatives in PSHE (Personal, Social and Health Education) and in citizenship are important examples of this process.

- Industry and commerce are becoming increasingly demanding. Globalisation is a part of this development. Education at all levels has had to respond to these new pressures. The 16–18 age group (tertiary) and post-18 education (higher and degree level) have been particularly important in this area.

- Growing levels of crime and public disorder since the 1970s have resulted in a new interest in the role of schooling. Whatever the causes of increased criminal behaviour, especially among the young, it is believed that education can play a key role in reversing the trend. This is particularly true of pre-school and primary education, which take place when children are developing their social characteristics.

- Education has been seen since the middle of the nineteenth century as an important vehicle for the principle of equality of opportunity. A good education is considered a gateway for all to seek success and prosperity. After World War II the pressure for true equality of opportunity (it had always been limited up to that time) grew. It was part of the broader philosophy of the Welfare State, as described in the 1942 Beveridge Report. The post-war consensus included the principle that a modern society must give *all* its citizens the chance of a decent standard of living.

THE TRIPARTITE SYSTEM

The system

The logical place to begin a review of modern education in Britain has to be the passage of the 1944 Education Act. This should be seen as part of the process of re-building post-war Britain, a task which was the subject of much agreement between the political parties. It was sponsored by R.A. Butler (and is sometimes known as the 'Butler Act'), the Conservative Education minister in the all-party coalition of the day. The principles and intentions of the Act were as follows:

1 The 'Board of Education' (of which Butler had been 'president') was dissolved and replaced by a Ministry of Education. This administrative device symbolised the desire, described in the introduction above, to bring education much more firmly under state control. It also raised the profile of education policy.

2 A firm dividing line was established between 'primary' and 'secondary' education. This had varied in the past, but it was now to be regarded as 11 years of age. All school children who were outside the independent sector, were to be tested in an examination known as the '11-plus'.

3 Free primary and secondary education was to be available for all between the ages of 5 and 15 (raised to 16 in 1973). Parents could still opt to send their children to fee-paying, independent schools, but there was no compulsion to pay in any state school. The actual 'type' of education offered at post-11 level, was to be determined by ability, not income.

4 Three types of secondary school were to be established. This is the origin of the term 'tripartite system'. Grammar schools were to take off the top 25 per cent (approximately) of the range. This was the group which came in the top levels of the 11-plus exam, based on literacy, numeracy and general intelligence (known as IQ: Intelligence Quotient). It was assumed that this group would go on to fill the professions, managerial posts, government service and other 'middle-class' occupations. Most of the rest would attend 'secondary modern' schools. These would be given a solid, but basic education in literacy and numeracy, but would also develop technical, manual skills. They would also not expect to take any examinations at the end of their school career. These pupils would probably go into manual occupations at various skill levels, or into lower levels of 'office work'. Girls at that time were, of course, largely prepared for parenthood and home-making at secondary moderns. A small number of technical schools were also set up. These were for children displaying special abilities in manual skills. It was hoped they would provide early training for more skilled workers. In the event very few technical schools were established. Much of the requirements for such skills training were left to post-16 colleges and on-the-job apprenticeships.

The importance of the tripartite system

Remnants of the system which was set up in 1944 still remain in British education. The split at 11 years old still endures, though there are also some 'middle schools' which span this age. Education remains substantially free. A few secondary schools have introduced 'voluntary' contributions from parents, but this is rare and no state school makes a compulsory charge for normal tuition. There are also some grammar schools still in existence. These select their pupils at 11, though there is no national examination. Grammar schools have their own selection procedures. Such schools are most common in Kent, Essex, the north west and parts of central southern England.

On the whole, however, the tripartite system has now been dismantled. It is, to some extent, symbolic of a class system which is fast disappearing. The grammar schools were filled almost exclusively with middle-class pupils and secondary moderns with the children of the traditional working class. Had it remained in place, it is possible that the more rigid class system which prevailed before the 1960s would have endured longer. Most economists and sociologists are agreed that this would probably have been an undesirable effect. Britain might have failed (even more than it did) to respond to the needs of an ever-more complex economy.

Nevertheless, the experience of the system has had a lasting impression upon British education. Some of its successes have endured even when most secondary schools had become comprehensive by 1980. These include:

- A legacy of excellence in education, especially at post-16 level, which had been established by the grammar schools.
- Many of the grammar schools formed the basis of comprehensive schools through a change in function or amalgamation with secondary modern schools.
- The system of selection at 11-plus provided the basis for the development of the debate about the effects of dividing children on the basis of ability.
- Several generations of working-class children were given the *possibility* of obtaining a highly academic education through the grammar schools. Though relatively few working-class children passed the 11-plus exam, those who did demonstrated the potential for an education system not based upon social class.

Yet the successes of the tripartite system proved to be insufficient to save it, when demands for much greater equality in education grew to a far higher level in the 1960s. The faults in the system were widely seen as follows:

- Although it was designed to provide genuine equality of opportunity, based purely on ability, it failed to do so. Most of the children passing the 11-plus were middle class. This was partly because these children had advantages based on their upbringing rather than their ability and partly because primary schools in working-class areas proved to be inferior to those in wealthier districts. So, rather than breaking down class barriers to equality of opportunity, the system tended to reinforce them.
- The system imposed an artificial threshold – the age of 11 – at which the ability of children was to be judged. Educationalists know, however, that children develop at various speeds. So-called 'late developers', for example, were being rejected simply because they were not ready for the exam at 11. There was a 'safety net' which allowed some children to

transfer to grammar schools at age 13, but by this age most such children had fallen too far behind their counterparts at the grammars to be able to transfer successfully.

- The secondary modern schools were often seen as schools for 'rejects'. Thus the quality of education in them varied greatly and aspirations tended to be low. At the same time the resources devoted to secondary moderns tended to be of lower quality than those enjoyed by grammars. Academic 'failure' tended therefore to be reinforced.
- Too few technical schools were established, so that children with the potential for developing higher skill levels were denied the opportunity to realise their full potential.

COMPREHENSIVE EDUCATION

The Labour governments of 1945–51 presided over the implementation of the 1944 Butler Act. They believed it did represent progress towards a more egalitarian society and so were content to see how well it would work. While out of office between 1951 and 1964, however, the party watched as the system, in their eyes at least, appeared to fail to achieve its stated aims.

Concerns about the effectiveness of tripartism were in other quarters too. The Conservative Minister of Education, David Eccles, was concerned about the lack of progress in standards. He presided over significant increases in education expenditure and introduced an examination – the Certificate of Secondary Education (CSE) – but neither proved to be effective. Meanwhile two investigative reports pointed out the deficiencies of selection at age 11. These were the Crowther Report of 1959 and the Newsom Report of 1963. Eccles was replaced in 1962 by Edward Boyle who set in motion the plans for the fundamental reform of education

The Labour party was also planning a revolution in secondary education. The idea was to introduce an entirely new kind of school – the comprehensive. There had already been some pilot schemes to investigate the idea of comprehensivisation and the early indications were positive. The principles of this were as follows:

- There would be no selection at age 11.
- All children in the state-run system would have the right to attend a school which was organised to cater for all abilities.
- Comprehensive schools would provide a wider range of educational experience than any of the schools in the tripartite system. The experience would include academic, cultural, technical, sporting and moral or religious content.

- They would create circumstances where children from different social backgrounds would mix together. This was believed to enrich the experience of all secondary pupils.
- The mixing of children with different ability levels would 'pull up' the attainment of the weakest without jeopardising the potential of the more able.
- It was assumed that comprehensive schools would usually be larger than existing institutions. Larger schools would provide a much wider range of experience and would benefit from 'economies of scale', thus making them better value for money.
- Above all they would provide genuine equality of opportunity for all.

When Labour won the 1964 election, the new Education Minister, Anthony Crosland, set about the task of abolishing the system of selection. To do so he had to persuade local authorities of the virtues of the new system. It should be pointed out at this stage that, in the 1960s, local government enjoyed considerably more independence than it does today. It was not expected that central government could dictate policy on education, and it was out of the question that legislation should be used to force them into action. Crosland, therefore, could only hope that they would respond to persuasion. He issued a circular (the traditional method of issuing a firm request to a local authority) known as 10/65, the month and year represented in the circular's title. This urged all local education authorities to produce plans for the replacement of selective education as soon as possible.

The circular was largely successful and by 1970 about one-third of all secondary pupils were in comprehensive schools. This represented rapid progress. It was also the result of a growing consensus around the principle of comprehensive education. It was not only Labour councils who were responding. Cajoled by a groundswell of public opinion in favour of reform, even Conservative councils were forced to abolish the grammar school system. Even when Margaret Thatcher became Education Minister (still not a cabinet post) in 1970 the process continued. She withdrew circular 10/65 but could not stem the tide. By 1974, when Labour returned to power, the proportion of children in comprehensives had risen to 60 per cent. A further five years of Labour administration saw only eight local authorities holding out against reform. They accounted for most of a remaining 150 grammar schools in existence. The year 1979, therefore, represents the high point of the comprehensive era.

We should not leave the comprehensive issue without reference to the Inner London Education Authority (ILEA). The ILEA was created in 1965 as a great experiment in the power of education to compensate social disadvantage. Comprehensive education was designed to create equal opportunity for all children. However, it was recognised that even this could not compensate for a child's deprived background. The ILEA was a single education authority comprising the twelve inner London boroughs, where deprivation was at its most severe. It was granted higher than normal levels of funding by central government to provide for smaller classes, additional resources and facilities for children with special educational needs. By doing this, it was hoped that a lavish educational provision would compensate children for poor home backgrounds including poverty, bad housing, broken families and low aspirations. In effect, it was comprehensive education plus. It was an attempt to provide *positive* discrimination in favour of the deprived and not just equal opportunity.

The ILEA experiment was never seen through to fruition. Its opponents regarded it as a product of left-wing education policies, while its supporters always felt it was not fully funded. Under the Conservatives in the 1980s it certainly lost its privileged status and it was finally dissolved in 1990 as one of the last acts in the consistent Conservative attack on local government independence.

Comprehensive schooling has remained the backbone of the British education system. In the 1990s a number of local authorities began to re-introduce selective education, although the number of grammar schools remained modest. Nevertheless, as standards in education continued to be criticised there were increased calls for the return of selection at age 11. The Labour party, preparing itself for government in the mid-1990s, declared through its spokesman, David Blunkett, that the party would never introduce selection. By 1997, however, Blunkett had to concede that public opinion in some areas was running strongly in favour of more grammar schools. The 1988 Education Reform Act, which is described more fully below, had allowed some schools to opt out of local authority control and become independent with funding direct from central government. This also allowed them to introduce a limited degree of selection. The new Labour government was forced to compromise on the issue. Blunkett allowed referendums among the parents of prospective pupils to determine whether selective grammar schools should be established. This quietened the demands for more selection, but had little effect. Most referendums failed to approve selective systems. The comprehensive principle, therefore, remained pre-eminent.

RAISING STANDARDS IN THE 1990s

The problem of falling standards

In 1997 a White Paper was issued by the new Labour government entitled, *Excellence in Schools*. The document declared that, *Standards matter more than structures*. This marked the end of the main debate about the structure of education. It confirmed an idea that had been growing steadily since the late 1960s. This was that educational standards were a more complex problem than had been appreciated before. Changing the nature of schools was not enough. A fresh outlook on the whole philosophy of how education was delivered was needed.

The opening shots had been fired in 1968 with the publication of a series of reports written by right-wing academics known as the 'Black Papers'. At first they were treated with scepticism. The Black Papers blamed left-wing ideas and so-called 'progressive' teaching methods which had taken root in the new comprehensives for declining standards. But they were seen as reactionary documents, out of touch with modern thinking. Yet these concerns would not go away. A report for the Conservatives, known as the 'Yellow Book' appeared in 1976. It reiterated many of the concerns of the Black Papers. The Yellow Book proposed a return to traditional methods of teaching and a return to increased discipline in schools. The Conservative party rejected its findings publicly, but their influence took root in the party.

When the Conservatives returned to power in 1979 the problems in education were perceived as follows:

- As the Yellow Book had suggested progressive teaching methods were blamed for poor levels of basic literacy and numeracy.
- Education had been run for many years by teachers and other academics. It was seen as preferable that some 'outsiders' should be brought in to bring a clearer perspective on the problems.
- There was too much interference in schools by local authorities, many of which were under left-wing control. These politicians were seen as more motivated by politics than by educational concerns.
- There was a great deal of variation in standards of education in different parts of the country and localities.

For much of the 1980s the debate on educational standards centred on the possibility of introducing competition among schools. The idea that competition creates the incentive to raise efficiency and equality was the preferred policy for other public services such as the nationalised industries (which were mostly being privatised), local government operations, health care and public transport. The question was, could the same principle be applied in the field of education?

In order to do so it would almost certainly be necessary to privatise schools in some way, but this would destroy the principle of free education for all children. The proposed answer was the so-called *voucher system*. Each parent would be given a voucher for the education of each child. This would be enough to pay for a standard form of schooling. However, parents with spare income would be able to 'top up' the voucher and send their children to a more expensive school. Since parents would have an entirely free choice of schools there would be competition for pupils. In this way the requirements of both free education for all and competition would be satisfied.

In the event the Conservative party rejected the voucher scheme. Even for a government fully committed to free market solutions, the voucher scheme was seen as too divisive and would not have enjoyed enough public support. Something different was therefore needed. This emerged with the *Education Reform Act of 1988*. This was probably the most important piece of educational legislation since the 1944 Act.

The Education Reform Act 1988

The Act was not just about standards, but its chief thrust was directed at the problem. Its main provisions were as follows.

- There was to be a **National Curriculum** (NC) established. This would apply to all state schools (independent schools were exempt) for children aged from 5 to 16. The NC prescribed a number of subjects to be taught to all to a specific standard. At certain **key stages** a number of educational objectives were to be achieved. These ages were:
  - Key stage 1:   7 years
  - Key stage 2:   11 years
  - Key stage 3:   14 years
  - Key stage 4:   16 years

- The traditional subjects of English, Maths, Sciences, Physical Education, Geography, Religious Education, Art and History were emphasised and only a small amount of time was made available for schools to choose their own variations. This was very much inspired by systems which are common in the rest of Europe.

- All secondary and primary schools would be taken out of the direct financial control of local authorities. Instead the budgets (and therefore effectively the management as a whole) would be handled by the head teacher and governors. This process, known as **Local Management of Schools (LMS)**, was designed to address the problem of schools being used by local politicians to further their own aims.

- All secondary and some large primary schools were given the opportunity to opt out of local authority control altogether. Instead they could be given **grant maintained status**. This would mean that they would receive funding direct from central government. In addition, they would be allowed to adopt some of their own practices such as a limited degree of selection at age 11.

THE EFFECTS OF THE REFORMS

The 1988 Act and the policies which flowed from it have had a profound effect on schooling in Britain. It has done what was intended, in that there is now genuine competition between schools. It has also created standards by which the performance of local authorities, schools, teachers and pupils can be judged. It has also wrested most control out of the hands of local authorities. At the same time schools are much more closely controlled by parents, governors and headteachers. This independence was seen as essential if schools were to pursue targets.

On the other hand the reforms also had unwanted effects. Some of these have been:

1 The teaching profession has been placed under enormous strain. Teachers complain about constant change in the way schools and the curriculum are organised and of greater workloads in recording test results and National Curriculum progress. The introduction of the Office for Standards in Education (OFSTED) has also been stressful on teachers and heads.

2 The variety of school curriculums has been reduced. Cultural, artistic and sporting activities have tended to be pushed out by traditional subjects and teaching methods.

3 While league tables and testing have allowed parents to judge between schools, the system has been divisive. Low-performing schools have been starved of better pupils and so find it difficult to improve.

4 Regular testing has placed increasing stresses on the children. It has been said that testing has introduced 'selection by stealth'.

NEW LABOUR: EDUCATION, EDUCATION, EDUCATION

On his election in 1997, Tony Blair declared that education was to be the flagship policy of New Labour. By talking about the three priorities, 'Education, education and education', he meant a number of things.

Firstly, he insisted that Britain needed a well educated workforce if it was to compete in an increasingly globalised world, where high levels of skill, knowledge and flexibility will be at a premium. Secondly, he felt that good education was the key to eliminating such problems as youth crime, long-term unemployment and poverty. Thirdly he argued that education was the key to equality of opportunity. In a just society, he asserted, everybody should be given the chance to make a good life for themselves.

Unfortunately, the tight economic stance which Gordon Brown adopted between 1997 and 2000 meant that progress on education was slow. However, by concentrating on primary and pre-school education, a start could be made. The measures which were introduced under Secretary of State for Education, David Blunkett were:

- Specific targets for schools to achieve. These involved bringing children up to minimum levels in standard tests for literacy, numeracy and science.
- Increased spending on information technology – seen as a key factor in improved education.
- The introduction of a 'literacy hour' and 'numeracy hour' in primary schools, ensuring that a minimum amount of time was devoted to English and Maths.
- Incentives for schools to improve their performance by introducing 'beacon' status. Beacon status schools may be rewarded with higher salaries and increased staff.
- Sanctions against failing schools and local authorities, including the ultimate threat of closure or transfer of management to state inspectors or even private management companies.
- Greater parental choice of schools to introduce an element of competition.
- A limited form of payment by results was introduced for teachers. Teachers with a good record could apply for substantial increases in salary.
- A guaranteed income, of at least £6,000 per year, was introduced for trainee teachers. This had the effect of increasing recruitment.
- There were general rises in pay.

Despite continuing problems with recruitment and retention and despite the continuing low morale of the teaching profession, improvements in the performance of most primary schools did follow. There were continuing concerns over truancy, behaviour of young pupils and racial difficulties, but the government could point to higher educational standards in 7 to 11-year olds.

EARLY YEARS EDUCATION

The idea of providing pre-school education for all children has long been a cherished goal of the Labour party. Blunkett was able to deliver this. Indeed, not only did all 4-year olds have a place in school by 2001, but progress had been made in supplying places in nurseries for 3-year olds.

A programme known as 'head start' became a key element in social exclusion policy. By taking children from deprived backgrounds, and starting their educational programme as early as possible – ideally at three – it was hoped to counteract the adverse effects of such an upbringing. It was hoped that this would have effects on youth crime levels as well as educational attainment. Its effects are yet to be assessed. In addition, summer schools were introduced so that those who were lagging behind would be able to catch up.

Early years education remains controversial. It is expensive and its effectiveness has yet to be proved. Indeed there are some who believe that early schooling can be positively harmful to some children. Nevertheless, the Labour government has placed much store by it.

HIGHER EDUCATION

It has been in the field of higher education, that Labour governments after 1997 ran into perhaps the greatest difficulty. A number of problems soon emerged:

- The new government in 1997 set itself a target of seeing 40–50 per cent of 18-year olds going on to degree or equivalent level courses. This may have been laudable, but the implications for expenditure on higher education were enormous.
- The costs of higher education were rising, irrespective of the numbers entering. Research and teaching facilities are becoming more and more expensive.
- The universities themselves were experiencing difficulty in recruiting suitable staff.
- The hope that universities would find alternative forms of income to tuition fees was proving to be unrealistic.

As a result of the financial crisis in higher education, the government made a momentous decision soon after coming to power in 1997. This was to introduce a fee of £1,000 per year for most students in order to make up the funding shortfall. Only the poorest families would be exempt. This proved to be exceptionally controversial.

Tuition fees broke a basic principle of the welfare state – that services should be granted free to all. It was also feared that many children from less well-off families would be discouraged from entering higher education. In the event total numbers continued to rise, but the fee burden was proving to be divisive.

So hostile has been the reaction to tuition fees, combined with the inevitable abolition of student grants, having been replaced by subsidised loans, that the whole future of the higher education policy was placed in doubt. By 2002 Scotland had abolished tuition fees and the government was considering restoring a form of student loans. Universities have been forced to find ways of providing better value for money, but there is no doubt that higher education is likely to be a growing financial burden on the Treasury.

CONCLUSIONS AND PROSPECTS

Education, despite the considerable progress which has been made, is riddled with seemingly intractable problems. The Labour government in 2002 was forced to commit growing levels of expenditure to all sectors of education. But money is not the only solution. We can summarise the continuing problems as follows:

- Teacher recruitment is proving very difficult. The numbers in training are growing, but not quickly enough.
- Morale in the teaching profession is stubbornly low. Even large pay increases have not helped. Teachers are concerned by the high general workload, excessive bureaucracy and paperwork, poor behaviour of both pupils and parents, the stress of competition among schools and the pressure to meet targets.
- Although performance of pupils in secondary schools is improving gradually, there are still insufficient numbers staying on at school beyond 16 or going into higher education beyond 18.
- There are major problems of poor behaviour in schools, including widespread truancy in some areas.
- There are wide variations in the standard of schools in different localities.
- The issue of how to fund the fast-growing higher education sector has yet to be solved.

On a more fundamental level, some key issues have yet to be resolved:

1 The issue of whether to allow some selection at 11 or older has not been cleared up. The Labour party has long been opposed to selective education, but is under increasing pressure from parents to allow it.
2 The major problems within the teaching profession, including low pay and status, poor recruitment and retention and career development have not yet been tackled successfully.
3 The Labour party and government (indeed all parties find this difficult) have not come to a firm conclusion on whether more single-faith schools are to be encouraged. In 2002 official policy was to encourage such forms of education and Tony Blair has given it his blessing. However, there are still disagreements between and within parties as to whether Britain should not be pursuing fully integrated education to improve the state of race relations in the country.

Despite the problems, it has to be said that there is a wide degree of political consensus on education. To summarise, we can identify the remaining points of general agreement and those which divide the parties: see table 4.1.

Table 4.1   Education: conflict and consensus

Consensus issues	Issues of conflict
Educational standards need to be raised	Whether to introduce more selective schools
Pre-school education is to be encouraged	How to fund higher education and provide funds for students
More 16-year olds need to be encouraged to stay in education	Whether to encourage or discourage single faith schools
Parents should be able to exercise a good deal of control over schools	Whether to encourage the growth of private education
Schools should be given a high degree of independence	How much private sector funding should be introduced

SAMPLE QUESTIONS

1 To what extent has education been the subject of consensus politics?

2 What have been the main effects of the introduction of the National Curriculum and testing?

3 To what extent has the Labour government since 1997 lived up to Tony Blair's call for 'education, education, education'?

4 What have been the main problems in raising educational standards since 1988?

5 Why, and in what ways, has selection been a major educational issue?

Social security

➤ The principles of social security in the Welfare State

➤ Review of how social security developed up to 1979

➤ Description and analysis of the reforms and new attitude to social security under the Conservatives after 1979

➤ Analysis of New Labour's attitude to social security after 1997

BEVERIDGE: FROM THE CRADLE TO THE GRAVE

The Beveridge Report of 1942 which heralded in the post-war Welfare State proposed a comprehensive **National Insurance** system which would look after people throughout their lives. Benefits were to be supplied by the state for all those who found themselves in need and who had no apparent means of helping themselves. Contributions, through National Insurance, were to be paid by all those in work, whether employed or self-employed. In addition, employers were given a duty to make a contribution for all those whom they employed. National Insurance payments were based on income, although there was an upper total limit on contributions.

> **National Insurance**
> A form of taxation levied on those in work and employers. Based on ability to pay, it has a ceiling so that nobody pays above a certain level. It is designed to pay for welfare benefits.

The Beveridge plan was not a completely novel idea. There was already a form of Welfare State which had come into existence over twenty years before, introduced by Lloyd George. However, the **Beveridge plan** was far more comprehensive and introduced the idea that membership was to be compulsory.

Once World War II was over, the Beveridge plan could be implemented. The system was indeed comprehensive and offered the following benefits:

> **Beveridge plan**
> Named after Lord Beveridge who reported on a future Welfare State in 1942. It proposed a comprehensive state system where all would contribute to services and benefits which would be available to everyone according to need. Benefits would be available to all critical stages of life.

- maternity grants upon the birth of a child;
- family allowances – a weekly payment to be made for each child in a family;
- unemployment benefit;
- widow's benefit;
- pensions for men over 65 and women over 60;
- death grant for the family of the deceased.

This was indeed a comprehensive system, far more than had been seen before in Britain. As time went by, it was added to by all governments. In principle what happened between 1945 and 1979 was that the system ceased to become merely a **safety net** and began, instead, to re-distribute real income from the wealthy, who contributed most, to the poor who contributed least but claimed more.

> **safety net**
> The concept that the state will be there for those who find themselves in need, providing benefits and services.

Additions and reforms of the system came thick and fast and are too numerous to be detailed here. A general review of the landmarks is therefore offered.

The developing social security system, 1945–79

- **1945 Family Allowances Act.** Benefits were to be paid for each child in a family, other than the first.
- **1946 National Insurance Act.** Introduced the basic system. Included pensions for all, sickness benefit for those prevented from working by illness, widow's pension, death grant and unemployment benefit.
- **1956 Family Allowance and National Insurance Act.** Provided for a comprehensive system of tax allowances for dependent children up to age 18.
- **1959 National Insurance Act.** Introduced a graduated system of pensions where both the contributions and payments could be made dependent on a person's income.
- **1966 National Insurance Act.** Introduced a system of unemployment benefit based on a person's earnings at the time they became unemployed. It also made sickness benefit dependent on a person's normal earnings.
- **1966 Ministry of Social Security Act.** Established a new Ministry of Social Security. It also introduced a comprehensive system of supplementary benefits for poor families.
- **1970 Family Income Supplement Act.** Gave a larger entitlement to benefit for poor families.
- **1975 Child Benefit Act.** Replaced tax allowances for families with children with a child benefit to be paid in cash direct to parents.

This extensive list of developments demonstrates the extent to which social security provision was changed and added to by both Labour and Conservative governments. As one would expect, most of the changes were made by

Labour, but the Conservatives played their part, with a key development being the introduction of the graduated, earnings-related pension.

Undoubtedly the most significant changes were made by Labour. The introduction of family income supplements, earnings related sickness and unemployment benefit and extensive child benefits were designed to alleviate poverty and re-distribute real income. They were not dramatic measures, but they demonstrated Labour's wish to use the Welfare State as a means of reducing inequality in society.

SOCIAL SECURITY AND THE CONSERVATIVES AFTER 1979

A new attitude to social security

When the Conservative party won power in 1979 the social security part of their expenditure commitments came under immediate scrutiny. There were five main reasons why this was so.

1 The new government wished to make inroads into the total level of public expenditure. Firstly, it placed a great burden on taxpayers – and they wished to reduce taxes. Secondly, it was seen as a deterrent to private investment as high government borrowing was thought to 'crowd out' funds which could be used by industry and commerce. The social security bill was the biggest single item in the public finances so it was an inevitable target.

2 Margaret Thatcher had pledged to 'roll back the frontiers of the state' when she took office. It was, therefore, natural that a number of social security commitments should be scrutinised with a view to allowing the state to withdraw its support.

3 Many Conservatives believed that a '**dependency culture**' had grown up in Britain. It was suspected that, as people grew to be reliant upon state benefits and learned to expect all kinds of financial support, they would cease to try to fend for themselves. In other words, excessive levels of social security benefit had become a deterrent to enterprise and hard work.

> **dependency culture**
> A Conservative belief that if the state provides too many benefits, people will come to depend on them. This will stifle self-reliance, enterprise and hard work. It also keeps people out of the workforce.

4 An important part of the Conservatives' economic policy was the creation of a more flexible labour market. This meant encouraging more people to seek work, if necessary at relatively low wages. High levels of benefit, it was thought, deterred many people from entering the labour market. As things stood in 1979, it was felt that benefits prevented people from taking low paid jobs.

5 The dependency ratio in Britain was inevitably worsening. This meant that an increasingly large number of people were depending on a shrinking number to contribute to benefits. To some extent this was caused by the ageing population, but it was also caused by high unemployment levels and increasing numbers of poor families. By reducing benefits, the effects of the high dependency ratio would be reduced.

New measures

During the 1980s there was a steady and prolonged attack on dependency culture. Many of the reforms which Labour governments had introduced were dismantled. The main measures were as follows.

The Social Security Acts 1980

There were two pieces of legislation in the new government's first full year of office. The rules for supplementary benefits for poor families were tightened up considerably. It also broke the link between a person's earnings and their level of sickness or unemployment benefit. In other words they reverted to a flat rate. Perhaps most startlingly, the first Act broke the link between the level of the old age pension and the average rise in the level of earnings. Instead, pensions would only be guaranteed to rise by the level of inflation. Since inflation rates are invariably lower than the rise in earnings, this was a major erosion in the level of pensions.

Social Security Act 1982

This required employers to pay a minimum level of sick pay to employees. In effect this eroded the state's responsibility to pay sickness benefit and transferred much of the responsibility to all but the smallest firms.

Social Security Act 1986

This restricted the payments of housing benefit, an important income supplement for poor families who found it difficult to pay rents, by reducing the numbers entitled and by effectively introducing a ceiling on payments. The Act also reduced unemployment benefits to those under the age of 25.

Social Security Act 1988

This took away the young unemployed's entitlement to income support. Instead, they were required to join youth training schemes in order to receive full benefit. This was the beginning of an attack on those young people, who, it was suspected, did not seek work enthusiastically enough.

Social Security Act 1989

This built on the previous year's Act. Entitlement was withdrawn from anybody who was unemployed but could be shown was not making themselves available for work. At the same time, anyone who was unemployed for three months was no longer entitled to turn down *any* job, no matter how poorly paid. This was the principal measure designed to free up labour markets at the lower end of the wage scale.

Statutory Sick Pay Act 1991

The employer's contributions to sick pay were increased and the contributions made by the state were reduced.

Job Seekers' Allowance 1993

This established the principle that unemployment benefit would only be paid to those who were genuinely looking for work and were willing to prove to civil servants that they were actually unemployed. Its effect was to make unemployment benefit more difficult to claim.

The legislation does not tell the full story. Through the 1980s and early 1990s the real value of many benefits was gradually eroded. We have seen that the old age pension was linked to inflation rather than earnings, but other benefits also fell in terms of their real value. Unemployment benefit, sickness and child benefits were all eroded. At the same time some of the benefits which had been paid largely by the state had become the responsibility of employers. For the disabled, too, the welfare regime became tougher. Important tests were introduced to ensure that only those who could prove to medical experts that they were unable to work owing ta a long term disability could claim benefit.

Nevertheless, the story was not all in one direction. Some additions were made to the welfare system. Cold winter payments were introduced for old age pensioners to help with fuel bills, family credits were introduced to allow people to borrow money to buy essential goods and the new income support system for the poor did improve benefits for some families.

ASSESSMENT OF THE CONSERVATIVE REFORMS

Opponents of these, and many other changes to the system of social security have argued that they fundamentally changed the distribution of wealth and income in Britain. The gap between rich and poor was widened and people spoke once again of 'two nations' being created. For some, the changes were seen as little more than an attempt to pay for tax cuts for the middle classes. For the left of the political system it was tantamount to class warfare.

The Labour party, which moved steadily to the left during the first half of the 1980s fought a bitter rearguard action against what they saw as the erosion of the Welfare State. But after their heavy defeat in the general election of 1983, they were powerless to stop the tide. A new pressure group – the **Child Poverty Action Group (CPAG)** came into existence to bolster opposition to the reforms, but they too fought a losing battle.

One of the objectives of governments of the 1980s and 1990s had been to reduce the Social Security Bill and so stabilise the public finances. This aspect of the policy, however, failed. The Social Security Bill rose during most of the 1980s. High unemployment in the first part of the 1980s and 1990s was the main culprit. The pensions commitment rose inexorably, even though the real value of the old age pension was falling. A higher and higher proportion of the population was falling into poverty and so needed support. Thus opponents argued that, while things might be improving for the majority, they were getting worse for a substantial minority and the state was having to foot the bill.

Supporters of the rolling back of the Welfare State and the toughening of the regime could, on the other hand, point to several improvements. The labour market was indeed made more flexible (aided by the successful attacks on trade union power) and unemployment receded during the 1980s. It was also argued that the dependency culture had been broken, that a new set of values was beginning to affect Britain. The 'work ethic' was strengthening and the performance of the economy, especially the so-called 'enterprise culture' had improved.

There was also a strong body of opinion that welfare benefits had become too easy to obtain. Therefore, by toughening the rules and forcing claimants to justify their dependence, a new kind of social justice had arisen.

NEW LABOUR AND SOCIAL SECURITY

There is no doubt that a key element in New Labour's philosophy was to attack poverty in the UK, especially child poverty. Gordon Brown, who was always slightly to the left of most of New Labour's leadership, held this belief especially strongly. Indeed one of the first measures introduced after 1997 was the national minimum wage. This device was to have a double effect. Firstly, it would obviously raise the earnings of a substantial number of workers. But secondly it was also expected to affect the social security budget. Fewer families, it was hoped, would have to claim extra support if they could earn a decent wage. Since its introduction, furthermore, the level of the minimum wage has risen faster than inflation – in other words its real value has increased. Having done this, Brown and the cabinet turned to the social security system.

Welfare to work

This idea was to change public and governmental attitudes to the use of welfare – social security, in particular, completely. The previous Conservative administrations had tried to reduce many benefits on the assumption that this would force more people into the workforce and so make them less dependent on the state. The New Labour plan was to use new welfare policies as an incentive instead of low levels of benefit as a sanction. There would still be a harder regime for those who refused to take up the system of incentives (perhaps even harder than the Conservatives had envisaged).

The change in policy direction came to be known as 'welfare to work' suggesting that the welfare system would help people back into the workforce rather than force them. It was, in other words, to be a carrot rather than a stick

The poverty trap

One of the main problems causing both poverty and unemployment in the UK has been the so-called poverty trap. This phenomenon occurs under a particular set of circumstances. Where nobody in a family is working and they rely on state benefits to live, there may be no incentive for anyone to find employment. If somebody did and began to earn money, the value of the earnings would be instantly eroded by taxation. At the same time the family would begin to *lose* many benefits which are means-tested. With some income coming in, such benefits as housing benefit, school uniform and meals allowances, income support and the like would be lost. The net effect of all this was often that a family was actually *worse off* by working than by not

poverty trap
A situation where families find there is no incentive to find work. The double effect of paying tax and losing benefits when they start work may result in a reduction in net earnings.

working. They were, therefore, in a **poverty trap**. It was a disincentive to work and, for those who nevertheless chose to find employment, it actually increased poverty.

There are essentially three ways to attack the poverty trap:
1 Raise earnings at the lower end of the wage scale. This was partly achieved by introducing the minimum wage.
2 Reduce or eliminate taxation at low earnings levels. To achieve this Brown introduced a new 10 per cent tax band to replace levels of 20 per cent or 22

per cent for low earners.

3 The most difficult measure concerns social security benefits. It was here that the most radical proposals were made by the new Labour government. Though many benefits would continue to be means tested, and therefore lost when a family raised its earnings, a system of **tax credits** could be used. Effectively this meant compensating such families for the loss of benefits and ensuring instead that their effective income level would be increased. This was designed, in the end, to ensure that anyone would gain by seeking and finding employment. It is discussed in more detail below.

> **tax credits**
> A system where the tax authorities actually pay back taxes to poor families. This improves their financial status and can reduce poverty.

The attack on poverty: selective universality

This apparently odd phrase (**selective universality**) has been used to describe the overall social security policies of the post-1997 Labour governments. It suggests a system which is designed to be of general benefit, but which targets action upon poor families, and especially those with children.

> **selective universality**
> A name applied to New Labour's Social Security policies after 1997. It refers to the idea that, although all benefits have been reformed, there is a focus on those groups who are especially in need through no fault of their own.

The main measures which are designed to achieve this targeting are as follows:

- The *working family tax credit* is a system of subsidising families where one or more of their members is earning. It compensates for the loss of benefits as earnings rise. It is designed to achieve an effective minimum level of income for such families. By 2002 this reached £214 per week. The family will actually *receive* money from the inland revenue, rather than simply paying to them.

- A *child tax credit* is also becoming available, again to ensure that working families are rewarded with extra income, rather than punished by the tax system.

- A new *stakeholder pension* scheme was introduced, specially for those unable to take part in private pension schemes. These are discussed below. A number of other measures to help pensioners are also described in the next section.

- Help became available to subsidise the cost of *child care* for working parents. Again this is described below.

- Higher levels of *income support* in general became available for families with children.

We can therefore see that benefits have tended to be aimed mainly at poor families, pensioners and those who have dependent children – traditionally the groups in society who are the poorest. We can now look at some of the measures in a little more detail.

Pensions

Gordon Brown decided at the outset to retain the link between the state pension and the rate of inflation. He resisted calls from his own party and pressure groups such as **Age Concern** and **Help the Aged** to restore the link between pensions and average earnings. This led to perhaps his greatest political error. In 2000, when inflation was at a particularly low level, the index-linked pension rise came to only 75p per week. It had been correctly calculated and Brown claimed that it was fair. But the psychological effect of such a tiny increase was devastating. At one point, indeed, it seemed to threaten the government's re-election prospects.

What had been lost in the political controversy which raged around the increase was the fact that Brown was attempting to target benefits on *poor* pensioners only. The state old age pension was not means tested and paid on an equal basis to all – from dukes to dustmen – as had been said. By raising means tested **minimum income support** for pensioners, he claimed to be helping those who needed the support, rather than everybody. So, even if the real value of the pension was falling, poor pensioners would be protected. By 2003 it is intended to raise the minimum income for a single pensioner to £100 per week, and £154 for a married couple. In addition benefits are available for those with disabilities and chronic illnesses.

But the Brown plan – another example of selective universality – did not convince the doubters. So in 2001 he was forced to give above-inflation pension increases. He also substantially increased the cold weather bonus (now available whatever the weather), the pensioners' Christmas bonus and a free TV licence for those over 75. These measures were successful in heading off opposition and the pensions issues did not affect the general election result.

Labour's other plan for the elderly has been the introduction of the **stakeholder pension**. For those who do not enjoy occupational pension schemes or cannot afford to have their private pensions, the state is now providing its own system. This is designed to 'top up' the state pension, which, as we have seen, is likely to continue to fall back below typical living standards. All large employers must organise a stakeholder pension

> **stakeholder pensions**
> A new system of old age pensions. People may start their own pension plan and will enjoy tax relief on contributions. Every large employer must offer such a scheme to their employees, though they do not have to contribute. It is needed because the value of the state pension is being eroded and the state cannot afford to meet the increasing demands of an ageing population.

scheme for their workers, though they do not have to contribute. The contributions to the stakeholder pension are tax free, though there is a ceiling as to how much can be put into the scheme.

Stakeholder pensions are not designed to replace private schemes – indeed the government encourages them. However, there is a recognition that the state cannot sustain the growing expenditure on the old age pension. Individuals will be forced to make their own additional contributions.

Child poverty

As we have seen, Gordon Brown's main priority has been child poverty. A significant number of measures have been introduced to try to alleviate the problem:

- The real value of child benefit has been increased substantially after over a decade of erosion.
- The state offers up to 70 per cent of the cost of child care to any poor parent who wishes to work.
- Child tax credits are available for poor families.
- Working families with children are now offered substantial income support
- The working families tax credit system, as shown above, is designed to have a major impact on children's welfare.
- Perhaps less directly, but nevertheless creating an impact on poorer families with children, especially lone parents, a place for all 4-year olds is not guaranteed at nursery school. In 2002 it was announced that the government also intended for places for every 3-year old to be available for all parents who needed it. The existence of such places for children is designed to help more parents with child-care responsibilities to seek employment.

Despite the measures and Brown's claim that he has taken hundreds of thousands of children out of poverty, his aim to eradicate the problem altogether is still very far off. Low wages and areas of high unemployment stubbornly refuse to go away and these may have to be the subject of future policies.

> **social exclusion**
> Part of New Labour philosophy. It refers to those who are deprived and have a variety of social problems with a variety of causes. Reforms to the social security system are a part of an overall strategy of reducing social exclusion.

Social exclusion

The term **social exclusion**, a key element of New Labour's philosophy, refers to those groups in society who have been seriously disadvantaged by a variety of circumstances. Some of Labour's Social Security policies have been directed at this problem. Four particular aspects of social exclusion can be used as examples of how welfare policy has been used to try to attack it.

1 **Youth unemployment** has been perhaps the most severe problem. It has given rise to high crime rates, drug use and poverty. To attack it, a new deal was introduced for the young unemployed. It basically gave young people four choices at age 16. They could stay on in education, in which case, if they were from a poor family, benefits would be maintained as an incentive. They could go onto recognised training schemes in which case, again, they would receive benefits. Thirdly, they could seek employment and would receive an allowance while doing so provided they attended training for job seeking and attended designated interviews. Finally they could do none of the above, in which case benefits would be withdrawn.

2 **Lone parents** created problems, both in terms of long-term dependency and the quality of care given to children. They were offered a new deal, like the young unemployed. Those who chose to look after their children would be rewarded with increased benefit. If they opted to seek work, the state would pay for up to 70 per cent of child-care costs so there would be no 'poverty trap' for them.

3 **Child poverty** is a further form of social exclusion. Not only is it seen as an evil *per se*, it also leads to other problems such as low educational attainment, truancy, crime and drug abuse. By eliminating child poverty it is assumed that many of these problems will dissolve.

4 **General unemployment** has been tackled by attempts to reduce the poverty trap as shown above. It is a cause of family poverty, of child poverty and of many other social problems. Clearly, the enduring health of the economy has helped ease unemployment since 1995, but the effects of 'welfare to work' policies may also have been a benefit.

NEW LABOUR: AN ASSESSMENT

In Labour's first term, and after their election victory in 2001, attention has tended to centre upon policies towards public services such as health, transport, education and crime. The failure of the party in these areas has put their future electoral prospects in doubt. This has tended to overshadow the progress they have made in the field of social security. There is no doubt that they have made some progress in reducing inequality and in dealing with poverty. The claims are grand ones and the party has very far to go. It may well be that Gordon Brown has overstated the achievements.

However, there remains some concern that the Labour government's refusal to use the tax system to re-distribute income from rich to poor will mean that progress will be limited. The role of welfare in bringing more people into the workforce and in reducing poverty can only go so far unless Brown is prepared to raise taxes at the top end. There is no immediate prospect of this happening.

Making fundamental social changes is a long-term project. The effects of ending child poverty and social exclusion will only be seen after a new generation has grown up. It is too short a time period to make a final judgement on New labour's performance.

AN OVERVIEW OF WELFARE AND SOCIAL SECURITY

We can usefully divide the post-war period into the folowing four main phases where welfare.

1 *1940s to 1960s*. In this period social security was largely seen as a safety net protecting those who were deprived through no fault of their own. It was also there to provide support for people at times when need is greatest – when children are young, when a person is unemployed, when there is sickness and when people are old.

2 *1960s to 1970s*. When Labour was in power in this period they attempted to use the Welfare State, in combination with direct taxation, as a means of re-distributing income and reducing inequality.

3 *1980s to early 1990s*. This saw the Conservative attack on the dependency culture and their attempt to create a more flexible labour market. Welfare benefits were reduced, partly to prevent too many people relying on the state and partly to prevent cash benefits being used to keep people out of the workforce.

4 *1997 to the present*. This period has seen New Labour's programme of welfare to work and its attack on poverty. Social security was to be used as an incentive for enterprise and for people to seek work, rather than as a safety net or a means by which people could continue to be dependent on the state.

SAMPLE QUESTIONS

1 To what extent have the principles of the Welfare State been eroded by social security changes since 1946?

2 How did the Conservatives seek to end the dependency culture after 1979?

3 How has New Labour attempted to attack poverty after 1997?

4 In what ways has the Labour government after 1997 sought to reduce child poverty?

6

Law and order

➤ Review of the problem of crime in recent decades

➤ Descriptions of the various attempts which have been made to reduce crime since 1979

➤ Analysis of different governments' attitudes to crime

➤ Descriptions of legislation passed to deal with law and order issues

➤ Analysis of theories concerning the causes of crime

➤ Speculation as to how law and order issues may be dealt with in the future

Before examining the political issue of law and order as it has unfolded since 1979, we need to define the scope of the subject. The following elements may be included under the general heading 'law and order'.

- **The system of criminal law**. How can it be kept up to date and used to combat law through conviction and deterrence.

- **Crime and punishment**. What are the most effective ways in which the sentencing of convicted criminals can be used to deter crime, to satisfy the victims of crime and to prevent re-offending.

- **The law courts**. How can they be organised to deal efficiently and effectively with crime.

- **The prison and probation system**. This needs to keep up with demand, ensure security from criminals for the community and to take measures to rehabilitate prisoners and try to avoid re-offending.

- **Policing**. How much should be spent on the service, how many officers should be employed, what equipment should be invested in and how should police forces be managed and deployed to combat crime.

- **How to deal with potential breaches of public order**. This concerns both the laws on public order and also how police are used. It also concerns the circumstances in which public meetings and demonstrations should be banned or curtailed.

- **How to deal with the social and moral causes of crime**.

From time to time all these matters come to the attention of policy makers. Some may be stressed more than others at times, but they are all facets of the same problem.

Although the maintenance of law and order is one of the oldest and most basic functions of government, it has not been one of the main subjects of partisan conflict for most of the modern era in Britain. Crime and public disorder are the concern of all, but usually stand in the background of party politics. This has been for two main reasons:

1 There was a perception that politicians do not have it in their power to control crime levels. Crime was seen as a social problem which is inevitable and whose causes are complex.

2 Until the 1970s, crime levels, or at least known and reported levels of crime did not rise seriously. Nor was fear of crime seen as a major problem. It was rare enough for people to be affected by crime or public disorder so that other issues, such as the economic well-being of the country, foreign policy and welfare policy, were uppermost in their minds when making political judgements.

This led to a circumstance where there was a general consensus on law and order issues. The causes of growing crime rates were social and moral, more the concern of the churches, the schools and the courts than of politicians. The way in which crime could best be combated, all major parties agreed, was to remove the social causes of crime. Prosperity, educational opportunity, high employment and better housing were all seen as the best way of dealing with crime. Breakdowns in public order were, meanwhile, rare events. There had been some race rioting in the 1950s, youth violence in the 1960s, political demonstrations in the late 1960s and some violence during large-scale strikes, but most people were unaffected. The police, too, seemed capable of handling the outbreaks. No special legislation was seen as necessary.

During the 1970s this situation began to change. Crime levels were rising inexorably, especially crimes against property and cars, and violent and sexual offences. This also meant that the fear of crime was growing. Public disorders also grew with large industrial strikes becoming more violent and football hooliganism growing.

An increasingly alarmed public turned to the politicians for solutions. Under this pressure the political consensus on law and order collapsed. The Labour party remained committed to policies which were designed to deal with the social causes of crime. The Conservative party, however, moved steadily towards a harder-line approach. For them the laws needed to be reviewed, police and law courts to be given greater powers' and public disorders controlled. The Liberals (later Liberal Democrats) shared a social view of crime with the Labour party, but also emphasised the threat to human rights of the Conservatives' increasingly severe policies.

The election campaign of 1979 marks a clear end to the consensus. The Labour party was still arguing that economic prosperity and reduced unemployment would solve many of the problems of crime. Restoration of communities, better housing and social services were also seen as basic answers. This was rejected by the Conservatives who actually blamed many of the policies of the Labour government of 1974–79 for the rising crime rate. Labour's 'soft' approach to trade unions led to public disorders. An extremely liberal approach to young offenders – largely replacing custodial sentencing with community work, probation supervision and the involvement of social services with young criminals – was criticised as failing to deal with delinquency. The electorate agreed. Conservative law and order policies were certainly one of the factors which brought them to power.

THE CONSERVATIVES IN POWER, 1979–97

The first seven years of the administration of Margaret Thatcher saw one of the greatest onslaughts on crime and disorder ever seen in Britain. The issue was attacked on all levels. The main developments were as follows:

- There was a steady increase in the size of the police force. Police pay was raised by 16 per cent to raise morale and boost recruitment. Between 1979 and 1984 expenditure on policing more than doubled. From 1979 to 1983 police numbers rose from 110,000 to 120,000 in the UK.
- To meet the demand for greater custodial sentences, eight new prisons and four youth detention centres were built between 1979–84.
- The **Criminal Justice Act** of 1982 gave magistrates much greater powers to imprison offenders and to lengthen sentences. More importantly a system of youth custody for very young offenders was introduced. This policy was known as the **short sharp shock** and was based on a belief that if a young criminal was given a short but strict period of custody it would nip their criminal tendency in the bud. The policy was highly controversial. Many sociologists were convinced it would not work and that the detention centres (sometimes known as 'boot camps') would only be breeding grounds were young offenders would learn crime from older inmates.
- The **Police and Criminal Evidence Act (PACE)** of 1984 marked a considerable increase in police powers. The ability to stop and search those suspected of committing or even contemplating crime was extended. It also became possible to question suspects for extended periods of time with the permission of a magistrate. The compulsory recording of interviews of suspects went some way to balance out the greater questioning powers, but the overall effect of PACE was to change the balance of power markedly in the direction of the police.

- In 1986 the **Public Order Act** was passed. This was a response to the inner city disturbances which had occurred in London, Liverpool, Bristol and other cities, and to the conduct of the miners' strike of 1984 when there was extensive violence around the pits and severe challenges to police peace lines. The Act gave the police extensive powers to prevent marches and demonstrations if they believed that breaches of the peace might result. Rioting itself became a special crime and curbs were introduced on the activities of trade union pickets who may try to prevent non-union workers entering factories and mines.
- New training was introduced for the police, enabling them to become almost a paramilitary force when facing serious public disorder.

These measures, and the general climate of policy makers being hard-line on crime issues, proved to be popular. However, the figures suggest they were unsuccessful. Crime levels continued to grow inexorably (see tables 6.1, 6.2 and 6.3). This led to a re-examination of policies after 1987.

Table 6.1 Crimes reported in the British Crime Survey (millions)

Year	Total crimes	Violent crimes
1981	11.0	2.2
1983	11.9	2.1
1987	13.3	2.3
1991	15.1	2.7
1993	18.6	3.6
1995	19.2	4.1
1997	16.4	3.4
1999	14.7	3.2
2000	12.9	2.6

Source: British Crime Survey.

Table 6.2 Total drugs seizures, 1981–99

Year	Cannabis	Heroin	Ecstasy	Cocaine	Crack
1981	17,227	819	n/a	503	n/a
1991	59,420	2,640	1,735	1,401	583
1995	91,325	6,468	5,513	2,210	1,444
1998	114,667	15,188	4,849	5,207	2,488
1999	97,356	15,108	6,438	5,619	2,436

Source: Home Office.

Table 6.3 Offences per 10,000 people, by age range

Age range	Male	Female
10–15	221	85
16–24	597	123
25–34	250	57
35 +	47	11

Source: Home Office.

1987–93: retreat from the hard line

By 1987 it was apparent that law and order policies, especially those designed to contain the crime rate, were failing. Furthermore there was a complete reappraisal of the hard line approach by policy makers. Attention switched once again to the social causes of crime and to the belief that severe custodial sentences, especially for the young, were ineffective. At the same time a new initiative was developed. This was a community-based approach to crime reduction. The changes which occurred in the period can be summarised as follows:

- Local authorities were given greater responsibility for crime reduction. Improvements in the condition of communities, neighbourhood watch schemes and the idea of **community policing** were all to be undertaken at local government level. Community policing was thought to be particularly important. The policy was that local police forces should become integral parts of their communities, with close links between officers and local agencies, schools, youth groups, tenants organisations etc. By so doing it was hoped that the police would be seen, not as outsiders, but as part of the fabric of local society. It was also expected that local authorities would create schemes for young unemployed and offenders which would provide employment or other projects to divert them from crime.

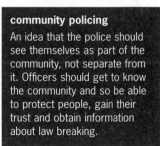

community policing
An idea that the police should see themselves as part of the community, not separate from it. Officers should get to know the community and so be able to protect people, gain their trust and obtain information about law breaking.

- Tough sentencing policies were relaxed. The courts and probation service were encouraged to find alternatives to prison and detention centres. The main device was to be community service and probation orders which were to be more active in attempting to rehabilitate offenders. This policy was legislated in the **Criminal Justice Act 1991**. Judges and magistrates were required to justify prison sentences and only give them in the case of serious crimes.
- There was a steady rise in the number of police officers and probation officers employed.

The course of policy and law and order was hampered considerably by a lack of consensus about how best to stem the alarming rise in crime statistics and by the fact that there was little continuity in policy. There were four different Home Secretaries in the period – Douglas Hurd (1985–89), David Waddington (1989–90), Kenneth Baker (1990–92) and Kenneth Clarke (1992–93) – reflecting the relatively low profile of the issue in the government's political programme. To make matters worse, an economic recession struck the country in 1990. Rising unemployment, which resulted, led to a further leap forward in the crime statistics.

So, by 1993 Conservative policy on law and order appeared to be in disarray. Both the hard line and the community-based approaches seemed to have failed. The party, which normally led Labour comfortably on this issue, began to lose public confidence. It was time for a radical initiative. This was provided by the appointment of Michael Howard as Home Secretary in that year.

The 27-point plan for law and order

When Michael Howard took over as Home Secretary he signalled a complete reversal of Conservative law and order policy. Cynics have argued that this was a response to the unpopularity of the government as it struggled to overcome the effects of a major economic recession. A more objective explanation is that it was the result of continued rises in crime rates and clear public demands for a tougher stance. Youth crime represented a main concern and Howard went a long way to addressing this particular aspect of the problem.

At the Conservative party conference in the autumn of 1993 Howard declared that 'prison works', and criticised his predecessors' policies as being too soft on crime. As the title '27-point plan' suggests his policy was broad and compre-hensive. Its main features were contained in the **Criminal Justice and Public Order Act of 1994** and were as follows:

- To tackle juvenile crime Michael Howard announced the introduction of secure detention centres for 12- to 14-year olds. This group had previously been placed into local authority hands for education and rehabilitation. At the same time magistrates were given powers to give longer custodial sentences to 15- to 16-year olds.
- It had long been a complaint of the police and the courts that the law was weighted in favour of accused persons. The main culprit was the ancient 'right to silence' which allowed suspects and defendants to remain silent without this being allowed to be used against them in court. So, a suspect who refused to answer police questions and/or who refused to testify in court was protected from suspicion on the grounds of silence. The absolute right was, therefore, removed. This marked a change in the criminal law which overturned a centuries-old principle allowing a person to refuse to

answer questions which may incriminate him or her (this is the famous fifth amendment of the United States Constitution). Accused persons who choose to remain silent may have the fact referred to in court and magistrates or juries may take the silence into account when judging guilt.

- The police were given increased powers to limit demonstrations and public meetings. Open-air 'rave' parties were effectively banned, squatting was made a criminal offence, as was trespass on private land. These measures extended police powers greatly and, most controversially, particularly affected young people. They were designed to control the activities of groups of homeless or travelling people who were often seen as a public nuisance and seedbeds of crime.

- The rules on bail were tightened so that it became very difficult for those who commit violent crime or are persistent offenders to be given bail. This resulted in a sudden increase in the numbers of people held on remand in custody. The police had asked for this measure on the grounds that accused people on bail very often committed repeat offences.

The Criminal Justice and Public Order Act of 1994 was an extremely controversial piece of legislation which received widespread condemnation as an infringement on human rights and a step backwards in the treatment of juvenile crime. But its author, Michael Howard, was unrepentant and continued his crusade to prove that a harsher regime would eventually make an impact on crime figures.

Also in 1994 the Police and Magistrates' Courts Act was passed. This made changes in the management of the police. It involved much greater central control over police policy, in the hands of the Home Office. By reducing the influence of local authorities, Howard hoped that policing could become more effective. It effectively marked the end of the experiment with community policing. More significantly, the Act introduced performance targets for police authorities. It was hoped that a system of targets for clearing up crime would concentrate minds and result in better detection rates.

Finally the **Crime Sentences Act of 1996** allowed for much higher minimum sentences, especially for repeat offenders, and those convicted of violent, drugs or sexual offences. For those already in prison the parole and early release system was severely reduced. More prisoners would now serve their full term. For younger offenders a system of curfews was allowed, permitting the police to impose movement restrictions of juvenile offenders.

The result of these measures was to increase the prison population from 47,000 in 1993 to 60,000 in 1997. On the positive side there were signs in 1997 that the rise in crime was slowing down and, in the case of some offences, was falling. Clear-up rates by the police also began to improve.

The post-1997 policies of the Conservative administration also have to be seen in the context of a marked shift in the party's moral outlook. Prime Minister John Major had announced in the early 1990s a new moral initiative which he titled 'back to basics'. The policy was designed to restore a stronger sense of moral responsibility and to try to re-establish Christian and family values. Criminals were seen as responsible for their own actions and the liberal notion that the causes of crime are predominantly social, was rejected. The term 'New Right', which has been applied to the more authoritarian policies of the Conservatives in the 1980s and 1990s, could be applied most directly to the law and order policies of Michael Howard.

They can also be viewed as a direct attack on many civil liberties which had been closely guarded in the United Kingdom for many years, even centuries. When added to the more draconian measures of the 1980s, they also mark a significant increase in the powers of the police. Citizens can be prevented from demonstrating in public or from forming any large gatherings which caused the police to believe there might be breaches of the peace. Individuals can routinely be stopped and searched by police officers. Accused persons may be held in custody for up to three days (longer still if suspected of terrorism). If they choose to remain silent, it may be held against them in court. Young people are much more likely to be given custodial sentences and these sentences may be for substantial periods. It is more difficult to obtain bail and prisoners are often denied the opportunity for parole or early release if they show signs of rehabilitation. Finally, judges and magistrates have had much of their power over sentencing reduced. There are now statutory minimum sentences for a range of crimes. This marks a significant shift in responsibility for the treatment of convicted criminals from the judiciary to politicians.

The Labour party, whose law and order policies were largely formulated by Tony Blair, the shadow Home Secretary until 1994, and his successor Jack Straw, opposed many of these policies. They, along with the resurgent Liberal Democrats, criticised the attack on civil liberties and the neglect of the social causes of crime. But it was clear that a new Labour government would not abandon all the Howard policies. Indeed, aware that a tough stance on law and order was a vote winner, Blair promised to be as hard on criminals as the Conservatives had been. But the traditional Labour view that crime has mainly social causes, meant that Blair had to promise that these too would receive the party's attention.

Tony Blair's 1993 assertion that Labour would be 'tough on crime and tough on the causes of crime' reflected this dual approach. However, when the party unveiled its programme of action on crime in 1995, the measures looked to be as severe as Michael Howard's had been. As the 1997 election loomed, the two main parties seemed to be engaged in a contest to see which of them could be seen as harsher line on crime in the eyes of the electorate. Thus, in many ways, a new consensus on law and order had emerged even though the two main parties *claimed* to have distinctive policies in the 1997 campaign.

TOUGH ON CRIME AND TOUGH ON THE CAUSES OF CRIME – NEW LABOUR'S RESPONSE

As Labour's policies on law and order began to unfold in its early years of office, it became clear that there was a great deal of continuity between the Conservative policies of Michael Howard and those of Jack Straw. There were, however, different emphases and it is certainly true that the Labour programme was more extensive than its predecessors.

Much of the programme was inspired by the experience of Mayor Giuliani of New York and his conspicuous success in reducing crime. His policy was commonly described as '**zero tolerance**', though it was much more than a drive against minor offences. The New York scheme suggested that 'low-level' crimes such as begging, minor drug dealing, drunkenness and general disorderly behaviour, if left unchecked, would soon grow into more general criminal behaviour. They

> **zero tolerance**
> An idea developed in New York. The police refuse to tolerate small crimes such as begging, graffiti and vagrancy. By doing so it is believed to discourage people from drifting into more serious crime. It also helps to reduce the fear of crime. In New York it has been dramatically successful.

exacerbated the fear of crime and socialised vulnerable younger people into a life of more serious offending. The effects on the crime statistics, especially violent crime, in New York were dramatic, with crimes falling by 15 per cent in 1995 alone. Murders fell from just over 2,200 to 990 between 1990 and 1996.

Jack Straw, who became Home Secretary in 1997, set about introducing a broad-based version of the New York experience. Youth offending was to be a priority as research indicated that most offences were committed by boys and men aged 15–25. The fact that government in Britain is able to make more social interventions than in the United States meant that a programme of attacks on the basic social causes of crime could be undertaken in a way which was less feasible in New York or America in general.

If we are to describe and assess policies since 1997, a summary of the policies is best divided into two sections, as suggested by Tony Blair's 1993 declaration, 'tough on crime and tough on the causes of crime'.

TOUGH ON CRIME

The Labour programme appears to be the most extensive set of proposals to appear in modern times. Of course, some of the plan is little more than a set of objectives, targets and pledges. But there is also a good deal of legislation and concrete action.

YOUTH CRIME

In 1999 a major experiment was introduced. **Anti-Social Behaviour Orders** could be made against youths who were suspected of causing widespread crime and disorder within a particular community. The youths were ordered to cease their activities and, if they failed to do so, would be liable to prosecution for ignoring the order. This represented a completely new kind of offence, based on generalised behaviour rather than specific crimes.

The central piece of legislation was the **Crime and Disorder Act of 2000**. This was aimed very much at young, repeat offenders who are responsible for the majority of crime. A **Youth Justice Board** was set up in order to co-ordinate the government's efforts and to advise on new legislation. However, immediate action was taken to speed up the legal process of bringing offenders to trial. The system of giving young offenders repeated warnings was ended. A 'final warning' system was devised after which young criminals were to receive a full-scale trial and sentence. Curfews were introduced for child offenders and restrictions placed on offenders, preventing them from entering certain districts where they were known trouble-makers.

The youth crime policies were further beefed up in the **Criminal Justice and Police Act of 2001**. The scope of curfews was extended and more youth detention centres were announced. The main thrust of this Act, however, was an attack on what Jack Straw described as Britain's 'yob culture'. The main innovation was a system of fixed 'on-the-spot' fines which could be levied by police against 'disorderly behaviour'. Eight relevant offences were identified including such actions as public drunkenness, threatening behaviour and general violence. The purpose of this development was twofold – to provide summary justice and to allow the police to deal with general street disorders more effectively.

General crime

Although there was little evidence that serious crime among the older age groups was on the increase, there were also measures which were designed to deal with criminals of all ages. Minimum sentences were increased for a range of crimes of violence as well as sexual and drugs-related offences. Mandatory drugs testing for all suspects was introduced in the **Crime and Public Protection Act** of 2001.

The Act also forced sex offenders to submit themselves to police orders on their movements after release from prison. A sex offenders register had already been set up, but the new regulations gave greater discretion to the police in informing communities of the presence of such individuals. In extreme cases sex offenders could be forced to re-locate. The laws preventing them working with children were also toughened.

For some prisoners 'tagging' was sanctioned, an electronic system for tracing the movement of offenders on early-release schemes. Such prisoners were also subjected to stricter probation conditions, while those given community service orders were subjected to greater controls over their work.

But adult crime was no longer seen as a key problem and the Labour government was less active in this area than the Conservatives had been. Instead, it was intended that more effective policing, higher detection rates and better social conditions would automatically reduce the overall levels of crime.

Football hooliganism

The main drive against this widespread range of offences was spurred by the behaviour of England football supporters in the 1998 World Cup and the European Championships of 2000. The two main devices introduced were International and Domestic Banning Orders.

The orders were applied not only to known, convicted offenders, but also to those who were merely suspected of being likely to commit crimes. The subjects of the orders could be banned from travelling to specific football matches, be required to report to police stations while matches were taking place and, most controversially, could be forced to surrender their passports when matches abroad were taking place.

The orders were largely at the discretion of the police and did not require sanctions by the courts. Thus some level of guilt was being presumed and the basic right of freedom of movement could be denied to individuals who had broken no laws, or at least had never been convicted of doing so.

Policing

Labour's attitude to policing was three-pronged. These concerned numbers, equipment and improving standards. Labour inherited a service which was suffering declining strength, low morale and a constant barrage of media criticism. The seemingly unstoppable rise in the levels of crime had sapped their confidence and, just as the crime statistics began to fall in the early 1990s, cuts in public expenditure began to bite.

While the new government wished to see an increase in police numbers after a decline during the 1990s, it was constrained by financial limits. Having committed itself to Conservative spending plans, the Home Office was forced to endure further reductions in police strength. It was not until 2000 that Gordon Brown was able to announce significant increases in spending. A plan to increase the service by 9,000 officers over three years was announced. By 2001 police numbers at last began to rise slowly. However, the increase was slow, being hampered by relatively low levels of pay and, in London especially, a reluctance among young recruits to locate in London or other expensive areas.

The second initiative promised to be more effective. The Home Office began to approve larger and larger numbers of closed circuit TV (CCTV) schemes, especially in inner cities and other crime 'hot spots'. The extensive use of speed cameras released officers from traffic duty and, as we have seen above, the force was given more powers to prevent public disorder I town centres. Disorderly behaviour in clubs or pubs could result in speedy closure on police recommendation and fixed penalties could be levied for offences of public disorder. In 2001 further measures were proposed to give the police a greater ability to secure convictions. The measures were promised a rough ride through parliament and widespread opposition among civil rights group, but David Blunkett, who took over as Home Secretary in 2001, seemed determined to push them through.

The right to trial by jury was to be removed for many 'medium level' offences under the **Mode of Trial Bill.** Apart from reducing the expense of the criminal justice system, it was also believed that juries were less likely to convict than magistrates. At the same time there were proposals to introduce 'double jeopardy', which would enable to courts to try a person more than once for the same offence provided new evidence was found. Like trial by jury, the double jeopardy rule was an ancient right, but was nevertheless to be dispensed with. A proposal which was to have similar effects was to allow courts to be told an accused person's past record before the verdict. Finally Blunkett decided that he would allow police forces to retain DNA records, not just on convicted criminals, bit also on anyone who had been a crime suspect, whether or not convicted. The overall effect of these proposals was, it was hoped, to tilt the balance of power decisively towards the police and away from accused persons. The Conservative Michael Howard's 1995 plea to 'take the handcuffs off the police' was being answered by a Labour administration!

The police were to pay a price for their increased powers. The **Crime and Public Protection Act** established the power of the Home Office to set performance targets for police authorities. League tables of performance based on crime reduction and conviction rates were to be published. Forces were also required to contribute to Local Crime and Disorder Reduction Task Forces, encompassing the probation and local authority social services as well as the police. In other words, the police were to improve their performance both in reducing crime and in tackling some of the basic causes of crime and disorder (see box).

Law and order legislation and increases in police powers

- **1984 Police and Criminal Evidence Act.** Increased police powers of stop and search. Extended allowed period of questioning without charge to 72 hours.
- **1986 Public Order Act.** Increased the power of the police to prevent demonstrations which might lead to criminal activity.
- **1991 Criminal Justice Act.** The courts were forced to justify custodial sentences, making it more difficult to imprison minor offenders.
- **1994 Criminal Justice Act.** Took away people's right to remain silent and not have their silence held against them. Created a new offence of criminal trespass. Increased police powers to prevent demonstrations and rave parties. Violent criminals were not allowed bail while awaiting trial.
- **1996 Crime and Disorder Act.** Forced courts to give longer sentences for serious offences.
- **2000 Crime and Disorder Act.** Required the police to bring more young offenders to trial. Introduced a new offence of racially aggravated crime.
- **2001 Criminal Justice and Police Act.** Introduced curfews for young offenders and instant justice for public disorder offences.
- **2001 Crime and Public Protection Act.** Allowed police to keep a register of sex offenders and to restrict their movements after release from prison.
- **2002 Terrorism Act.** Gave wide police powers to detect international terrorists, including inspecting bank accounts, mobile phone records and to search premises.

THE CAUSES OF CRIME

Principles

The Labour government subscribed to the view of Liberals and many sociologists that much crime has its roots in the very young. The seeds of criminal behaviour, they believed, were sown very young. They also accepted that the causes of crime were multi-faceted. Attempts to attack these causes, therefore, would also have to be pluralist. Strengthening the powers of the police and the courts could do so much, but it was not enough.

Three basic New Labour principles were applied to the crime problem. The first concerned **social exclusion**. This phenomenon was identified as the tendency for some deprived portions of the population to become excluded from the normal benefits of the welfare state and so become alienated and disaffected. The sources of social exclusion included poor parenting, bad housing or homelessness, family unemployment, low educational attainment and truanting, drug misuse, general lack of opportunity, teenage pregnancy and chronic poor health. Clearly, many of those suffering from such exclusion are likely to turn to criminal activity.

> **social exclusion**
> A New Labour expression. It refers to those people, often young, who are excluded from mainstream society because of a variety of problems including low educational standards, unemployment, drug use, homelessness, petty crime, bad housing.

The second idea is **joined-up government**. Here, it is seen that, if social problems have many and varied causes, the solutions must also be pluralist. In practice this implies that a number of agencies, rather than just one, should be involved in solving the problems, Crime, especially among the young, should therefore not just involve the police and the courts. Social services departments, probation offices, schools, education welfare departments, community groups and youth organisations were also to be involved.

Finally, we should refer to the **communitarian** and **active citizenship** philosophies which are an important element of the New Labour programme. These approaches to all social policies are designed to promote the belief that individuals should feel responsible for what occurs within their own communities. 'Communitarianism' as a principle stresses that communities are largely responsible for their own welfare. While this includes such features as the physical environment, education, care of the elderly or needy and cultural life, the central element concerns law and order issues. Thus the existing neighbourhood watch schemes have received additional funding and publicity, while

> **active citizenship**
> Another New Labour idea. This suggests that people should take responsibility for their own communities. This includes helping to control criminal behaviour.

residents are encouraged to report possible law-breaking (especially drugs offences) to the police and to become actively involved in preventing juveniles becoming involved in crime. Active citizenship, too, implies that we are not only responsible for ourselves and our families, but also have a social duty to involve ourselves in social action to make our communities better and safer to live in.

MEASURES

The most dramatic of the measures has been the **Surestart** programme with a budget of £540 million for three years. This identifies children, mostly below the age of 4, who are at 'multiple risk'. The agencies, working together as described above, are to intervene to try to prevent later trouble. Parents of such children are encouraged to take up parenting classes. Special nursery education is provided to try to ensure that children can integrate successfully into mainstream education. Children with special needs are to be subject to remedial action by all the agencies described above. As a corollary to this, negligent parents may be subject to criminal prosecution, especially for failing to ensure the children attend school.

On a broader front than Surestart, the **New Deal for Communities** was granted £800 million to be spent regenerating some of the most deprived communities in Britain, in which crime has been prone to ferment. Schemes for improved environments, housing, schools and remedial education schemes for habitual truants were introduced in selected districts.

Truancy, indeed, has been identified as a key factor in youth crime. Schools have been given targets for the reduction in truancy and league tables, similar to those for examination results, are being published. As we have seen above, parents are liable for prosecution if their children miss too much school. At the same time persistent offenders may be provided with special schooling designed to make education more relevant.

These and other schemes are supervised by **Youth Offending Teams**, staffed by multiple local agencies. These teams are charged not only with the task of improving the detection of criminals, but also with reversing criminal behaviour among individuals. This latter objectives involves a more active approach to punishment. Ways are to be found to force offenders to face up to their crimes and their victims. Thus, community service orders, special education and counselling may be used as well as custodial sentences.

SOME THEMES

Civil liberties

There is no doubt that, since 1979, all governments have been engaged in a consistent drive to halt the seemingly inexorable rise in crime and, hopefully, to start bringing the figures down. It is also clear that this drive has meant that a number of civil liberties, some of them very ancient, have either disappeared or come under serious threat. Indeed, in an interview with the author in the 1988, the then Home Secretary, Douglas Hurd, admitted that a major part of his role as a minister was to balance the community's desire for security from criminals and public disorder with individuals' right to civil liberty. He also accepted that this role was almost impossible, though it had to be undertaken. A review of these threats includes the following features:

- The position of those accused of crimes has been significantly altered. Above all the right to remain silent without this incriminating them has been removed by the Criminal Justice and Public Order Act of 1994. The police may question suspects for longer, in the case of suspected terrorists for seven days. DNA and fingerprint samples are routinely taken and are now retained, whether or not the suspect is convicted. Rape victims cannot be forced to confront their accused attackers directly in court and children are heavily protected in sensitive cases, being able to give evidence by video.

- On our streets, the police have also gained considerable powers. There is now an almost unrestricted right for the police to stop and search suspects. Summary justice may be meted out to those who are committing public order offences, with fixed-rate fines applying. Young offenders may have orders placed against them, preventing them from entering specific districts where they have committed crimes in the past. Many city streets are now scanned by closed circuit TV (CCTV) systems and many more such schemes were announced in August 2001.

- It is now more difficult to hold public demonstrations as the police have increased powers to prevent such events if they believe breaches of the peace may result. The right to hold open air parties and to gather on common land has also been curtailed.

- Motorists are regularly photographed or video'd if they are speeding and may be fined on the basis of this evidence alone. There are now proposals to extend video and photographic evidence to illegal parking. These measures are seen by civil rights groups as important infringements on the right to privacy.

- Severe restrictions may now be applied to individuals who are merely suspected of habitual criminal behaviour. Both convicted and suspected football hooligans may be prevented from travelling both at home and abroad and may have their passports confiscated. Known youth offenders may be excluded from certain districts even after they have been punished for their crimes.

- Convicted prisoners are now more likely to have to serve their full terms and have had their right to parole and early release curtailed. Released prisoners may be tagged or curfewed to restrict their movements. Children up to the age of 15 may also now have to observe a curfew, again in addition to any other punishment.

These, and many other less severe measures represent both a large extension in police powers and a loss of personal liberty. If, on the other hand, we test these developments against public opinion, there is little doubt that they have received the backing of the majority of the public as well as the law enforcement community.

Are measures working?

One of the problems of making an assessment of the Labour government's two-pronged attack on both crime and its causes is that it is difficult to establish how far success has been achieved.

The significant reductions in crime levels which began in the mid-1990s coincided with Michael Howard's tougher approach. It is therefore tempting to suggest that the approach works. On the other hand, the same period saw the onset of rising prosperity and falling unemployment, both of which might have a similar result. To further muddy the waters of this debate, police numbers were falling at this time while police powers were being extended.

Under Labour administrations the same dilemma exists. Most crime statistics continued to fall after 1997, but whether this was due to the even stricter policies of Jack Straw or whether more sympathetic social policies are having an effect may never be known, certainly not in the short run. If we are to assess whether New Labour has indeed been 'tough on crime and tough on the causes of crime' we may take a straightforward approach. In terms of the depth and variety of measures adopted, Labour's programme certainly looks more extensive then anything seen before. On the other hand we must also point once again to the better economic health of the country. This alone could be solely responsible for the lower crime statistics. It must also be noted that crimes of violence, which contribute so greatly to the public fear of crime, have continued to rise.

It is clear that both the main parties place a huge significance upon the law and order issue. It is also true that Labour has stressed the social aspects of the problem more than the Conservatives, but they have extended police powers as much as their predecessors. Labour places great store by police numbers and closer monitoring of police performance as a means of bearing down more forcibly on crime and disorder. Thus, Labour policies have certainly represented toughness on known criminals and an attempt to reduce the numbers of new ones by attacking the causes of crime. The extent to which tough talk is converted into success remains unclear.

Terrorism

During 2001 the attention of the Home Office was drawn to the problem of terrorism. Two pieces of legislation emerged. The first was the **Terrorism Act** of February 2001. This had two main effects. Firstly, it broadened the definition of a 'terrorist'. It could now include anyone, who in the opinion of the law enforcement authorities was planning any damage to the state. Civil Rights campaigners suggested it could be used against anyone who was planning any form of demonstration which *might* lead to damage to property. In other words, all pressure groups planning direct action might be under suspicion. Secondly, it allowed the police to hold for questioning a terrorist suspect for up to seven days with the permission of a minister. In other words, the government could create its own definition of a terrorist.

After the 11 September attack on the USA, stiffer measures were proposed.

Future proposals

Terrorism

The terrorist attacks on the USA in September 2001 and the anti-terrorist movement which followed them has given rise to a number of new possibilities. The most important suggestion has been the introduction of identity cards. On a broader front, there have been calls to increase police powers of property search or seizure, surveillance, internment of suspects and deportation. It seems likely too that police will be given even greater freedom to question terrorist suspects before bringing them to trial.

Double jeopardy

The Stephen Lawrence murder trial, when the police case collapsed for technical reasons gave rise to proposals to allow suspects to be tried twice for the same crime. In the Lawrence case further evidence emerged after the case had been heard, but could not be used because of the ancient double jeopardy rule. The police and Crown prosecution Service believe that more criminals would be brought to justice if the rule were to be removed.

Trial by jury

It is Labour government policy to reduce, though certainly not abolish, the right to be tried by a jury in medium-level offences (minor offences are already tried by magistrates only). This will, it is believed, speed up the process of law, reduce expense and ensure the conviction of more guilty offenders. It has been successfully fought off by civil rights campaigners, especially in the House of Lords, but government seems determined to change the law.

Previous offences in trials

Until now, an accused person's previous offences are not revealed in the course of a criminal case until the jury have delivered a verdict. The Home Office, with strong police backing, is considering changing this rule, again in order to secure more convictions.

Sentencing

The Labour administration would like to extend Michael Howard's programme of introducing longer mandatory sentences for serious offences. This would further erode the judiciary's control over punishment, placing it instead in the hands of political ministers. Though the Labour party stresses the causes of crime, they also accept in part Howard assertion that, in many cases, 'prison works'.

Whichever, if any, of these measures are introduced it seems likely that the process of extending police powers, reducing the rights of accused individuals and coming down harder on serious offenders will continue for the foreseeable future. It is also inevitable that civil rights campaigners will continue to resist such policies.

SAMPLE QUESTIONS

1 'Tough on crime, tough on the causes of crime.' What did Tony Blair mean by this 1994 assertion? In what ways have his governments since 1997 attempted to meet this commitment?

2 What special measures have been taken to combat youth crime since 1979?

3 How have police powers increased since 1979?

4 To what extent have the increases in police power since 1979 eroded human rights?

5 Describe and analyse the different approaches to crime adopted by Labour and Conservative governments.

Issues concerning women

7

> The development of the women's movement

> Descriptions of the legislation passed to improve the status of women

> Review and analysis of remaining issues concerning the status of women

BACKGROUND

Women's emancipation

Although the cause of improvement in the status of women can be traced back into the nineteenth century, the effective story must begin with the time when women achieved the right to vote after a sustained campaign of civil disobedience and parliamentary campaigning. Women over 30 years old were allowed to vote in 1918 and 21-year olds (the age of male suffrage) followed in 1928.

But women's suffrage was not the breakthrough which it might at first appear. It had been hoped, and even assumed, that once women were given a political voice many other benefits would automatically follow. With politicians now accountable to women and seeking their votes, surely they would begin to listen to demands for further concessions. Furthermore, the movement had been almost exclusively middle class in character. There was little interest in the plight of women in working-class families such as lack of education, poor career prospects and the common burden of large families in poor circumstances of health and housing.

The truth was that, in the first half of the twentieth century, the problems of women, their rights and status, were too deeply rooted to be solved merely by access to the political system. The political parties did not, as had been expected, place women's issues on their political agenda, there was no avalanche of women entering the House of Commons and the extra-parliamentary movement seemed to wither after it achieved its primary goal.

Sandwiched between the two stages in the enfranchisement of women came an Act which had almost as much potential significance. This was the Sex

Disqualification (Removal) Act of 1919. This legislation opened up both the universities and the professions to women. There had previously been a range of prohibitions on women's ability to pursue advanced careers. In the event, relatively few women entered politics for many years to come, but the opening up of higher education and the professions had a more immediate impact.

Nevertheless, progress in the early part of the twentieth century remained slow. Between 1928 and the 1960s, therefore, the women's movement retreated into the background of British politics. When it re-emerged in the 1960s, the impetus came from the USA.

Radical feminism and the New Left

A crucial event in the development of the modern women's movement was the publication of an American book – *The Feminine Mystique* – written by Betty Friedan in 1963. Friedan's work was a devastating criticism on a culture which had come to be completely dominated by men. She demonstrated that 'patriarchy' was in fact a complete system of oppression of women. Women suffered not only discrimination in fields such as employment, education and the arts, they were also being denied opportunities to realise their full potential. From the moment of birth, she complained, gender stereotypes are encouraged which suggest that men are superior. This went much further than the women's movement had ever gone before, representing a radical analysis of a male-dominated society and implying similarly radical measures to combat patriarchy.

In the early 1960s the infant women's movement was part of a broader phenomenon which came to be known as the 'New Left'. This essentially left-wing political philosophy saw society as polarising into two large groups. The first contained those who were enjoying all the benefits of the prosperous consumer society. They were in the mainstream of a mass culture which was the result of fully developed capitalism. The other was a collection of groups who had become alienated from the mass culture. They were denied many of its benefits and made to feel outsiders. The principal examples of alienated cultures were ethnic minorities, the poor, disaffected youth, gays and, of course, women. In each case radical, often revolutionary, movements grew up in the 1960s.

The women's movement, inspired by Friedan's work spread into Europe. Its key figures were Kate Millet and Shulamith Firestone in the USA, Germaine Greer in Britain and Simone de Beauvoir in France. In varying degrees these campaigners recommended militant measures to liberate women from the control of the men. They suggested women should separate themselves entirely by forming their own communes or should engage in subversive activities to undermine patriarchy very much as the suffragettes had done fifty years before. These radical feminists, as they came to be known, argued that legislation to grant women equal opportunities and higher status would not be adequate. The problem of women's status would require a radical transformation of society.

During the 1970s the radical feminist movement began to weaken and become dissipated. This was, to some extent, part of a general decline in the strength of the new left. However, it was also overtaken by the fact that a wide range of concessions were appearing. These were designed to meet some of the clearer demands of the women's movement, but also had the effect of splitting the women's movement. In the 1970s it was a new liberal kind of feminism which was gaining the ascendancy.

Liberal feminism

Liberal, as opposed to radical, feminists were not revolutionaries. They wished to see reform, but did not challenge the fundamental order. In other words they believed it would be possible to achieve equal status and liberation for women through changes within the *existing* social order. Three important developments in Britain (all of which were also supported by the militant feminists) occurred in the 1960s and 1970 to give a boost to the liberal movement and set it on the way to further successes.

The *birth control pill* became widely available after 1967. This heralded in a period of sexual liberation for women, which became the centrepiece of a more general youth liberation movement (the so-called 'hippy' or 'flower power' era). It resulted in two developments. The first was that married women were able to take control *themselves* of family planning and so rely less on men. This meant that women were able better to control the size of their family and/or delay childbirth to a later age, thus enabling them to pursue a career. The second was that unmarried women were more sexually liberated as they could protect themselves easily from fear of pregnancy. Of course, for many this was an undesirable result, but it was welcomed wholeheartedly by all feminists.

Also in 1967 the **Abortion Act** was passed. For the first time abortion became legal in Britain (England and Wales only at first). This had an immediate effect on the illegal abortion industry which resulted in many health problems and even deaths for young women. More importantly here, however, abortion became the flagship issue for women. In practical terms it stood alongside the birth control pill as a liberating force. But it was much more than that. Abortion became symbolic of women taking control of their own bodies and health. Feminists saw the prohibition on abortion as a feature of a male-dominated society. Put simply, it was men deciding what was best for women on their behalf. So the legality of abortion became a vital gesture of liberation.

The **Divorce Law Reform Act** of 1970 made it much easier for women (incidentally as well as men) to obtain a divorce. It established that there was only one ground for divorce which was the irretrievable breakdown of the marriage. The Act established that a two-year separation (five years if the divorce was contested) constituted a breakdown. Not only did this liberate many women who were trapped in unhappy and unfulfilling marriages, it also helped to take away the social stigma which used to surround divorced women. Like the other two reforms described above, easier divorce had its opponents who saw it as a retrograde step in terms of morality and social stability. But also like the other two feminists welcomed the liberalisation of the divorce laws as a key step forward for women.

In the same year the **Matrimonial Proceedings and Property Act** gave courts the power to grant property to divorcing women and to force husbands to make financial provision for ex-wives and their children. So, not only was it easier for women to obtain a divorce, but the financial consequences would also be less severe.

The scene was now set for even more important battles to be fought by the feminist movement. These were the issues of equal pay and the outlawing of sex discrimination in a wide variety of fields.

EQUAL PAY

By 1970 there had developed a crescendo of women's protests against unequal treatment of women in the workplace. There were significant differences in the pay of women compared with men. The **Equal Pay Act** of 1970 attempted to correct this situation. At first sight it seemed to have solved the problem, but it turned out to be a flawed measure.

The Act stated that women should be paid the same wage as men if they were doing the same job. However employers were able to avoid the legislation simply by giving women different job titles or by slightly altering the nature of their work. In this way it could be claimed that men and women were not doing the *same job* in the strict sense of the word. Two more Acts were needed to tidy up the equal pay legislation.

The **Sex Discrimination Act** of 1975, which is described more fully below, established that if a woman's work was effectively the same as that done by a man then she was entitled to equal pay. In 1984 the **Equal Pay**

(Amendment) Act was a final attempt to close up all the loopholes. It was passed to bring Britain into line with European Union legislation (which was to be binding in the UK). This introduced a new test for equal pay. Provided work is *of equal value*, even if it is different in nature, women should be paid the same as men (and vice versa, of course). The 1984 Act was the most radical of all the measures on pay as it was an attempt to establish total equality for women in the workplace

But equal pay was only one of the issues concerning the status of women. It was seen as a symbol of wider discrimination which was taking place, but on its own it was inadequate. A broader, all-embracing measure was needed. This arrived in 1975.

THE SEX DISCRIMINATION ACT 1975

The new Labour government which came to power in 1974 was determined to complete the radical reforms concerning equal opportunities which had been started in the 1960s. It therefore passed the landmark Sex Discrimination Act as a priority. The Act contained two main elements as shown in the box.

Sex Discrimination Act 1975

1 Outlawed discrimination on the grounds of sex (i.e. for either men or women, but not including homosexuals) in a wide variety of activities.
2 Established the Equal Opportunities Commission whose role was both to administer the existing legislation and to further the issue of sexual equality into the future.
   Since 1975 many cases have been brought by individuals and by the Equal Opportunities Commission which have 'filled out' the basic laws. This body of 'case law' has established some of the following principles:
   - Even when an employer is not discriminating *directly* against women, he may be accused of engaging in practices which *have the effect of discriminating*. For example if an employer will not employ people who are lone parents, this will have the effect of tending to discriminate against women. It is also not permitted to refuse to employ a woman on the grounds that she is likely to become pregnant and so take too much time off work.
   - If a woman can prove that she has equal qualifications to men and yet is continually passed over for promotion, a case may be made that the employer is discriminating.
   - If women are doing the same work as men, but have a different job title, they must not be discriminated against in terms of pay.
   - In the provision of services such as insurance, bank loans, mortgages and rental agreements, women must be treated on an equal basis to men.

These cases are a sample of the way in which the sex discrimination laws work. They are also reinforced by the European Court of Justice and the European Court of Rights which ensures that women are given equal treatment at work, in terms of working conditions and in welfare benefits. The passage of the Human Rights Act in 1999 made it easier for women to claim discrimination under the European Convention on Human Rights. They may, since then, bring a case in the British courts. This saves both time and money.

REMAINING ISSUES

The battles for equal treatment for women in most aspects of life have been won. However, there remain a number of areas, often which are less clear, where women do not feel they have achieved equality or justice. The main examples are described below:

Sexism

The term 'sexism' refers to a cultural attitude towards women which implies that they are inferior or that they have a limited role to play in modern society. Sexist attitudes are, claim campaigners, carried in such institutions as schools, TV and radio, the press, sport and entertainment. It is further argued that, as long as sexist attitudes persist, real, concrete examples of discrimination will follow. Furthermore, the more extreme examples of sexism may lead to the degradation of women.

Pornography, hard and soft, and the gratuitous display of women in sexual poses to advertise goods are seen as particularly undesirable examples of sexism. Led by Cabinet Minister Clare Short, women's groups have sought stricter laws against pornography and so-called 'page three girls'.

The problem with sexism is that it is difficult to tackle it with legislation. All that can be done is that women's groups, including the Equal Opportunities Commission, to raise awareness of the problem and seek to combat it through education and public campaigning. Moreover, the anti-sexism movement has had to face accusations of 'political correctness' by Conservatives and liberals who see it as a form of cultural coercion.

DOMESTIC VIOLENCE

Until the 1970s the existence of widespread violence by men against their female partners was scarcely recognised. It was almost impossible for women to persuade the police to prosecute in such cases. Furthermore, it was recognised that many women were suffering systematic violence but were trapped by circumstances – usually poverty and responsibility for children – and so could not escape.

These problems were attacked on two fronts. The first was to force the police to accept that domestic violence is a serious crime and to begin prosecutions. This campaign has yielded results and all police forces now have special domestic violence units. The second problem – women being trapped in a cycle of violence – was tackled by the opening of a network of refuges. In these 'safe' houses women and their children were able to escape from violent partners, their location being kept secret. Social and voluntary workers who are attached to these refuges are also able to attempt to find long-term solutions for the women.

RAPE

Legislative action is not required to strengthen protection against rape. The problem has been that too few cases have reached successful prosecution. The reasons for this are that:
- Women are constrained from reporting rape because they have feared they will not be treated sympathetically by the police.
- It is difficult to prove a charge of rape, especially when the defence is that the woman consented.
- Also in cases where consent is the main issue, women may find cross-examination in a trial a gruelling experience.
- In cases where the alleged rapist is a close friend, perhaps boyfriend (so-called 'date rape') it is especially difficult to secure a conviction.
- Wives have long claimed that it is possible to be raped by one's own husband. Until recently courts did not accept this.

Considerable progress has been made. Many police forces now have special rape units and officers trained to deal with women. In court women receive some protection by judges when giving evidence, especially when they may be cross-examined by the alleged rapist. The importance of date rape has now been recognised and it has become possible for husbands to be convicted of rape.

Nevertheless, women's campaigners continue to argue that rape is not taken as seriously as other crimes by either the police or the courts. This involves a change in attitudes, rather than any change in the law. In particular, it is argued that the past life of a woman should not be taken into consideration when she has accused a man of rape.

POSITIVE DISCRIMINATION

Women are still considered to be suffering from discrimination. This occurs especially in employment. The law says that discrimination must not occur, but it is happening in subtle ways which avoid prosecution. The main concern is the so-called **glass ceiling** which is said to exist in many occupations, mainly the professions. The glass ceiling theory says that there is a level of promotion above which women find it very difficult to rise. The main culprits are said to be law, medicine, teaching, business and government.

The more extreme campaigners suggest that the answer to the glass ceiling is positive discrimination. Such a scheme requires that quotas should be established, so that a minimum proportion of women should be promoted to higher levels. This is, of course, a highly controversial proposal as it is suggested that some 'inferior' women may be promoted simply to fulfil a quota. Supporters, on the other hand, claim that positive discrimination will change the 'culture' in many organisations. With better opportunities, more able women will enter such professions so that the quotas will be filled by able people.

POLITICS AND PARLIAMENT

Just as it was assumed by the suffragettes that obtaining votes for women would lead to further examples of emancipation, modern campaigners see increased participation of women in politics as vital for the movement. The election of Margaret Thatcher as Conservative leader in 1975, and then as Prime Minister in 1979, may have been a key development. However, women's groups tended to disown her, partly because she was extremely unpopular in some sections of the community and partly because she refused to champion any women's causes.

Attention since has centred on having more women elected to parliament. Aided by a Labour party policy of insisting on more women candidates in winnable seats, a breakthrough seemed to have been made in 1997. A total of 120 women were elected, 101 of them from the Labour party. More women were also seen in the cabinet and by 2001 there were 7 and many more in junior ministerial posts. In 2001 fewer women were elected, but the number remains high. Women do play a key role in politics – far more than previously.

There remain some issues in politics. In particular the rules and procedures of parliament are considered unsympathetic to women MPs. Long hours, a lack of childcare facilities and the sheer nature of the job which involves much travelling, does not lend itself to motherhood. It is hoped that proposed reforms to the House of Commons in 2002 will address some of these concerns.

There is also lack of a specific cabinet post which deals with women's issues. There is a junior minister in charge of policy for women, but the fact that it is a junior post indicates how low it is on the political agenda.

SAMPLE QUESTIONS

1 Why has it proved so difficult in modern times to advance the cause of women's rights?

2 What are the main legislative and non-legislative initiatives since the 1960s which have been designed to raise the status of women?

Racial issues and the multicultural society 8

➤ The background to racial problems in the UK

➤ Descriptions of the main pieces of race legislation

➤ The features and importance of the Stephen Lawrence case

➤ The importance of the Macpherson and Ousley Reports

➤ The work of the Commission for Racial Equality

➤ The broad issues of racial discrimination

➤ Forms of non-legislative race relations initiatives

➤ The issue of multiracialism

IMMIGRATION

Although Britain has, throughout its history, assimilated large numbers of different ethnic groups from abroad, the issue of race was not a particularly significant element in politics until the 1950s. There were two reasons for this: Firstly, the incoming groups were small and tended to lose their own cultural identity quickly, becoming, within two or three generations, effectively British. Apart from the small Jewish community, many of whom do retain a strong separate identity, most immigrant groups until the 1950s were thoroughly absorbed. Secondly, skin colour had not been a factor until that time. There were small communities of Afro-Caribbean descent, a few residents from the Indian sub-continent and groups of Chinese immigrants, but they had been insignificant in size or impact. Then everything began to change in the second half of the 1950s.

The first significant wave of non-white immigration occurred in the 1950s. This was a time of full employment and there were significant shortages of labour in such fields as the health service and public transport. To meet the shortages, the government introduced a system of subsidised immigration, most from the West Indies. With expenses paid, the new immigrants were promised good wages, decent housing and guaranteed employment. Many thousands took up the offer. Immigration from the West Indies has continued ever since, though strict quotas have been set and the cash incentives no longer exist.

The second wave of immigrants arrived in the 1960s and 1970s. These were of Asian descent, either from India and Pakistan (later also Bangladesh), former members of the British empire and therefore British passport holders. In addition to these economic migrants seeking a better life, there were refugees from East Africa, mostly Uganda and Kenya. These groups, also originally from the sub-continent, but largely running businesses in Africa, suffered persecution at the hands of newly independent regimes. Forced out of their adopted countries, and often having their businesses confiscated, these Asians found a natural home in the UK.

Since then immigration has become more diffuse. The numbers are less than in the 1950s to 1970s, but the origins of immigrants have widened. The immigration 'mix' now includes Africans, West Indians, Sub-continent Asians, Hong Kong Chinese and refugees and asylum seekers from all over the world. In the 1990s and early twenty-first century, there has been a large inflow from the Balkans, East Africa, Eastern Europe and even Afghanistan.

IMMIGRATION CONTROL

In the 1950s there was no thought of the need to control immigration. Indeed, as we have seen, most of the immigrants had actually been invited to settle in the UK. However, as unemployment began to rise in the 1960s and the flow of immigration showed little sign of abating, demands grew for some controls on the numbers entering. In 1958 race riots in London, Nottingham and Liverpool broke out, demonstrating the fears that were beginning to emerge, especially among white members of the working class in cities, where jobs were under threat.

The response of governments of both the main parties was to introduce numerical controls to stem the flow. Commonwealth Immigration Acts in 1962 and 1968 introduced quotas. The Immigration Act of 1971 broadened the controls to non-Commonwealth countries. However it was the 1981 British Nationality Act which represented the most stringent measure to date. This Act remains the basis of immigration policy to the present day. The Act stated that possession of a British passport no longer entitled the holder to residence in the UK. At a stroke many millions of people all over the Commonwealth – i.e. former British colonial possessions – who believed themselves to be partly

British, were no longer allowed to come to the UK. Residence in the UK would only be allowed to those who could show that they, a parent or a grandparent were born in the UK. The only other way to obtain full nationality and residency rights was to apply for naturalisation after seven years living in the country.

The Nationality Acts of 1962 and 1968 were highly controversial and were the first pieces of legislation which were thought to be 'racist' in their effect (though governments argued they were not racist by intention). The reason was that their effect mostly fell upon Afro-Caribbean and Asian peoples – i.e. so-called 'coloureds'. Would-be white skinned immigrants from Australia, New Zealand, Canada or South Africa could usually find at least a British born grandparent to give them residency rights. This was more rarely the case with black and Asian immigrants.

THE RACIAL QUESTION

In the 1950s and 1960s racial tensions in Britain grew, very much in proportion to the quantity of immigrants entering the country. Immigrant groups were openly attacked in the race riots of 1958, especially in the Notting Hill district of London. Discrimination against black immigrants was becoming a major cause for concern. Thus was most common in employment, housing, education and social life. But matters reached a head in 1968.

In that year immigration of Asians from East Africa was reaching a peak. The government was proposing more controls on the numbers. A leading Conservative, Enoch Powell, during the debate on the new Immigration Bill, gave a speech in Birmingham (where many of the new immigrants were settling) which was to echo throughout Britain. With a dramatic piece of imagery he claimed, 'like a Roman I seem to see the river Tiber foaming with much blood'. The reason for his vision, he said, was the result of excessive immigration leading to racial violence. The speech, which has come to be known as the 'rivers of blood speech', created a furious response.

On the one hand, Powell claimed to receive 100,000 letters of support for his views. The right-wing press seized on the statement in their campaign to see strict limits on immigration. The Conservative party (led at the time by Ted Heath), where Powell did have a certain degree of support, was forced to sack him from the shadow cabinet. In parliament, where the second Race Relations Act was being debated, MPs on both sides of the divide were galvanised into a major conflict over immigration policy. The speech contributed to the effective end of Powell's political ambitions, but he had set the scene for debates on race for many years to come.

The Conservatives remained split on the issue, but official policy remained that while immigration quotas should remain, there was to be no repatriation of immigrants. Repatriation was a policy of both the right wingers in the Conservative party and extremists such as the National Front, but it was never seriously considered by political parties. Labour and the Liberals, meanwhile, were committed to improving the state of race relations in the country.

Immigration attitudes

- **Liberal Conservatives and Labour.** Support the idea of a multi-racial society with tolerant attitude to racial minorities and accepting racial diversity. Tolerant attitude to asylum seekers. Immigration to be continued, but controlled to reduce over-population and to import people who can reduce skill shortages.
- **Centre Conservatives.** Support controls on immigration, but allowing some to enter under strict quotas. Insist that racial minorities should learn to integrate.
- **Right-wing Conservatives.** They have opposed immigration and supported repatriation of immigrant groups. Suspicious of the idea of a multi-racial society, they take a hard line on asylum seekers.
- **Liberal Democrats.** Strongly believe in a tolerant, multi-racial society. They have an open policy towards asylum seekers and economic refugees. They favour stronger race discrimination laws.

LEGISLATION ON RACE

The Labour party which came to power in 1965 was committed to improving race relations in Britain. It therefore passed two pieces of legislation.

The Race Relations Act 1965

This set up the Race Relations Board. The board was to perform two main tasks. Firstly, it was to investigate ways of improving race relations in the country. Secondly, it received complaints from individuals and organisations concerning **racial discrimination**. It could investigate the claims and recommend measures to overturn the discrimination (**positive discrimination**).

The board lacked legal powers to enforce its recommendations. However, it did place race

racial discrimination
The systematic practice of disadvantaging members of an ethnic group in such fields as employment, social life, supply of service, housing.

positive discrimination
A system which actually favours members of ethnic groups. For example some jobs or housing will be reserved for such groups. Known as affirmative action in the USA.

relations on the political agenda and did highlight the worst examples of **racism** or **discrimination**.

Race Relations Act 1968

This Act gave the Race Relations Board some enforcement powers, in particular it could bring to an end any systematic examples of discrimination. A Community Relations Commission was also established. This commission was to look at the broader picture of race relations. It made recommendations concerning education, employment and housing to try to ensure that members of ethnic minorities received fair treatment.

racism

A generalised attitude which views some racial groups as inferior. It leads to discrimination and sometimes race hatred.

racialism

Scientific or quasi-scientific theories about race. Most theories suggest that some races are superior to others. The German Nazis and South African white supremacists were examples.

The two Race Relations Acts were certainly progressive on the issue of race. However, in both cases they lacked teeth and failed to make serious inroads into public attitudes. Labour had lost power by 1970 so further progress was put on hold. The Conservatives were not so concerned with racial issues and so relied on the board and the commission to try to keep the lid on race relations. When Labour returned to power in 1974, race appeared high on the agenda again. A third piece of legislation was therefore introduced.

Race Relations Act 1976

The Commission for Racial Equality

Firstly, this tidied up the confusion over the existence of two bodies concerned with racial issues. The Board and Commission were replaced by the Commission for Racial Equality (CRE).

Role of the CRE

- To advise and assist people and organisations, including the media, on racial issues.
- Investigate discrimination policies by companies, the media and other organisations, requiring them to change as necessary.
- To take legal action against specific discrimination incidents.
- To sponsor judicial reviews by individuals and groups where they feel they have suffered discriminatory practices by a public body.
- To advise the government on possible future legislation and race policy.
- To liaise with local **Racial Equality Councils**, which have been set up to foster good community race relations.

The Commission has 15 members and a staff of over 200. It has regional offices and is headed by a chairperson.

The Act and racial discrimination

For the first time the Act was specific in making certain discriminatory practices illegal. Any action which is considered to be discriminatory (either directly or in its indirect effect) on the basis of race, colour, nationality or ethnic and national origin, is deemed to be illegal. The CRE may prosecute any individual or organisation which contravenes this provision.

Certain areas of activity were specified as applying to the law. These were:
- *Employment:* in pay, recruitment, promotion or training practices.
- *Housing:* applying to the allocation of housing by local authorities and housing associations. This also applied to private landlords or estate agents and solicitors involved in sale and purchase.
- *Education:* schools could not refuse entry on the grounds of race etc. Nor could any racial group be excluded from specific subjects or activities.
- *Provision of goods and services:* discriminatory practices when selling goods or providing services.

Summary of the Act

The 1976 Act was undoubtedly the most important development in race relations since World War II. It was important for the following reasons:
1 It established discrimination as a crime.
2 It established the Commission for Racial Equality as a key part of the British political establishment.
3 It widened the areas in which racial discrimination was to be outlawed.
4 It created a powerful pressure group which could campaign for better race relations in the UK.

But the Act had its weaknesses. A number of institutions were exempt, most notably the police. It also could not enforce the law with regard to private organisations such as sports or social clubs. Perhaps most significantly, the Act could only really deal with very specific examples of discrimination. It could not deal effectively with *attitudes* to race. Nor was it concerned with some of the *social* causes of racial conflict. Thus, when serious inner city disorders broke out in London, Liverpool, Leeds and Bristol in 1981, the racial undertones were left largely untouched.

Legal measures undoubtedly help to lead public opinion towards a more tolerant society. However, they are insufficient on their own. It was not until the 1976 Act was amended in 2000 that the broader aspects of the race problems were tackled by legislative action.

ARTICLE 13 OF THE AMSTERDAM TREATY

This was agreed in 2000 by all EU members. It asserts a minimum standard of legal protection for all ethnic minorities. When the Article became compulsory in 2003 ethnic minorities throughout the European Union were offered the same protection.

The British government take the view that the law in the UK already conforms to Article 13 in most respects, but there may have to be some toughening up of the regulations on policing and the conduct of trials where race is an issue. The additional measures are due to be announced later in 2002.

THE RACE RELATIONS (AMENDMENT) ACT 2000

This Act came into force in April 2001. It was in part an updating and extension of the 1976 Act, but was also a response to growing concerns about the state of race relations in Britain at the end of the twentieth century. In particular it had to deal with the conclusions of the Macpherson Inquiry into the Stephen Lawrence murder case. The incident and inquiry are described in more detail below. Macpherson uncovered deep problems in race relations in Britain. It had six main measures.

1 It established a code of practice which the CRE tries to promote in public bodies. It applies mainly to the criminal justice system, the police, education, the health service, housing, local government, politics and sport. Best practice is not a statutory (i.e. legally compulsory) requirement, but the CRE is charged with the task of trying to implement it.

The kind of measures included are the education and training of staff on racial equality, eliminating practices which might cause racial discrimination, directly or indirectly, the reporting of racial incidents and future prevention. There was also an implication that ethnic minorities should be given fair representation in recruitment and promotion. However, the last measure was to be beefed up when the Act was amended in 2000.

2 There was a statutory duty imposed upon all public bodies to *promote* equality of opportunity and race relations. Government, education, the police and local authorities were the principal examples.

3 Where crimes were considered to have a racial element (such as an assault based on racial conflict) they would be considered to be more serious and the sentences would reflect this.

4 Incitement to racial hatred (whether or not leading to violence) was made a serious offence. This was particularly aimed at publicity produced by such extreme groups as the British National Party.

5 Police officers were made *vicariously liable* for racial offences committed by the police. In other words more senior officers can now be held legally responsible for the actions of their subordinates, whether or not they are directly involved.

6 A race legislation unit within government was set up to oversee the implementation of the Act

The 2000 Act did, therefore, attempt to fill in some of the gaps left by the 1976 legislation. It extended the provisions, outlawed more general examples of racial conflict and introduced statutory duties on organisations to improve their race relations record. Its main effect will be felt by the police. This is because the Act had to respond to the Macpherson Report (see below). Nevertheless it has created a climate in which *all* public bodies now feel they have a responsibility to improve race relations and racial equality.

Above all, however, the 2000 Act has shifted the whole emphasis on race relations. In the past the stress has been placed on dealing with racism by making discriminatory activities unlawful. Following the Macpherson Report and the 2000 Act there is a statutory duty upon many organisations to advance good race relations in a *positive* way. As we shall see below too, non-legislative measures have tended to concentrate on positive measures and not just negative prevention.

THE STEPHEN LAWRENCE INQUIRY (MACPHERSON)

At first sight the Stephen Lawrence case and inquiry represented a tragic incident which had little impact outside south London. In fact, the case proved to be something of a turning point in race relations in Britain.

On 22 April 1993 Stephen Lawrence, a black teenager, was murdered in south London by a group of white youths. The murder seemed to have no motive, but it was later established to be racially motivated. Though the guilty men were widely known in the area, the police failed to secure a prosecution. It was claimed that the police had made insufficient efforts to secure a conviction, had failed to offer sufficient protection to witnesses and had failed to understand the racial nature of the crime. The Lawrence family, encouraged by the CRE and other race relations campaigners, called for an inquiry into the case and the government acceded to the request by convening a commission under Sir William Macpherson to investigate.

His report in February 1999 had an extraordinary impact. Its effects can be seen on two levels:

The police and institutional racism

Macpherson declared that the Metropolitan Police, who had investigated the case, were characterised by what he called **institutional racism**. Thus a new phrase entered the vocabulary of race relations. The definition in the report was as follows:

---

institutional racism

'[Institutional Racism] consists of the collective failure of an organisation to provide an appropriate and professional service to people because of their colour, culture or ethnic origin. It can be seen or detected in processes, attitudes and behaviour which amounts to discrimination, through unwitting prejudice, ignorance, thoughtlessness and racial stereo-typing which disadvantages minority ethnic people.'

There had long been strong suspicions that the police contained racist elements, but Macpherson went further. He suggested that racist attitudes were deeply ingrained in the force and in its institutions. In other words it was part of the *culture* of the institution. The implications for race relations were, of course, very serious. The CRE had already pointed to lack of trust between ethnic minority communities and the police. Macpherson confirmed this and demonstrated how deeply established the problem was. Indeed Macpherson suggested that, as the police were part of the problem, they also had to be part of the solution.

There was also an implication that other institutions might also suffer from institutional racism. He therefore made a general statement with them in mind:

> It is incumbent upon every institution to examine their policies and the outcome of their policies and practices to guard against disadvantaging any section of the community.

The Race Relations (Amendment) Act of 2000 responded to this conclusion. The police service was required to introduce a number of measures, known as the Police Action Plan. They included:
- Education for police officers to prevent racially motivated actions. Awareness of possible racial problems in policing to be raised.
- Efforts were to be made to ensure that recruitment, retention and promotion policies are non-discriminatory.

- The recording of all racial incidents.
- Logging of all 'stop and search' incidents to ensure that there was no systematic discrimination against ethnic minorities.
- Strict disciplinary procedures were introduced against officers guilty of racial prejudice.

Community race relations

The Lawrence murder had once again drawn attention to the sorry state of race relations in poorer districts of big cities. To some extent, Macpherson asserted, this was due to lack of trust between the community and the police. His recommendations were designed to reduce such suspicions. However, the report went further.

Macpherson recommended that racially motivated crimes should be singled out for special attention. Where there was a racial element, sentencing was to be more severe. Furthermore all racial incidents, whether or not they resulted in a crime, were to be recorded by the police. A racist incident was defined by Macpherson as: 'any incident which is perceived to be racist by the victim or any other person'.

The police were not the only body to be singled out as playing a crucial role in community relations. Macpherson also stressed the need for a multi-agency approach to improving race relations at local level. Local councils, schools, social services, community leaders and the police were urged to work together to build trust among different ethnic groups.

On a national level the government's Race Equality Unit of the Home Office responded to Macpherson by producing 'public service agreements' with a variety of institutions. The central plan was to see progress towards 'representative' workforces (i.e. containing appropriate proportions from members of ethnic minorities). The institutions concerned included the police, fire, probation and prison services. These bodies stand at the forefront of race relations so that their race policies are crucial.

As we have seen, the impact of Macpherson was far-reaching. As the twenty-first century dawned, therefore, there were renewed hopes for race relations in Britain. Sadly these hopes were dashed in the summer of 2001 by racial conflict in a number of northern cities.

THE 2001 RIOTS AND THE OUSELEY REPORT

In July 2001 serious rioting broke out in a number of cities including Burnley, Oldham and Bradford. The problem was largely confined to white and Muslim youths who engaged in organised fighting and damage to property. The former Chairman of the Commission for Racial Equality, Sir Herman Ouseley, was immediately asked to make an inquiry and he reported rapidly on the incidents. His report was entitled, ' Community Pride, Not Prejudice'.

Community pride, not prejudice

Ouseley was addressing an issue which had become central to race in Britain at the beginning of the twenty-first century. This was a twofold problem:

1 Assuming that a multi-racial society is desirable, how should we define the term 'multicultural'?

2 Having established the nature of a multicultural society, how should we go about achieving it?

The answer to the first question was that a multicultural society is one where all ethnic groups feel integrated and included. In other words, although cultural differences should be tolerated and protected, it is desirable for all groups to integrate into mainstream British culture. This image is very much how traditional Jewish communities in Britain have dealt with the problem. Ouseley was also suggesting that the reason why youths from ethnic minorities (mainly Muslim in the case of the 2001 riots) were so disaffected was that they felt alienated from British society. It was not so much that they experienced direct discrimination, but that they felt excluded.

The second question is clearly more complex. However, in general terms Ouseley was proposing that each community had a responsibility to promote full integration and to prevent any group feeling excluded. In practical terms this would mean finding ways of bringing ethnic communities together, but more importantly, it required a widening of opportunity for those members of ethnic minorities who experience the alienation. If these objectives could be achieved, all members could share in 'community pride'.

An alternative view

An alternative view of what a multi-cultural society is, which can be broadly described as 'liberal' in nature, is rather different. This view suggests that, in a truly multicultural society, cultural differences should be preserved and celebrated. Within such a scenario, each ethnic group should tolerate the different cultures which flourish, but should not seek full integration.

This vision sees diversity as a positive force, increasing the richness of society and actually encourages tolerance. In practice, it implies the creation of more single-faith schools which preserve different cultures and the strong protection of minority rights against discrimination and antagonism.

Members of so-called 'ethnic minorities' should still be required to be good citizens, with all the responsibilities which that carries. However, as far as possible, cultural differences should be protected by the law (notably the European Convention on Human Rights) and positively encouraged.

THE RACE EQUALITY UNIT

This is a government body which was set up to implement Labour's race relations policy. Its view of a **multicultural** society is very much along the lines of the second vision described above – that ethnic differences should be allowed to flourish, but that each group should have an equal stake in society and should be free from discrimination. The 'mission statement' of the race equality unit very much epitomises the Labour government's view of good race relations. It says that Britain should be a country where:

> **multiculturalism**
> Ideas which suggest that society should tolerate ethnic diversity or should encourage full cultural integration.

- Every colour is a good colour.
- Every member of society is able to fulfil their potential.
- Racism is unacceptable.
- Everyone is treated equally according to needs and rights.
- Everyone recognises their responsibilities.
- Racial diversity is celebrated.

This is a clear enough statement of what is considered to be a fair and healthy multicultural society. A particularly practical step has taken place within the Home Office where there is an agreement to create 'representative' workforces in the police, fire, probation and prison services.

NON-LEGISLATIVE RACIAL MEASURES

Most of the attempts to outlaw racism and racial discrimination in Britain have involved legislation, either to prohibit discriminatory practices or to require institutions to improve race relations. However, dealing with this issue is too complex to be handled through the law alone. There have also been a number of initiatives designed to change attitudes, consciousness and behaviour. In other words there is a need to create a new culture of race relations. Some of the objectives of these programmes have been:
- to create equality of opportunity for all racial and national groups;
- to eliminate racist attitudes and so reduce racial violence;
- to foster better relations between different ethnic groups;

- to make Britain an inclusive society in which all groups feel they have a stake;
- to create a climate of tolerance towards an ethnically diverse society.

A wide variety of measures are in place to try to achieve these objectives, mostly under the auspices of the Commission for Racial Equality. However many other agencies are involved. These include the football authorities who have instituted a programme to remove racism from the game, local authorities, educational bodies and the Civil Service itself.

Ironically it is in the field of politics where there has been a noticeable lack of progress. There are still very few MPs from ethnic minority backgrounds (though the number is creeping up). The battle to have separate 'black sections' within the Labour party failed. This would have ensured guaranteed representation on party bodies for ethnic minority members. It would also have increased the number of parliamentary candidates and therefore MPs. The House of Lords, which is supposedly a socially representative chamber has also lagged behind. The new Appointments Commission is, however, charged with the task of ensuring the nomination of more peers from different ethnic groups. The Civil Service code of practice also now demands progress towards more racial equality in recruitment and promotion.

However, it is likely that education is the main field in which better race relations and equality of opportunity will be achieved. The National Curriculum recognises this and every local education authority has a duty to improve race relations. Unfortunately, by 2002, there was still no clear policy on whether schools should be more ethnically mixed or whether it was better to encourage the creation of more single-faith schools. There are many who believe that the latter will reinforce ethnic tensions, while others suggest that such schools actually prevent them.

Table 8.1 Britain's ethnic mix, 2001

Ethnic group	Millions
White	53.0
All black groups	1.3
Indian	1.0
Pakistani/Bangladeshi	0.9
Chinese	0.1
Others	1.5
All non-white	4.8

SAMPLE QUESTIONS

1 Discuss the significance and impact of the Macpherson Report into the Stephen Lawrence case.

2 What have been the main barriers to improving race relations since the 1960s?

3 Differentiate between legislative and non-legislative methods of improving race relations.

4 What have been the attitudes of the main parties in Britain towards race relations and immigration?

5 Describe the role of law in the field of race relations.

The environment

9

➤ The background and origins of the environment as a political issue

➤ A review of the ways in which the environment became a more prominent issue

➤ Description and assessment of New Labour environmental policies after 1997

DEFINING THE TERM 'ENVIRONMENT'

The term 'environment' is a broad one and we need first to establish which aspects are covered here. For the purposes of this chapter, we will recognise the following meanings.

● Matters concerning the physical environment, including air and water quality, climate, noise, traffic congestion, health issues and the physical beauty of landscapes etc.

● Long-term concerns about bio-diversity, preservation of endangered species, the effects of earth changes which affect climate etc.

● Issues concerning the safety of foods etc., mainly dealing with the implications of genetically modified foods.

● Environmental issues which affect safety, such as the use of nuclear energy or mining.

● The question of preserving sources of energy and other resources, including the development of alternative forms of energy and recycling schemes.

These examples may omit some environmental concerns, but they represent a selection of the most important matters which have been considered by the British political system.

PRINCIPLES

Environmental policy is very different to other issues in British politics. There are a number of reasons for this.

As a policy issue, it is very densely populated with pressure groups. Greenpeace and Friends of the Earth are well known examples, but there are many others concerned with a wide range of specialised areas. Furthermore, some of these groups have extremely large memberships. The National Trust and the Royal Society for the Protection of Birds (RSPB) are prominent examples. But there are many others such as the Council for the Protection of Rural England, the Countryside Alliance and Woodland Trust. If we consider local levels of political activities, there are still more, many of them temporary in nature. Groups exist to promote or prevent traffic management measures, airport building, changes in countryside use, building developments and the like.

Issues affecting the environment concern the political system at different levels. There are, as we have seen above, many local campaigns constantly being fought. In addition, issues may be regional or national, but, more often than not, are European and global in nature. Most environmental problems do not recognise political boundaries, so action by governments is rarely simple and cannot be conducted in isolation.

The environment is not normally considered to be a subject which is a vote winner or loser in elections. Although environmental issues remain on most people's list of concerns, it is not normally high and rarely influences voting behaviour. Political parties know this, so they do not consider it a high priority. Meanwhile, the British Green party has failed to gain a significant toe-hold in British political life, largely as a result of the first-past-the-post electoral system which discriminates against small parties. As we shall see below, some progress has been made in recent years, but this is slow and relatively modest.

THE ORIGINS OF ENVIRONMENTAL CONCERNS

Until the 1960s the environment scarcely appeared at all on the political agenda. There had been concerns about the health implications of pollution in the nineteenth and early twentieth century, but they were largely seen as isolated examples. They tended to be dealt with by the creation of inspectorates, which were set up to regulate the activities of individual industries.

Two early pieces of legislation which signalled the end of an *ad hoc* approach to environmental issues were the **Clean Air Acts** of 1956 and 1968. This legislation applied to both individual households and to industry. They were concerned solely with air quality, but were the first signs of a national policy emerging.

In 1974 the **Control of Pollution Act** marked a further step towards a more comprehensive policy. This was both national and dealt with a wider variety of forms of pollution, adding water quality to air. At the same time the issue of pollution was brought onto the agenda of the European Community, with Germany leading the way in demanding European-wide anti-pollution standards.

These were some of the opening shots in the war against pollution and in the battle to bring environmental concerns to a higher place on the political agenda. During the late 1960s and 1970s a number of developments were important:

- Part of the New Left movement of the 1960s, which was concerned with the alienation of marginalised groups in society, became interested in environmental issues. Left-wing opponents of free-market capitalism, mainly among youth protest movements, saw it as exploiting the earth's physical environment as well as its workers and consumers. As members of this youth movement grew older, many of them retained the environmental concerns which they had developed in the 1960s.
- A larger amount of scientific evidence was emerging. Information gathered about links between air pollution and diseases such as cancer and asthma. Concerns about the increasing danger to many animal and plant species were growing. Scientists began to suspect that long-term changes in climate were taking place and were possibly the result of environmental degradation.
- The two oil price crises of the 1970s alerted the developed world to its over-reliance on a single source of energy. This led to a search for new sources of energy which would be both environmentally friendly (i.e. not fossil fuels) and renewable.
- New political groups were coming into existence in this period. The British Ecology party appeared and soon transformed itself into the Green Party. Friends of the Earth appeared as a world movement and soon became a huge pressure group with extensive funds and a large organisation for campaigning, publicity and scientific research. Greenpeace soon followed. Meanwhile, existing organisations such as the National Trust were turning themselves into campaign groups.

THE ENVIRONMENT BECOMES A MAJOR ISSUE

Having drifted around the margins of British and European politics in the 1960s and 1970s, the environment moved closer to centre stage in the 1980s. The environmental concerns of the past were becoming more obviously acute and political action was clearly needed.

In Britain the issue was brought to the forefront of the agenda by the Conservative government of Margaret Thatcher. They seemed to be an unlikely candidate as guardian of the environment. As an apparent friend of capitalism, which was seen as the main culprit in environmental degradation, one would not have expected radical policies in this area. Yet progress was made in the mid-1980s.

In 1987 **Her Majesty's Inspectorate of Pollution (HMIP)** was set up. This was the first national organisation created to deal with environmental maters. They had powers to deal with both industry and local authorities in controlling air, water and waste pollution. In 1988 Thatcher herself made a landmark speech to the Royal Society, accepting that global warming was a serious problem for the future.

The years 1989–90 proved to be landmark ones in Britain. In 1989 the **National Rivers Authority (NRA)** was set up. In 1990 the **Environment Protection Act** was passed. This was the first piece of legislation to set universal standards of pollution control. They were to be administered by the NRA and the HMIP. Private and public bodies were bound by the targets and sanctions were introduced against transgressors. Any organisation which felt it could justify breaking the targets was forced to apply for special dispensation. Also in 1990 the Conservative government published a document entitled **This Common Inheritance**, the first comprehensive policy document to appear concerning sustainable development.

While these initiatives were taking place, the European Community were placing the environment onto their agenda. In 1987 the **Single European Act** was implemented. This Act made environmental protection one of the responsibilities of the Community, with voting on the issue in the Council of Ministers requiring unanimity to protect national interests.

In 1993 John Gummer became Environment Secretary. This was a key event as Gummer was an important environmental campaigner. He wished to build on the progress made in the 1980s. Gummer introduced air pollution targets, which began the process of reducing harmful car emissions, and instituted a policy for farmers to create environmentally sensitive areas, with grants to support them. Most importantly, however, he created the **Environment Agency** in 1995 by amalgamating the NRA and the HMIP. This large powerful body was to carry forward environmental policy and had extensive powers to enforce standards. Any developments which might have environmental consequences had to submit plans to the agency for approval.

NEW LABOUR AND THE ENVIRONMENT

Part of New Labour's 'third way' philosophy was to accept environmentalism as a key political issue. Although Blair's party is committed to supporting business, it argues that this can only be done provided environmental concerns are addressed. In other words, it contains a belief that industrial development and environmental concerns can be compatible, an idea which many campaigners see as impossible. The diversity of New Labour policies reflects the breadth of the issue in itself.

Global involvement

Two international treaties have set the scene of global concerns. These were the agreements at Rio de Janeiro in 1992 and the Kyoto agreement in 1997. The former was negotiated by the Conservative government of John Major and the latter by the Labour government, with John Prescott representing Britain, interestingly assisted by John Gummer who had led the Conservative environmental initiative earlier.

These two agreements aimed to make progress in cutting harmful emissions, known as greenhouse gases. The Rio accord, known as **Agenda 21** placed a requirement on all participants to take measures to reduce emissions. However, the targets were too imprecise. At Kyoto, however, it was agreed that greenhouse gas emissions should be cut from 1990 levels by the following levels:
- USA: 7 per cent
- EU: 8 per cent
- Japan: 6 per cent

There is little doubt that the British government representatives played a leading role in these negotiations. Furthermore, the British commitment has been in excess of the targets set. New Labour sees itself as a more internationalist government than its predecessors and has attempted to move both the EU and the USA to a more radical position on the environment. In the case of the USA this has not been successful and President George Bush junior repudiated the Kyoto treaty early in 2002. His administration also largely ignored the 2002 Johannesburg conference on poverty and the environment.

Traffic and car pollution

Although the Labour government since 1997 has claimed to be interested in reducing traffic levels and congestion in cities, its policies have failed to make significant progress. Road building programmes have not been cut back (despite fierce opposition from a variety of local anti-roads campaign groups). Indeed, when London Mayor Ken Livingstone announced the introduction of congestion charges in the city centre and proposed parking taxes, the government seemed remarkably hostile.

Labour has also dragged its feet on such issues as road tolls to reduce motorway traffic and a taxation system designed to reduce the use of large-engined cars which produce most pollution. Its **1998 Transport White Paper** promised more spending on public transport to get cars off the road, in combination with a variety of proposals to introduce charges on motorists to deter car use. By 2002 little progress had been made and a new crisis in public transport threatened to de-rail (literally!) policy.

But the government's anti-emissions policy was most severely tested in the autumn of 2000. At that time there was a sharp rise in oil prices, and therefore also petrol prices. This caused a massive campaign against the high levels of duty on fuel which the government was levying (in its defence, the government could argue that the rise in fuel taxation had started under previous Conservative governments).

Gordon Brown was now in a dilemma over how to deal with the crisis. Fuel depots were being blockaded by protesters: the farmers and other rural interests were applying huge pressure and motorists were running out of fuel as the blockades prevented petrol getting to filling stations. Brown argued that high petrol duties were a key part of an integrated emissions policy. Indeed, he added, it was part of the country's Agenda 21 commitments.

In the event Brown made concessions to the protesters. Fuel duties were reduced and he gave a commitment to hold them down in the immediate future. Environmentalists were dismayed by Brown's apparent climbdown. Motorists, however, were pleased that the crisis had passed. Most agree that the government, Brown in particular, had failed its greatest environmental test.

Farming and the countryside

The Labour government reluctantly became mired in problems with the countryside after it came to office. It was dealing with the aftermath of the BSE crisis, which had devastated livestock farming when two further problems emerged. The first was the outbreak of foot and mouth disease in 2001. It took nearly a year before the epidemic subsided. During this period rural interests claimed that the crisis had been badly handled and was a sign that the government did not understand the problems of the countryside. The second was very much of the government's own making. It decided to allow parliament a free vote on whether to ban hunting with hounds (mainly foxhunting). This was seen as an attack by urban dwellers on the countryside.

The three problems which the government faced threw into focus the whole issue of the British countryside and rural life. John Prescott had already established a so-called 'right to roam', forcing landowners to open up footpaths and rights of way. The measure had been greeted with mixed feelings. It had also placed the countryside and the environment together by creating a new government department – the Department for the Environment, Food and Rural Affairs (**DEFRA**). Now the whole issue of the Common Agricultural Policy (CAP) had to be addressed.

Expenditure on the CAP was becoming excessive. Furthermore British agriculture was not benefiting greatly from it, while it seemed to be of most interest to the French, who were seen as being at the centre of the beef industry's problems over BSE. It was, therefore, decided in 2002 to tie together the two issues of agricultural subsidies and environmental measures in the countryside. Rural Affair Minister Alun Michael announced that some subsidies would be phased out. Under a new EU directive he is free to replace up to 20 per cent of subsidies with government grants to farmers in return for their becoming responsible for environmental protection. Such issues as the conservation of endangered species, river water quality, maintenance of meadows and hedgerows are to be included in the scheme.

At the same time the new department has additional funds available for the encouragement of organic farming. It is recognised that large-scale industrial farming is unlikely to have a future in the UK. Farmers here cannot compete in an increasingly free world market. Industrial farming is also seen as a danger to the countryside environment.

The issue over which Labour has created most difficulty for itself in this field concerns research into genetically modified (GM) foods. In 1998 the government decided to ban its commercial use and brought in regulations (which apply throughout the EU) to force food processors to declare whether GM ingredients have been used. However, Tony Blair himself is committed to the continued approval of research. This has angered campaigners, especially Greenpeace and Friends of the Earth, who want an outright ban.

NEW LABOUR: AN ASSESSMENT

Despite its rhetoric, the Labour government which came to power in 1997 has a very mixed record on the environment. It has shown considerable global concerns and is widely praised for its attempts to preserve the Rio and Kyoto agreements on climate change. On the other hand its policies on transport have been less coherent. The commitments to reduce road traffic and improve public transport have not been maintained.

The main problems concern the government's difficulties in reconciling competing interests. The conflict between environmentalists and the motorists' lobby is a typical example. So too are those issues which create heated debate between farmers and rural interest groups and, in some cases, within the farming community itself. Its difficulties over what to do about GM foods is a typical example of the latter.

It may be that it will need a further advance by the Green Party and its allies to stimulate fresh interest. The Greens made an apparently famous 'break-through' in the elections to the European Parliament in 1995 by winning 15 per cent of the popular vote. It has also won seats in the Scottish Parliament and Welsh Assembly where proportional representation (PR) is being used. But these advances have been small and short lived. In terms of the popular vote the Greens have achieved little. Until they do, the government is unlikely to renew its commitment to the environment. As things stand, environmental campaigners are pleased by what they hear but are disappointed by what has been achieved.

THE EUROPEAN UNION

As we have seen, environmental protection, became an EU concern in 1987. Its jurisdiction lies in the following areas:
- The preservation of fish stocks in the seas around Europe. This is part of the Common Fisheries Policy (CFP).
- Control over sea pollution. Member states must conform to regulations concerning sewage and other potentially harmful releases into the sea.
- There is a scheme in place to encourage clean beaches. Coastal towns which can demonstrate minimum standards of cleanliness receive European awards.
- Under the Common Agricultural Policy, farmers must agree to certain environmental regulations in return for subsidies.
- Emissions controls over industries, notably chemicals and metals, are set by the EU.

- There are European emissions control regulations on cars, lorries and all forms of transport.
- European targets for the cleanliness of rivers have been agreed.
- There are European controls over the hunting of species which are considered to be endangered.

SAMPLE QUESTIONS

1 Why has environmental policy remained relatively low on the British political agenda?

2 In what ways has membership of the European Union affected environmental policy in Europe?

3 Assess New Labour's claim to be a friend of the environment since 1997.

Northern Ireland

10

➤ The background to the Northern Ireland problem

➤ The build up to and the importance of the Good Friday Agreement

➤ The effect of the devolution process on Northern Ireland

➤ The workings of the Northern Ireland Assembly

➤ The effects of decommissioning of arms and demilitarisation

➤ The future of Northern Ireland

BACKGROUND TO THE PROBLEM

How Northern Ireland came about

Until 1921 Ireland was a single political entity under British rule. It elected MPs to parliament in London, but was directly ruled by the British government. Between the 1880s and 1921 there was an ongoing campaign among nationalist Irish politicians, British Liberals and the new Labour party. At the more extreme end of the nationalist movement Sinn Fein, a political party dedicated to Irish independence and the Irish Republican Army (IRA, originally the 'Irish Volunteers') were formed to fight for independence.

The momentum for independence gradually built up to something of a crescendo when there was an IRA-led uprising in 1916 – the so-called 'Easter Rising'. Though the revolt was easily crushed, Britain's new prime minister, David Lloyd George, became convinced that a settlement had to be reached. However, there was a major obstacle to the independence process.

In the north of the island there was a concentration of Protestants who formed a majority in the so-called 'six counties' which comprised most of the ancient province of Ulster (strictly speaking, Ulster and Northern Ireland are not the same thing. Ulster is slightly bigger than what later became Northern Ireland). However, the Protestants were a minority in Ireland as a whole. These Protestants were the descendants of people who had been settled in Ireland since the seventeenth century. They had been given large tracts of land and so, by the twentieth century, they formed a high proportion of the middle classes in the north. In other words they enjoyed considerable economic, political and social power in those northern counties. Most of the Protestants were totally opposed to Irish independence. By the end of the twentieth century, many of their descendants were equally horrified by the prospect of a united country.

The Protestant fear and opposition of a united Ireland are complex emotions, but two main features stand out. The first is that this group, usually known as 'Loyalists', consider themselves culturally British. They are loyal to the monarchy and believe they have more in common with British people than with the Irish. The second issue concerns religion. The religious question in Northern Ireland requires separate consideration and is described fully below. In short, however, the Protestant minority in the north totally opposed absorption into a new Catholic state of Ireland.

It was therefore decided by government and parliament in London that Ireland would have to be partitioned. Six counties in the north would remain part of the United Kingdom, while the rest of the island was to become a separate state. In 1922, therefore, the 'Irish Free State' and 'Northern Ireland' – a province of Great Britain – came into existence. At first, the Irish Free State remained part of the United Kingdom. It had its own independent parliament and government, but accepted the authority of the British Crown. This fact prevented excessive tension from growing in Northern Ireland. All the Irish people owed allegiance to the Crown, so there was little to fear for the Protestants. But this situation began to change after 1937.

In that year the Irish Free State broke its close links with Britain and became 'Eire', though there was still a weak link with the crown. More importantly, however, a new constitution was developed under the influence of the Irish president, Eamonn de Valera. The new constitution incorporated a number of principles based on the Catholic religion (described below). This created a wide cultural and religious division between Northern Ireland and Eire. In 1949 Ireland became a full republic (known since as the 'Republic of Ireland) with no links to Britain. (It can be noted here that the term 'Republican' which is still applied to modern campaigners for a united Ireland, arises from the movement which had always opposed continuing links with the British Crown.) The schism between the north and the south was now complete.

Religion

The religious divide in Northern Ireland can only be understood in relation to the events of 1688–90. It may seem strange to consider history which is over three hundred years old when explaining a modern political problem, but that is part of the mystery of the province.

In 1688, the Catholic King of England, James II (of the Stuart dynasty), was removed from the throne. He was replaced by the Protestant William III (of the family of Orange). William knew he had to quell the Catholics of Ireland and so sent an army to crush a revolt led by the exiled former King James. At the Battle of the River Boyne in 1690 the Catholic army was defeated and Protestant ascendancy in the north was established. King William's family title, of course, gives its name to the Protestant Orange Order which was founded to celebrate the victory of protestantism in Ireland. When the Orange Order marches in the north today it is a demonstration of triumphalism which is well understood by both sides of the political divide.

So history continues to play a major role in the troubles. But it is not just an ancient tribal feud. The Protestants in the north fear the domination of the Catholic religion in various aspects of their lives. Education is a prime example of this, but there is also a fear that artistic and cultural life will be suppressed by the dominance of strict Catholic values. Until 1998, indeed, the constitution of the Irish Republic contained principles of law which were effectively religious rules. Divorce, abortion and contraception, for example, were all outlawed in Irish law. On a stricter religious level, some Protestants also fear the authority of the Pope which Catholics accept. This is now a more extreme view, but is held by some such as the reverend Iain Paisley who leads the extreme loyalist party, the Democratic Unionist party.

As religious observance has declined, it might be thought that the so-called 'sectarian' divide in Northern Ireland might disappear. This has not been the case. Strict religious belief may be less significant, but religion still represents culture and the conflict is, to a great extent, cultural in nature. There is an old joke in Northern Ireland which illustrates the strange place of religion in the troubles. It runs like this: A Jew was walking along a Belfast street. He was stopped by a threatening group of youths. 'Are you a Protestant or a Catholic?', they demanded. 'Neither', said the man, 'I'm Jewish'. 'Yes,' said one of the youths, 'but are you a Protestant Jew or a Catholic Jew?' The spiritual side of religion is less important than its cultural and political significance.

To many in Northern Ireland, therefore, being Protestant is synonymous with being 'British', while Catholics are seen as 'Irish'. The religious labels have become convenient ways in which we can identify the political and cultural divide, even though there is nothing intrinsically Protestant about loyalism or Catholic about republicanism.

The onset of the modern 'troubles'

When the province of Northern Ireland was granted its own devolved government in 1921, it was given political institutions which were, in effect, a smaller version of the Westminster model. A small parliament (known as 'Stormont' after the building where it met) was elected by first past the post after a brief flirtation with proportional representation. From the majority at Stormont an executive government was drawn, with a prime minister and a cabinet. It operated very much like the government in London, though its jurisdiction was limited to domestic affairs. Foreign policy, defence and overall economic management were set in London. There was also a full local government system put in place.

This seems uncontroversial at first sight. However, it transpired that all the institutions of government came to be dominated by the Protestant Unionists. This was reinforced by the practice of 'gerrymandering' where political boundaries were manipulated to favour one political party – the Unionists. Although the Unionists represented about two-thirds of the population of the north, they exerted 100 per cent control over Stormont, the government and most local government. The Catholics felt effectively 'disenfranchised'. But the problem ran deeper than this. It was also the case that Catholics suffered widespread, systematic discrimination at the hands of state institutions.

This discrimination existed in education, housing provision, employment in public service, the granting of official contracts to local firms and, perhaps most seriously, in the law enforcement system. The Northern Ireland police – known as the Royal Ulster Constabulary – was almost exclusively Protestant, and so was much of the judiciary. It was therefore suspected (with varying degrees of justification) that Catholics were also discriminated against in the criminal justice system. As the 1960s wore on, the Catholic minority found it could less and less rely on the forces of law and order. Indeed many actually felt directly threatened by them. This is a key ingredient in the recipe for conflict

To add to the political and religious strife, Northern Ireland Society is also culturally divided. Most schools, sports clubs, pubs, clubs, newspapers and housing estates are associated exclusively with one side of the sectarian divide or the other. The two communities, therefore, rarely mix. The opportunities for mutual understanding and compromise are, thus, limited.

Tension within the Catholic community mounted steadily during the 1960s. A largely middle-class civil rights movement was formed in 1968, a year when protest movements of various kinds had emerged all over Europe and the USA. This began to demonstrate against discrimination against Catholics. It became ultimately allied to a working-class movement in the Catholic housing estates whose grievances were not only economic and political. In hard economic times in the mid-1960s it was clear that the Catholic workers suffered more than their Protestant counterparts. The chemistry between the two movements proved to be explosive.

THE MODERN 'TROUBLES'

The flashpoint for conflict occurred in 1968 when a march by the new Civil Rights Association – a largely Catholic, Republican organisation – was attacked by Loyalists in Londonderry. The Royal Ulster Constabulary restored order, but at the expense of some violence, which antagonised the civil rights campaigners. During 1968 and 1969 there were growing outbursts of conflict between Loyalists and Republicans. Extra British troops were drafted into Belfast to keep the peace. From then on, the British army presence in Northern Ireland steadily grew.

The year 1971 proved to be a critical one. A bomb, planted by the Protestant paramilitary organisation – the Ulster Volunteer Force – killed fifteen Catholics in a Belfast bar. This was in response to what the Protestant community saw as an increasing threat from the Irish Republican Army (IRA). The IRA had mobilised its forces and was recruiting new members rapidly. The response of the British government was to introduce internment.

The process of internment had last been used in World War II to remove people of enemy nationality from society by placing them in special camps. In Northern Ireland it was applied to anyone who was *suspected* of being engaged in terrorist activity. No trial was held, though the authorities had to convince a judge that there were grounds for suspicion. Three hundred were interned in the summer of 1971, nearly all Catholics, who were suspected of IRA membership. This angered the civil rights campaigners who saw it as imprisonment without trial. More seriously, it convinced the Catholic, Republican, community that the British government was firmly on the side of the Loyalists.

Demonstrations, sporadic rioting and bombings continued through 1971, culminating in the most serious incident of the troubles to date. In 1972 a relatively peaceful civil rights march in Londonderry was broken up by members of the Parachute Regiment. Thirteen people, some merely bystanders, were shot dead by the troops. The explanation of how this occurred is still not resolved. However, it was seen by the Catholics and Republicans as the clearest sign of British intent – that they would resist political reform at all costs. The British embassy in Dublin was attacked and a bomb was set off at an army barracks in Aldershot. The transfer of violence to the British mainland was a particular shock, as it now became clear that the Northern Ireland problem was about to involve everyone in Britain.

The reaction of the British government was to institute direct rule in Northern Ireland. The devolved institutions in Belfast were suspended. It was clear that the Northern Ireland government had lost its authority in the province and could not maintain order. Furthermore the Unionist-dominated institutions only served to antagonise the Catholic minority. Laws were from now on to be made by the Westminster Parliament and government was to be carried out by the Northern Ireland Office, headed by the Northern Ireland Secretary (the first being William Whitelaw).

DIRECT RULE

The period of direct rule from London lasted from 1972 until 1999 when devolved government took over in the province. For 27 years Northern Ireland suffered from violence, disruption, political initiatives bringing hope followed by disappointments, and renewed sectarian conflict. The story of direct rule is best divided into three themes – the course of sectarian violence, the fragmentation of the party system and the various attempts to find a lasting peace.

Sectarian conflict

Violence continued to dominate life in Northern Ireland through the 1970s. This was characterised by rioting, bombings, attacks on security forces, tit-for-tat killings and punishment beatings. In 1974 the Prevention of Terrorism Act was passed, giving the security wide powers to stop and search people, property and vehicles, to ban marches and demonstrations and to detain terrorist suspects for extended periods.

Political assassination was added to the litany of violence in 1979. Lord Mountbatten, a member of the royal family, was killed by an IRA bomb and Airey Neave, Conservative Opposition spokesman on Northern Ireland, was killed in Westminster by the Irish National Liberation Army (INLA). This second death marked the arrival of a new Republican group which was even more committed to violence than the IRA.

By the early 1980s Northern Ireland's main prison, the Maze, was full of terrorist prisoners. Seeking a special 'political' status, the republican prisoners started a campaign to gain privileges normally accorded to such detainees in 1981. Several went on hunger strike and fasted to death. The most celebrated of them was Bobby Sands who actually won a parliamentary by-election while in prison and close to death. Sands entered the mythology of Republicanism and became one of its most revered martyrs. His death brought a new wave of rioting and general violence.

Dramatic bombings continued, the best known of which destroyed part of the Brighton Hotel which housed many leading members of the Conservative party who were in town for the party's annual conference in 1984. Prime

Minister Thatcher only just escaped, but four others were killed. Eleven people were killed by an IRA bomb at Enniskillen, and 10 Downing Street suffered a mortar attack in 1991.

A crescendo of violence seemed to have been reached by 1993. There were now a number of groups operating all over Britain, each of which was capable of wreaking havoc. On the Republican side there was the IRA and the INLA. The Loyalist cause was served by the Ulster Defence Association (UDA) and the Ulster Volunteer Force (UDV). The politicians who spoke for these groups were incapable of controlling them. It was at this point, however, that political forces had gathered sufficiently to break the deadlock. An IRA ceasefire was declared in 1994 (following the Downing Street declaration – see below) and the Loyalist paramilitaries followed suit. Apart from the bombing of Canary Wharf in London in 1996, the ceasefire held. Only the INLA and the 'Real IRA' – an extreme breakaway group – continued the campaign of violence.

Party fragmentation

Up to 1970 Northern Ireland politics was completely dominated by the Ulster Unionist party which won most of the seats in Stormont and at Westminster. They were opposed by Nationalist parties and Sinn Fein, but these had little or no hope of breaking Unionist control. Everything changed, however, with the onset of the troubles.

A moderate party was formed to represent the Nationalist community. This was the Social Democratic Labour party. Its domestic policies were similar to the British Labour party but it was also committed to the uniting of Ireland by peaceful, political means. This party had no connection with terrorists and did, indeed, shun all forms of violence. A non-sectarian, neutral party, the Alliance also came into being in 1970. This party gained an immediate following within the Northern Ireland middle classes and hopes were high that it represented the future. After a brief early flurry, however, the Alliance has failed to make a significant impact. Meanwhile, Sinn Fein, which was considered to be the political wing of the IRA, was increasing its support, especially among working-class Republicans.

The Unionists were also not immune from internal dissension. The unionist Party split almost as soon as violence broke out. The main schism, then and ever since, lies between the more moderate centre of the party and the extremists led by the Reverend Iain Paisley. Paisley is a militant in both the religious and political senses. His brand of Protestantism is totally opposed to Catholicism (he describes Catholics as 'papists') while, as a Unionist, he is opposed to any compromise with Nationalism. His party became known as the Democratic Unionists (DUP) in 1971.

Since Paisley's defection from the Ulster Unionist party (UUP), others have followed and there is now a varied collection of Unionist parties including the UK Unionists, Progressive Unionists and the United Unionists Assembly. These groups vary in their attitudes towards the peace process from extreme to moderate. There is also a Women's Coalition party which is dedicated to a peaceful solution and claims to be non-sectarian. The other non-sectarian group – the Alliance party – has survived but with very little influence.

Party fragmentation has brought with it a number of problems. Firstly, it is extremely difficult to reach general agreement on any new initiatives, so many factions have to be satisfied. The pressure to ensure that all groups are represented in any political system means that complex electoral systems have to be adopted. Some of the groups, furthermore, have their own military wings which they only partially control. Failure to satisfy them all may result in a continuation of violence, even from very small splinter groups. Above all, however, the multi-party nature of Northern Ireland politics means that there is always likely to be a lack of coherence in any of the various movements which jockey each other for influence.

Peace initiatives

Throughout the 1970s, 1980s and 1990s British governments produced a series of initiatives to try to find a peace formula. The essential details of the most important stages in this process are described below.

POWER SHARING AND THE SUNNINGDALE AGREEMENT, 1973–74

With hindsight it may seem naive that the British government should believe that the political problem of Northern Ireland could be solved simply by creating a system which appeared to give representation to both the loyalist and nationalist communities. But back in 1973 this was perceived to be the main problem. The idea that conflict was more deep rooted was simply not understood at the time.

So, in 1973, a new assembly was elected and an executive was drawn from it. This 11 person government was comprised of 6 Unionists, 4 Nationalists from the SDLP and 1 'neutral' member from the Alliance party. This was a reasonably fair reflection of the divisions in the community, but it still meant that the Unionists held a clear majority. Furthermore, the head of the executive – Brian Faulkner – was soon rejected by his own Unionist party. Sinn Fein, who now claimed to represent nationalism, was also excluded on the grounds that it was a terrorist organisation.

Despite its problems the government continued to hope for a settlement. The following year the Sunningdale Agreement was signed with the government of the Irish Republic. This allowed for regular consultations between the British and Irish governments over Northern Ireland affairs and a good deal of cross-border co-operation, especially over security. The agreement was seen as a 'sell-out' to the Irish by the Nationalists while the new executive was seen as no more than a continuation of Unionist domination by the Nationalists.

In 1974 a general strike by Nationalist, Catholic workers was called and it was very soon realised that this was a clear demonstration of a withdrawal of popular consent from the new arrangements. The government of Britain conceded defeat and dissolved the new assembly. Direct rule was re-established.

ROLLING DEVOLUTION, 1982–86

The Labour government of Harold Wilson had investigated the possibility of a new settlement by calling a **Constitutional Convention** in 1975, but there was still insufficient common ground for meaningful discussion. The convention collapsed after less than one year. Undaunted, a renewed attempt at settlement was begun in 1982. This was a process known as 'rolling devolution' and was introduced by the Conservative Northern Ireland secretary, James Prior.

The idea here was to elect a new assembly, but to give it little power at the beginning. As time went by and the community got used to the idea of having its own government, the powers of the assembly were to be gradually increased until self-government for the province could be established. The SDLP and Sinn Fein boycotted the assembly, so that its early signs were very pessimistic. Some hope for its future were revived by the **Anglo-Irish Agreement** of 1985. By this convention, the government of the republic of Ireland accepted that Northern Ireland could not be united with the rest of Ireland without the consent of its people. This agreement, it was expected, would allay the fears of the Unionists of a Catholic takeover. But it proved to be insufficient. Unionists wanted a complete surrender by the republic of ireland and this was not forthcoming. The failure of the Anglo-Irish Agreement contributed to the demise of the rolling devolution process and the assembly was dissolved in 1986.

THE DOWNING STREET DECLARATION AND THE IRA CEASEFIRE, 1993–94

The so-called Downing Street declaration – the brainchild of John Major – changed the Northern Ireland situation dramatically and marked the beginning of the modern peace process. The declaration stated that the British government had no 'strategic interest' in Northern Ireland remaining part of the United Kingdom. What this meant – and its significance was not lost on the Nationalist community – was that Britain became a truly neutral player in the game of Irish politics. In the past Britain had always been seen as an ally of the Loyalists. Now it portrayed itself as a neutral arbiter between the two communities.

The following year the IRA called a ceasefire and most of the other paramilitary groups followed suit. An uneasy peace descended and serious talks began. President Clinton of the USA threw his weight behind a settlement and sent Senator George Mitchell as a neutral envoy to try to broker a new political agreement. Sadly for John Major, who had put all his efforts into a permanent peace, he was ousted from office before a new agreement could be reached. It was left to Mo Mowlem, the new Labour Secretary of State to reach a settlement in 1998. This was the Good Friday agreement.

Reasons for failure before 1998

Why had all these attempts to find a lasting settlement failed before the Good Friday Agreement? This is a complex question, which must involve considerable speculation. Some of the reasons which have been offered are as follows:

- Political agreement could not be reached until there was some certainty that sectarian violence was over. There was always a fear that if either side could not achieve its aims politically it would simply resort to violence. There was no prospect of a lasting ceasefire until after 1997.
- The British government was treated with suspicion by both sides of the sectarian divide and could therefore never negotiate with both sides on an equal basis.
- The government of the Irish Republic was seen as a malign influence on Northern Ireland affairs by the Loyalists. Until it showed a determination to allow Northern Ireland to command its own destiny its motives would always be suspected.
- The security forces in Northern Ireland were not seen as even-handed. Ironically, both sides of the sectarian divide believed the British army favoured their opponents. The Royal Ulster Constabulary (RUC) was also viewed as a Protestant force by the Catholic community.

- However sincere attempts were to achieve genuine power-sharing, there was always a suspicion that the majority – i.e. the Protestant Loyalists – would always be in political control.

THE GOOD FRIDAY AGREEMENT

The conditions for peace

Having established the reasons why so many previous attempts at peace-making had failed, we can now examine the circumstances which allowed a convincing agreement to be reached in 1998. Again these must inevitably be speculative, but there is considerable evidence to support them:

- The British government needed to convince both sides that it was a neutral player. The new Labour government was able to achieve this to some extent. In addition the intervention of the United States, President Clinton and Senator Mitchell in particular, went some way to establish trust on both sides.
- The new Secretary of State for Northern Ireland – Mo Mowlem – enjoyed the trust of the Republican community more than any of her predecessors.
- The Unionist Leader, David Trimble, had the necessary respect to carry forward a more moderate Loyalist position. His willingness to negotiate – albeit indirectly – with Sinn Fein was a huge step forward.
- Possibly, the return of some degree of economic prosperity in the second half of the 1990s may have reduced alienation among the working classes.
- The rapid and dramatic growth in prosperity in the Republic of Ireland, together with a distinct loosening of religious influence there, may have allayed some of the fears of Protestants in Northern Ireland.
- The death of 27 people in Omagh (albeit after the Good Friday Agreement was signed) confirmed the community's desire to see an end to violence. Sinn Fein and the IRA, neither of whom were responsible for the Omagh bomb (it was the act of the extremist 'Real' IRA), repudiated violence of this kind. The revulsion within Northern Ireland renewed determination to make the agreement work.

The nature of the agreement

The Good Friday Agreement can be divided into five main strands. These are as shown in the box.

Good Friday Agreement

1 There should be a devolved government in Northern Ireland along strict proportional lines with all elements of the community properly represented.
2 There was to be real progress towards the solving of sectarian issues such as the decommissioning of terrorist weapons, reform of the Royal Ulster Constabulary, the gradual withdrawal of British troops and reform of the criminal justice system.
3 There was to be increased co-operation and some power-sharing between the governments of the United Kingdom, the Republic of Ireland and the devolved government of Northern Ireland.
4 All sides in the agreement should renounce the use of violence once and for all.
5 The Republic of Ireland should give up its historic objective of uniting Ireland and should amend its constitution and laws to remove specific terms which were offensive to Protestants.

DEVOLUTION

The electoral system

The devolution process in Northern Ireland had to be very different from its counterparts in Wales and Scotland. In particular, the electoral system to be used had to be such that all minority groups were represented. A form of proportional representation was used in Scotland and Wales, but this was not a radical system and it eliminated the very small parties which might have sought election. In Northern Ireland even very small factions had to have a chance of winning seats in the new assembly. For this reason, the Single Transferable Vote (STV) was introduced. STV allows both small parties and individuals to win seats as it is one of the most proportional forms of electoral system known to politics. The results of the first assembly elections reflect the success of STV in this regard (see table 10.1). Local government elections were held on the same basis and the results were similar.

Table 10.1   Northern Ireland Assembly election, 1998

Party	Seats won
Ulster Unionist party	28
Social Democratic and Labour party	24
Democratic Unionist Party	20
Sinn Fein	18
Alliance party	6
Northern Ireland Unionist party	3
United Unionist Assembly party	3
Northern Ireland Women's Coalition	2
Progressive Unionist party	2
UK Unionist party	1
Independent Unionist	1

We can see that Loyalist parties (all the Unionist factions together) won over 50 per cent of the seats, but the political system is so fragmented that no group enjoys a dominant majority. This contrasts with the traditional political system in the province, which was completely controlled by a large, single Unionist party

The Assembly

The election result demonstrates that the new assembly, containing 108 members, represented a multi-party system, very much along the lines of most European systems. In order to pass legislation, coalitions of support have to be built. No single group can bulldoze any measure through the legislature.

Its powers are extensive. A wide range of primary legislation can be passed. However, such areas as foreign policy, the economy, finance and, above all, security matters, cannot be left to the assembly. Security (mainly policing) and criminal law are the most sensitive of issues in the province (unlike Scotland and Wales where sectarian conflict is not an issue). It also oversees the administration of such services as health, education, housing, transport and agriculture. It is expected that these policy issues, which were formerly run on sectarian basis, will be conducted in a neutral fashion so that no section of the community will suffer discrimination. A strong committee system, which scrutinises the work of the devolved government, helps to prevent such possibilities from re-emerging.

The idea of cross-community agreements in the assembly was a key innovation. It is completely different to anything known either in the British political system, or the devolved arrangements in Wales and Northern Ireland. Essentially, the safeguards work as follows:

- All Northern Ireland legislation must conform to the European Convention on Human Rights. This ensures that no sections of the community or individuals may suffer discrimination. Though this provision is in place in Scotland, it does not apply to primary legislation for England and Wales.
- The committees of the assembly, which consider both proposed legislation and the operation of government, are formed in direct proportion to party strengths in the whole assembly. Again, this ensures proportionality.
- Legislation must command not only an overall majority of the assembly, but must also be approved by a majority of *both* communities, i.e. Unionists and Nationalists. This unique provision is a vital element in the arrangements. It ensures that a majority cannot govern without the consent of both sides of the sectarian divide. This is, of course, not the case in Westminster, nor does it apply in Scotland and Wales where the nationalists have been excluded from power.

What we see here is a new model for proportional forms of government. It may not work in the long run, but, as a constitutional innovation, it may serve as a blueprint for the settlement of similar conflicts here or elsewhere.

The executive

This is effectively the government of Northern Ireland. Powers which have not been devolved, such as defence, security, finance, the economy, remain in the hands of the UK government or the Secretary of State for Northern Ireland. It is headed by a first minister. This will be the nomination of the largest party in the assembly. Accordingly, David Trimble was the first holder of the post, the nomination of the Ulster Unionist party. It is assumed that his deputy will be from the biggest party on the other side of the sectarian divide. Thus Seamus Mallon of the SDLP became Trimble's first deputy.

An executive of ten members works with the first minister. Places on the executive are awarded in proportion to the strengths of parties in the assembly. The parties which qualify nominate those whom they wish to serve. Again this ensures that all sections of the community are represented in the government. It was, for example, a radical and dramatic development when Sinn Fein found itself in a position to nominate two members. One of them, indeed, was a former senior member of the IRA, Martin McGuinness, who became education minister. We therefore saw the amazing reality of Unionist politicians sitting down in government with former Republican terrorists. It was an uneasy partnership, but it did take place. Unsurprisingly, the radical anti-Good Friday Agreement party, the Democratic Unionists, led by Iain Paisley, did not take part. As a safeguard, all Northern Ireland ministers must publicly renounce the use of violence to achieve political aims.

Once again the arrangements for the executive were radically different from those at Westminster, Cardiff or Edinburgh. The Northern Ireland executive does not feature collective responsibility – each minister is independent and answers directly to the assembly – and it is not controlled by a single party or a partial coalition. Its critics point out that it has a very narrow jurisdiction so that its existence is very much a token of power-sharing. This may be the case, but, if so, it was an important symbol of reconciliation.

EXTERNAL RELATIONS

Northern Ireland had been seen as a British problem within the province. Any attempts at interference from the rest of Ireland was viewed with great suspicion. The agreement, however, accepted for the first time that the Republic did have legitimate interests in the province. Three new institutions were therefore set up:

The north–south ministerial council

A regular opportunity for ministers from both sides of the border (i.e. from the Republic and Northern Ireland) to discuss matters of mutual concern. It meets twice a year at the most senior level but more junior ministers may discuss specialised issues at any time. The meeting cannot make binding decisions but is expected to make influential recommendations to member governments. The issues it discusses regularly include security, transport, economic development, agriculture, tourism, fisheries and European affairs.

The British–Irish council

This has also been described as the 'council of the isles'. Representatives from all over the British Isles meet twice a year. Thus, not only are Britain and Ireland represented, but also all their constituent parts – Scotland, Wales, the Isle of Man, Channel Islands and, of course, Northern Ireland. To a large extent this is a token organisation, designed to give equal status to all parts of the British Isles and to express some kind of common heritage and interest. Its range of concerns is inevitably limited. Such matters as drugs enforcement, crime and the environment are discussed in a generalised way.

The British–Irish inter-governmental conference

This involves representatives from the main British and Irish governments, with the intention that heads of government should try to meet twice each year. The issues it is expected to address give us clues as to its purpose. They include, for example, cross-border policing and security, human rights and terrorism.

To some extent in recognition of this open involvement of the Irish government in the affairs of the province, the Republic made a key concession. It had been placed in the Irish constitution of 1937 that an objective of the Irish state was to unite Ireland, i.e. to take possession of the north at some time in the future. This territorial claim was dropped (following a referendum to amend the Irish constitution). Instead, both the British and Irish governments agreed to respect the will of the majority of the people of Northern Ireland. The removal of the Irish 'threat' to the 'Britishness' of the province allayed some of the Protestant fears of a Catholic takeover.

THE RESOLUTION OF REMAINING ISSUES

It was recognised that the creation of political institutions alone could not result in a lasting peace. The other sources of conflict had to be addressed too. The main issues which were reserved for additional negotiation were as follows.

The Royal Ulster Constabulary (RUC)

As we saw above, the RUC was regarded as a major stumbling block to security by the Nationalist community. Most of its members were Protestant (Catholic members were persecuted and even shot by terrorists) and it was seen by Nationalists as a Loyalist force which was not even-handed in its dealings with the community. Even the title 'Royal' suggested to them that it served the British Crown, rather than all the people of the province. Although, by the 1990s, it had been reformed and had become a more neutral body, the Nationalists wished to see the creation of an entirely new police force which could serve both communities equally.

An inquiry was set up under former Conservative minister and governor of Hong Kong, Chris Patten. His proposals, which were presented in 2000, suggested a change of name, completely new recruitment policies, with a minimum quota of Catholics and a new set of safeguards to be introduced. However, they were quickly rejected by the Loyalists, who objected especially to the change of name to the 'Northern Ireland Police Service' or something similar. They insisted on it remaining 'Royal'. They also objected to the enforced membership of large numbers of Catholic officers. The issue of the RUC remains unresolved.

Prisoner releases

The existence of large numbers of terrorists in Northern Ireland prisons remained a potential source of friction on both sides. As an act of good faith by the British government and in recognition of the ceasefire which was holding on both sides of the sectarian conflict, it was agreed that some long-term prisoners should be released early. This was on the understanding that they should renounce violence. In other words they were set free 'on licence'.

Although both Loyalist and Republican paramilitaries benefited from the scheme (which also applied to prisoners in the Irish Republic), many Unionists opposed this part of the agreement, especially when some of the released men committed crimes for which they were re-arrested. The policy was, however, retained as it was seen as an important factor in maintaining a lasting peace.

Demilitarisation

The hard-line Republican movement saw the presence of large numbers of British troops, together with road blocks, watch towers and armed bases, as an occupying army. By 1998, too, the need for such a tight security system, had diminished. There was, therefore, added to the agreement a loose commitment to troop reductions.

In the event, largely symbolic gestures were made towards de-militarisation. A few army bases were closed and troops were less evident on the streets, being confined mainly to barracks in case hostilities broke out. Three years after the agreement was signed, little progress had been made. Indeed, by the summer of 2001, when there was an increase in sectarian violence, the need for the retention of a large British force remained undiminished.

Weapons decommissioning

This issue remained the central feature of the search for a lasting peace. The Good Friday Agreement quoted the following resolution from the talks which preceded it:

> the resolution of the decommissioning issue is an indispensable part of the process of negotiation.

In order to deal with the process a commission was set up (under General John de Chastelaine) which would organise and verify the removal of weapons. In addition the agreement set a deadline for decommissioning at two years after its ratification by referendum. In the event, this date passed without a solution, so the problem rumbled on.

One of the difficulties with decommissioning is that the agreement did not define it precisely. In the months and years which followed, indeed, it became increasingly apparent that the Unionists and the Nationalists defined it in different ways. Unionists wanted to see the final destruction of all weapons held by terrorist organisations. This was to be a clear public gesture that violence was to be renounced for good. The Republican Nationalists, specifically Sinn Fein and the IRA, refused to accept such a tight definition. To them decommissioning meant 'taking weapons out of use'. They were prepared to accept public demonstrations of this concession, but stopped short of actual weapons destruction.

But this dispute was not just a question of words and definitions. Weapons decommissioning had powerful symbolic significance for both sides. To the IRA it potentially meant surrender to the Loyalists and to the British government. Though they were prepared to hold a cease-fire and to demonstrate that weapons were out of use, they were not ready to accept their destruction which would suggest capitulation and would create a permanent situation. The Unionists, on the other hand, wanted a firm assurance that the IRA had renounced violence for good. The mainstream Unionists added that they were not prepared to sit down permanently in government with Sinn Fein, as long as they were backed by a military force. They feared that, if a political conflict were to appear, the Republicans could resort to violence again if the weapons were still in existence. The hard-line Unionists, such as Paisley's DUP went further, seeing decommissioning as a sign of defeat, ironically, the same view as that of the IRA.

In August 2001, as the deadline for decommissioning was running out, the IRA and the de Chastelaine commission announced an agreement to put weapons out of use once and for all (still stopping short of full destruction). However, in the absence of details and a timetable of action, the Unionists rejected the plan and the decommissioning process was back almost at square one. Sinn Fein continued to protest that they did not control the IRA and could therefore not be blamed for slow progress on the issue. But this was not enough for the Unionists who remained cautious and suspicious.

Standing, as it does, at the centre of Unionist concerns, decommissioning remains the main stumbling block to final agreement. It cannot guarantee peace as there will always be extreme splinter groups of both Loyalists and Republicans, but a successful agreement would lead to the opportunity for a lasting political settlement. Sinn Fein would no longer be seen as a front for terrorists and the withdrawal of a large British military presence may become a possibility. Peaceful politics might take centre stage at last.

WHY THE GOOD FRIDAY AGREEMENT WAS POSSIBLE

If we wish to answer this question we need first to consider why previous attempts at a settlement failed. The following problems may be included.

1 They were seen as a token attempt at power sharing, but they were perceived as little more than devices to give the Catholic community some representation, but not equal status. The power-sharing assemblies and executives which had existed before 1998 still allowed the Unionists to dominate the political system.

2 There was a lack of trust, mostly among Republicans, of the motives of the British government. Most negotiations had taken place in secret so that suspicions were inevitably aroused that private deals had been made by ministers and other officials.

3 There had never been sufficient political will among Northern Ireland

politicians to reach a long-term agreement. The cumulative effect of atrocities played its part as the population, weary of continual grief and disruption, put pressure on elected representatives to end the violence.

4 The motives of the government of the Irish Republic were suspected by the Loyalist community. Interference by the Republic was always seen as an attempt to persuade Britain to give up the province to them.

5 Perhaps above all, previous attempts at settlement had taken place within the context of continued violence. Politicians on both sides of the divide felt that any political progress was likely to be undermined by the terrorists. Furthermore, whenever there was a political deadlock, the paramilitary wings of the parties simply chose to commit acts of violence in pursuit of their aims.

The preparation for the Good Friday Agreement was designed to overcome most of these problems. The key elements were as follows:
  • The Downing Street declaration, which stated that Britain was neutral in its attitude to Northern Ireland sovereignty, allayed the suspicions of the Republicans.
  • The ceasefire meant that negotiations could take place in good faith and without pressure from terrorists.
  • The intervention of representatives of the USA was important. The involvement of President Clinton and Senator George Mitchell both inspired the people of the province to search for peace and provided genuinely neutral go-betweens who could move the peace process forward. Senator Mitchell, indeed, was the key figure in bringing Republican and Unionist politicians together.
  • The declaration that Sinn Fein was willing to renounce the use of violence was a key development.
  • The statesmanship of leading politicians, notably David Trimble for the Unionists, John Hume for the SDLP and Gerry Adams of Sinn Fein must receive credit. These men showed a willingness to make some concessions and so find common ground. In the past, sectarian politicians had sought outright victory, but Trimble, Hume and Adams understood that any final settlement would need a consensus. Similarly, British ministers, such as Patrick Mayhew, Mo Mowlem and Peter Mandelson, showed greater vision than in the past in understanding the difficulties of Republican and Unionist politicians.

HOW SUCCESSFUL HAS THE AGREEMENT BEEN?

Events in Northern Ireland move quickly. Any assessment of the Good Friday Agreement must, therefore, be very tentative. But some assessment can be made.

Successes

The assembly and the executive have survived for longer than any of their predecessors since 1972. This is, in itself, an achievement. The longer political institutions can survive, the more chance there is of a lasting peace. Apart from sporadic outbreaks of rioting and some atrocities by extreme groups who do not support the agreement, the ceasefire has also held.

The institutions of devolved government also seem to have worked well. It was certainly a triumph that the foot and mouth epidemic which decimated farming in the rest of Britain was dealt with decisively in the province. The committees of the assembly have made a great deal of progress in making the Civil Service more accountable and in creating more open government. There are also signs that the health and education services are being sensitively run. The education service, already felt to be stronger than its English counterpart, abolished school league tables and is moving further towards independence. In general, therefore, the ideal that devolved government should create a 'real' and independent sense of regional government may be succeeding.

Public support for the institutions is also high. Opinion polls show a good deal of confidence being expressed on a non-sectarian basis. The fact that Unionists and Republican politicians, once implacable enemies, have been able to sit together in the assembly and the executive does inspire confidence and may help to reduce tension.

Finally, and perhaps most importantly, devolved government is providing lasting protection of human rights and the maintenance of equality. The agreement itself built into Northern Irish politics safeguards which ensured that executive action could never be seen to be sectarian in nature. The assembly cannot pass sectarian legislation and the cross-party committees keep a careful watch over institutions to ensure that they do not fall into the pre-1968 situation when they were unionist dominated.

Problems

The agreement has certainly not removed the threat of sectarian violence. There have been regular outbreaks of rioting, the worst example of which were the attacks on young Catholic children being taken to school in the Ardoyne district of Belfast. There have also been punishment beatings by paramilitaries, a few sectarian assassinations and attacks on security forces.

By the autumn of 2001 the problem of decommissioning had still not been solved. Clearly the IRA did not have sufficient faith in the long-term success of the political process to give up weapons permanently. Until the issue of armed terrorism is solved it seems unlikely that the Good Friday Agreement, or any other such settlement, will succeed in the long run.

Though the agreement has seen politicians from across the sectarian divide finally meeting openly, its real test is whether it can start to bring the communities together and prevent the polarisation of politics which has occurred in recent decades. By 2001 there was little sign of this. As we have seen, a constant level of violence remains. The Orange Order marches in the summer also continue to cause tension. More worryingly, however, the 2001 general election saw advances made by the two main extremist parties, the Democratic Unionists (who are still refusing to take part in the Northern Ireland executive) and Sinn Fein. They won more votes and seats at Westminster than in 1997, an indication that voters were losing faith in the moderate, pro-agreement parties such as the UUP and the SDLP. Hopes that progress could be made in such areas as reform of the Royal Ulster Constabulary and reduction of troop levels have been dashed and look remote with the two communities seeming to move further apart.

SUMMARY – THE FUTURE FOR NORTHERN IRELAND

At the end of 2002, as this book is written, the future remains uncertain as it has done for over thirty years. It is impossible to predict what will happen over the course of the next few years. A number of possible scenarios do, however, present themselves.

1 The most optimistic view is that the people of the province will become weary of the conflict and pressure will build up on all sides to make the Good Friday Agreement and devolved government work. This must, it seems, depend on a resolution of some kind of compromise on weapons decommissioning and on a reduction in sectarian tensions. In the very long term this must involve reconciliation between the two communities and an effective programme of education so that future generations will not inherit the entrenched views of their parents and grandparents.

2 More realistically it may be that devolved government will survive, but that sectarian tension and violence will continue to affect the province. In such circumstances it seems unlikely that Northern Ireland government will be effective. Devolution may become something of a symbolic gesture. In such circumstances there may also be periodic suspensions of the assembly and the executive. There had already been two suspensions by 2001 and direct rule may certainly have to be imposed again.

3 The most pessimistic scenario is that the remaining problems will not be resolved in time to save devolved government. Direct rule may be imposed and tight security regulations maintained. In such a case violence will

continue. In the long run it seems likely that continued conflict will result in economic decline and large-scale emigration from the province (to Ireland or mainland Britain).

4 Finally we can consider a longer-term vision. This concerns the development of closer integration in Europe. The issue of sovereignty has always been one of Northern Ireland's main problems. Republicans challenge British sovereignty, while Loyalists will not accept any diluting of British political authority. As long as the majority of the people wish to be considered British, there will always be some conflict (either violent or political) with the Catholic minority. A more closely integrated European Union, however, will reduce the importance of national sovereignty.

In such circumstances Northern Ireland will become a European region and British rule will become a less important issue. There will always be a *cultural* division between Protestant and Catholic communities, but there will be some blurring of sovereignty between Ireland, Britain, Northern Ireland and the EU itself. Furthermore, regional aid is increasing. Northern Ireland may well enjoy a similar economic renaissance to that of the Irish Republic, underpinned by EU subsidies. Since some of the 'troubles' have their origins in economic deprivation, growing prosperity can only ameliorate sectarian conflict.

SAMPLE QUESTIONS

1 Explain the nature of the sectarian divide in Northern Ireland.

2 To what extent can the Good Friday Agreement be considered a success?

3 Why did the Good Friday Agreement apparently succeed where previous attempts to achieve peace had failed?

4 What problems remain to be solved in Northern Ireland following the implementation of the Good Friday Agreement?

5 What are the main distinctive features of the devolution settlement in Northern Ireland? Why did it differ so much from devolution in Scotland and Wales?

Constitutional reform

11

➤ Review of constitutional reform before 1997

➤ Analysis of the reasons behind the Labour reform plan of 1997

➤ Descriptions of the main reforms

➤ Analysis of the reforms

➤ Prospects for future reforms

CONSTITUTIONAL REFORM BEFORE 1997

Attitudes to reform

The attitude of most governments towards constitutional reform during the twentieth century has been essentially conservative. This has, of course, partly been the result of the dominance of the Conservative party for most of that century. But when Liberals or the Labour party have been decisively in power there have always been other policy issues which have tended to dominate. There are few votes in successful constitutional reform so it has often been squeezed off the political agenda. At the same time Liberals and Socialists in Britain have rarely been able to agree among themselves on what reforms are desirable. So the Conservatives have had a relatively clear field in the constitutional arena. The dominant 'conservative' view can be described in the following terms:

- There has been a reluctance to make changes to the constitution on the grounds that this is likely to be disruptive to the political process.
- Change has largely been the result of a breakdown of the system, rather than from any conscious policy decisions. For example, the powers of the House of Lords were reduced as a result of the Liberal government budget crisis in 1909, Ireland was partitioned in 1921 in order to avoid a civil war, the institution of life peers was developed in 1958 to head off growing demands for abolition of the House of Lords. In all these cases, reform was *forced* on government.

- It has always been assumed that the uncodified, flexible nature of the British constitution has allowed it to adapt *naturally* to the need for change. So, for example, the non-political role of the monarchy has gradually evolved for over a century. Similarly, parliament has rarely experienced any dramatic changes to its powers and procedures, but has adapted itself to the nature of modern government cautiously and gradually.

Reform before 1997

The main changes in Britain's constitutional arrangements have consisted of the severance of political links with the Republic of Ireland and the dismantling of the Empire, mostly after World War II. *Internal* reform, on the other hand, has been relatively modest. Three areas of internal change are identified below.

Without any legislation the political role of the monarchy has been gradually eroded. This process has its origins in the eighteenth century, of course, but it has been the last hundred years that have seen its final demise. It is now accepted that the monarch plays no active part in policy making, even in times of war, and will only become involved in government formation if all other systems have failed. Outright republicanism is weak in Britain so there have been only limited calls for abolition. But it is true that the monarchy has little more than a symbolic role in Britain today.

The role of the House of Lords has been gradually eroded after 1911. Its delaying power was set at two years in 1911 and reduced to one year in 1949. It was not allowed to interfere in the financial affairs of government after the 1911 Parliament Act. In the 1940s the 'Salisbury Convention' was developed – a classic example of how the constitution has evolved without legislation. The convention (developed by a Conservative peer after whom it was named) suggests that the House of Lords cannot challenge a manifesto commitment of the elected government. In essence the Convention accepts that the unelected Lords has a much weaker degree of political authority than the elected Commons. The decline in the influence of both the House of Lords and the monarchy represented important examples of how *traditional* authority has been replaced by *elective* authority.

Particularly after 1979 there was been a steady 'drift' of power away from local government towards the centre. This has been achieved by the transferring of powers and responsibilities. There has also been a huge increase in the amount of political or financial control which central government exercises over local authorities. The fact that Britain has no codified and superior constitution has meant that the process has occurred gradually, through individual pieces of legislation. No individual statute caused a major change, but the accumulated effect has caused a significant change in the distribution of power.

The sum total of these changes is not very great. When we think of how much change there has been in the constitutions of other European powers during the twentieth century, we realise how conservative Britain has been over the period. This comparison can be viewed in two ways: either it is symptomatic of the deep-seated conservatism of the British political establishment which has contributed to Britain's relative economic decline, or it is a powerful demonstration of stability.

LABOUR'S AGENDA IN 1997

Why Labour came to support radical constitutional reform

Significant constitutional reform was a key element in the New Labour 'project' which was developed by Neil Kinnock, John Smith and Tony Blair in the 1990s. The party, which had been transformed by the three leaders and their allies, was essentially a 'modernising' force. It was committed to reforming economic policy making, industry, foreign and defence policy and the public services. Partly for its own sake and partly to pave the way for pushing through reforms, it was seen as necessary to make significant constitutional reforms. The following three factors made a constitutional reform programme possible and desirable when Labour took power in 1997.

1 The Labour party has always wished to promote constitutional reform but has rarely had sufficient political control to be able to do so. As a party, Labour has always sought to promote popular democracy, equal rights and the reduction of traditional 'establishment' powers. By the mid-1990s it was clear that the party was going to win the next general election comfortably and, what is more, had the prospect of at least two consecutive terms in office. Reasonably secure in this knowledge, the party could include constitutional change in its political programme.

2 Despite the prospect of power, the Labour party had experienced two long periods of Conservative government – 1951–64 and 1979–97 – during which they had felt totally excluded from influence. The constitutional reforms proposed were, therefore, partly designed to prevent a situation where one party would be able to dominate the political agenda so completely. It is, of course, ironic that Labour's hold on power had become, by the end of the century, so secure that the constitutional changes it proposed could be directed against themselves when it had been developed to break Conservative hegemony.

3 There was clearly considerable public support for reform. Public opinion polls had long since indicated that a majority would be in favour of change, but this support had always been considered 'soft'. In other words it was not high on anybody's list of concerns. By the mid-1990s, however, it was becoming obvious that demands for reform were hardening. This was demonstrated by growing support for the Liberal Democrats, who strongly advocated reform, for campaign groups such as Charter 88 and for Scottish and Welsh Nationalists.

The principles of Labour's reform

We can divide Labour's reform programme into the following processes.

- *Democratisation*. Too much of the British political system was seen as undemocratic. The prime targets were the unelected House of Lords, and the notoriously unrepresentative electoral system.

- *Decentralisation*. As we have seen above, Labour had been scarred by the experience of watching powerlessly as successive Conservative administrations gathered increasing amounts of power into the centre. Part of the programme was, therefore, designed to disperse power away from central government to the regions and localities.

- *Restoration of rights*. During the 1980s there had been consistent fears that the rights of citizens in Britain had been consistently eroded. In fact the process could be traced back to earlier periods, but Labour concentrated on what had occurred under the Conservatives. In addition, Labour wished to bring Britain more into line with European practice in constitutional matters. They therefore proposed the incorporation of the European Convention on Human Rights into British law. In addition a Freedom of Information Act was seen as essential.

- *Modernisation*. As we have seen above, the Conservative party had done much to modernise the Civil Service during the 1980s and 1990s. The Labour party wished to extend this programme further, but also turned their attention to parliament. Changes in the composition of the House of Lords were a key element in this, but there were also hopes that reform of the House of Commons to make it more efficient and effective could be undertaken.

We can now see how extensive the Labour proposals were in 1997. Of course, experience tells us that the new government fell some way short of implementing the whole plan. However, in order to evaluate the process, it is important to be able to compare Labour's original aspirations with its subsequent actions. These can now be considered in more detail.

DEVOLUTION

The details of the devolution settlement are described in a separate chapter. Labour had attempted to introduce devolution in the late 1970s but had been foiled by a combination of two factors. Firstly, the government of the day did not have a parliamentary majority and so could not push the legislation through. Secondly, forced to rely on referendum approval, with more than a simple majority in favour required, the government could not summon enough support in either Scotland or Wales for the proposals. The Welsh voted decisively against. The Scots did vote yes, but the turnout and majority were too low to satisfy parliament.

By 1997, however, the political tide had turned decisively in favour of devolution. Labour had a huge majority and so had a clear field. The Scots were very much in favour and voted for devolution in 1997 by a large margin. Support was lukewarm in Wales, but a narrow referendum vote in favour was enough to persuade the new government to go ahead.

Though falling well short of the aspirations of Scots and Welsh Nationalists (who want either full independence or at least a federal arrangement with extensive sovereignty transferred from London) devolution represents a huge shift in power away from London. The Scottish parliament became a centre of power away from London which had not been seen in Britain since it had last been abolished in 1707. The Welsh, meanwhile, had never had a true government of their own, so this was a unique political development for them.

Devolution of power to Northern Ireland was part of the wider Good Friday Agreement of 1998. It was essential for the possibilities of a long-term peaceful settlement there. All the sectarian groups needed some political representation and this was provided. At the same time it was important for the British government to withdraw from most Northern Ireland affairs, as it had come to be seen as a mistrusted element in the sectarian conflict.

THE HOUSE OF LORDS

The jewel in New Labour's constitutional crown was undoubtedly devolution. However, the introduction of a codified set of rights and reform of the House of Lords followed close behind. Over many years Labour governments had suffered from obstruction from a house which had always had an in-built Conservative majority. In the past, attempts at abolition and reform had failed so it was not surprising that, when the party did have a decisive majority and time to spare, it should decide to take the opportunity while the going was good. Reform has occurred in two stages.

Stage 1

Immediately after taking office the Labour government took steps to remove the voting rights of hereditary peers. These eight hundred or so members of the nobility were either permanent absentees or were invariably committed to the Conservative cause. The number of Labour or Liberal Democrat hereditary peers was extremely limited. The party had also been severely affected by an incident in 1988 which was to spell the ultimate demise of the political role of the hereditary peerage. The incident entered the collective memory of the Labour party so that, when they returned to power, it was hardly surprising that it should occupy their immediate attention.

In 1988 Margaret Thatcher's government was trying to force through legislation to introduce the poll tax into local government. The poll tax was extremely controversial, being seen in many quarters as unfair as it was not based on ability to pay. The whips forced the Bill through the House of Commons with relatively little difficulty. The Lords, on the other hand, were threatening to thwart the government's will. It was at this stage that the government, with its back to the wall, decided to persuade large numbers of hereditary peers to come to London to vote through the new tax. Many of these peers – sometimes known as 'backwoodsmen' – never normally voted. Some did not even know where to go to vote. However, the plan worked and the legislation was passed. Labour, as we have said, never forgot the incident. The days of the hereditary peerage were numbered, though no one knew it at the time.

At first the legislation to remove the voting rights of hereditary peers was held up. Not surprisingly the large Conservative majority there were unhappy with the proposals. Many meetings were held behind closed doors to find a compromise. Conservative leader, William Hague, feared that the obstruction would lead Labour to even more radical reform. He therefore persuaded his colleagues in the Lords to accept a limited reform. Ninety-two hereditary peers – less than an eighth of the total – were to remain on a temporary basis. These peers were to be elected by the rest of the hereditaries. They were still a Conservative majority, but the government now had the opportunity to redress the political balance by creating many new Labour-supporting life peers.

It was always asserted that this was only the first stage of reform. The next stage was initiated with the appointment of a commission to consider a long-term solution. By appointing a Conservative peer – Lord Wakeham – Tony Blair signalled the fact that he did not expect any radical change. Wakeham obliged with a moderate report. Its main principles were as follows:

- The powers of the House of Lords were to remain substantially unchanged. It was to be clearly subordinate to the House of Commons.
- A minority – possibly as few as 20 per cent – was to be elected by proportional representation on a regional basis.
- There were to be no more hereditary peers in the House.
- The rest of the House was to be appointed.
- An independent appointments commission would ensure that appropriate people were appointed and to prevent the excessive use of political patronage by party leaders.
- The political balance of the house would prevent domination by any one party. Independent 'crossbenchers' would hold the balance of power.

Stage 2

After a second decisive election victory in 2001, the Labour government was encouraged to complete its reforms. Its proposals, however, proved to be more controversial than the government had expected. The plan unveiled in late 2001 was as follows:

1 20 per cent of the chamber would be elected by proportional representation.
2 20 per cent would be independent peers, appointed by the appointments commission. These would be crossbenchers without political allegiance.
3 60 per cent would be appointed through party patronage.
4 The appointments commission would ensure that nominations were people of 'suitable character'. They would also ensure a political balance so that party nominations would be apportioned in proportion to their strengths in the House of Commons. Overall, the balance would be maintained so that no single party would have an overall majority.
5 The appointments commission was to appoint representatives of religious and ethnic groups in society.
6 The powers of the Lords would remain largely unchanged.

A storm of protest from all sides greeted the plans. In general terms, the counter-proposals looked like this:

- *Liberal Democrats:* A fully elected chamber.
- *Conservatives:* 80 per cent elected and the rest appointed by parties.
- *Charter 88 and other constitutional reform groups:* Fully elected.
- *Substantial Labour backbench opinion:* Variations between 50 per cent and fully elected.

So the government's policy had few friends. Even the cabinet was undecided about how to proceed. The proposals were therefore put on the back burner.

By autumn 2002, no further progress on reform had been made. Two alternatives were envisaged. One was a shelving of further reform. The other was a revised plan to meet some of the demands of the backbenchers.

THE HOUSE OF COMMONS

New Labour also pledged to make reforms to the House of Commons in order to modernise it. In the event, however, this proved to be one area of reform which appeared to be stillborn. This was despite widespread and growing concern that the Commons was becoming, at best, ineffective and, at worst, impotent and irrelevant. It was in need of streamlining certainly, though whether it needed more power was problematic.

A modernisation committee was set up early in Labour's administration, but it has had little effect. A few cosmetic changes have been made, including the reduction of Prime Minister's question time from two short sessions to one longer one. The facilities for MPs have been improved with a new office block and there are increased allowances for secretarial and research backing. But nothing *substantial* has altered. Indeed, after 1997, most commentators saw the Commons as declining in importance, especially as Labour won two thumping majorities in succession.

Robin Cook, who took over as Leader of the House in 2001, has shown some willingness to promote change, but experience of the past suggests that any of his proposals are unlikely to be given much prominence by the government. The one major change which Cook has made was, in fact, forced on him by his own backbenchers. They insisted that membership of the departmental select committees should be placed in the hands of MPs rather than the party whips. In the long term this may prove to be a significant reform, but as long as the government has a large majority, the balance of power is likely to remain firmly with the executive.

Ironically, it has been the Conservatives who have made most of the running on Commons reform. It was Margaret Thatcher herself who had backed the creation of departmental select committees in 1979, perhaps the most important parliamentary development of the twentieth century. These committees certainly improved the Commons' ability to call ministers to account and are still the main way in which our representatives are able to scrutinise the work of government. In fields such as foreign policy, defence spending, health administration and police matters they have been especially effective in throwing extra light on official or unofficial policies.

More recently the Norton Committee, chaired by a Conservative peer, has led the calls for further changes. His report, published in 2000, contained many recommendations, the most important of which included:

- the restoration of two Prime Minister's question times;
- longer ministerial question time sessions with more in-depth questions;
- more opportunities for backbench MPs to raise issues;
- debates should have shorter speeches so that more members can participate;
- more research resources available for the Opposition parties;
- more research facilities for select committees;
- the MPs should control their own select committees rather than the party whips;
- standing committees which consider legislation should have more time to use outside witnesses, along the model of the US Congress;
- more resources for the Commons to consider EU legislation;
- select Committee chairs to be paid a minister's salary so that there is an alternative career option for MPs to being a minister. This would break much of the influence of the prime minister and the whips.

These recommendations represent something of a consensus on how the Commons' work could be made more effective. However, Blair's government shows no enthusiasm for them, especially as it had been too busy struggling with a rebellious House of Lords to worry about the Commons. We may also reflect on the comments of former Cabinet secretary Lord Butler in a 2001 lecture to the Politics Association. He suggests that only the reform of the electoral system could bring about any truly meaningful change in the role and influence of the Commons.

HUMAN RIGHTS

A brief description of the events surrounding the introduction of the Human Rights Act needs to be included here.

Why the Human Rights Act was proposed

A number of factors led the Labour party to incorporate the European Convention on Human Rights into British law. These were:

- A general desire to bring the British constitution into line with the rest of Europe, all of whose states have special arrangements to protect individual rights.
- The increase in the powers of the police and the courts which had occurred in the 1980s and 1990s were now seen as a major threat to our rights.

- The British government had been brought before the European Court of Human Rights (which seeks to enforce the Convention) over fifty times since 1966 and had lost most of the cases. Although the decisions of the court are not legally binding, these cases had been an embarrassment to the government.
- New Labour stressed the idea of active citizenship. This concept included the principle that citizens have responsibilities to their communities and to the country as a whole. In return for these responsibilities it was believed that rights should be better understood and safeguarded.
- It was part of the devolution settlements that the Welsh and Northern Ireland assemblies and the Scottish Parliament should be bound by the Convention. This was designed to reassure the citizens of these nations that devolution would not threaten their rights.

So it was that the Human Rights Act made the European Convention part of British law in 2000.

How the Human Rights Act works

The Human Rights Act states that the European Convention on Human Rights is binding on virtually all public bodies in virtually all circumstances. Furthermore, it can be enforced by any British court of law. In essence, therefore, the following individuals and bodies are bound by the Act:
- the Welsh, Scottish and Northern Ireland political systems in their entirety;
- local authorities;
- government ministers, civil servants and their departments;
- all government executive agencies;
- all quangos (non-government public bodies);
- any other organisation engaged in 'public business' – this includes the media, all schools and colleges, charities etc.

Any regulation or action by any of these bodies can be scrutinised in a court of law and may be declared unlawful. This will result in the action being cancelled and may result in compensation.

The main exception to this law concerns parliamentary legislation. In order to preserve the constitutional principle of parliamentary sovereignty, the Convention cannot be considered superior to parliament. A minister who introduces proposed legislation in parliament must make a declaration. This declaration will state whether the government believes the proposal to be either compatible or incompatible with the Convention. If it is thought to be *incompatible* the fact will be taken into consideration when parliament debates the Bill. However, if a Bill received parliamentary approval it will be enforced by the courts.

The European Court of Human Rights may still hear appeals against UK national legislation and may declare an Act to be in breach of the Convention, but its judgments are still not binding in Britain.

The Human Rights Act in context

In some senses the Act can be considered to be an extremely radical example of constitutional reform. Indeed some commentators have suggested that it is the most important development since the Great Reform Act of 1832 when parliament began the road to democratisation.

Certainly it is the first example of the codification of rights in British history. What is familiar to most Europeans and all Americans – a clear statement of enforceable individual rights – has not been seen here since Magna Carta in 1215. It also represents a huge advance in the protection of individuals against the power of the state.

On the other hand, critics suggest that the Human Rights Act does not go far enough. By preserving parliamentary sovereignty and making parliamentary legislation an exception to its jurisdiction, the Act fails to deal with a fundamental problem in the British constitution. That is the enormous power of central government and its almost complete control over parliament. Had the Human Rights Act been binding on parliamentary legislation it would have represented a major check on governmental power. But it stopped short of this.

ELECTORAL REFORM

Background

Both the Labour and Liberal (now Liberal Democrat) parties have long since espoused the cause of electoral reform in the UK. The Liberal (Democrats) have been more consistent in their support and, by the 1960s, it was firmly at the centre of their political beliefs. The Labour party's interest, on the other hand, has ebbed and flowed.

Cynics suggest that the interest of both these parties has been fundamentally self-motivated. The decline of Liberalism after the 1920s meant that they could not hope to recover their strong position under the first-past-the-post system. Once the party had lost most of its seats in the House of Commons, a vote for them was seen as wasted. Furthermore, the Liberal (Democrats) have always had a very dispersed support. The lack of any concentrations of voting power has also meant that the traditional electoral system works against them. With a more proportional system, the party believed that it could reverse its fortunes and challenge for at least a share of power again.

Similarly, Labour has watched while the electoral system has tended to exaggerate the support for the Conservatives. It has tended in the past to convert votes into parliamentary seats more generously for the Conservatives than for Labour. Three election defeats in a row from 1951 to 1964 and an even longer period in opposition from 1979 to 1997 both resulted in renewed interest in electoral reform within the Labour party. Certainly after their 1992 defeat many in the Labour party began to believe they might never win again under the first-past-the-post system.

Both parties have refuted these criticisms, of course, arguing that their support for electoral reform is, in fact, *principled*. In other words, they argue that first-past-the-post is unfair, undemocratic and unrepresentative. The Liberal democrats add that it results in governments which have large parliamentary majorities and are therefore able to dominate the policy agenda excessively. It also means that the House of Commons fails to make government properly accountable.

Two groups have maintained implacable opposition to electoral reform. These have been the Conservative party and most elements of the traditional left wing of the Labour party. The Conservatives take a pragmatic view. First-past-the-post guarantees a two party system and governments with decisive parliamentary majorities. This means stability and certainty, key aspects of Conservative philosophy. Traditional sections of the Labour party have set great store by the power of the state. This power, they have argued, has been essential to make the necessary reforms to create social justice. A multi-party system, which would result from electoral reform, would weaken state power and so jeopardise any future socialist programmes.

New Labour and electoral reform

In truth, the Labour party which prepared itself for power in the 1990s, was completely split on the issue of electoral reform. From a pragmatic, self-interested point of view, a change looked attractive. The dominance of the Conservative party since 1951 showed no signs of disappearing, especially after their 'against-all-odds' victory at the 1992 general election. If this hegemony could not be broken by political means, argued many in Labour, perhaps electoral reform would do the trick. But this was not the only factor.

As we have seen, New Labour was committed to modernising elements of the British constitution. The old electoral system was beginning to look out-of-date, whatever the consequences of reform. There were powerful voices in the party who suggested that Britain had become fundamentally undemocratic.

The doubts within Labour were demonstrated by the party's indecisive approach to possible reform. In Opposition they had commissioned Lord Plant to recommend a course of action. The Plant Committee did opt, albeit unenthusiastically, for reform, suggesting something like the German Additional Member System as an alternative. Still unconvinced, Tony Blair offered the electorate a referendum on the issue if Labour won power in 1997. Labour duly won, but no referendum was forthcoming. Instead another Commission was appointed, this time under Liberal Democrat Lord Jenkins.

Jenkins reported in 1998. He strongly advocated a more radical system than Plant had done. This was known as AV plus (alternative vote). Its basic operation is described below. The party leadership demonstrated little enthusiasm for the Jenkins proposals and they have effectively been shelved. Labour continued to delay and, having won again in 2001, were far from ready to consult the electorate. However, this did not mean that electoral reform was a dead issue. On the contrary, various forms of proportional representation were steadily creeping into the political system.

Electoral reform since 1997

While little progress has been made by the electoral reform movement in terms of *general elections,* there has been great progress in other forms of election. Indeed, Britain since 1997 has resembled a great experiment in how different electoral systems can work. The descriptions below demonstrate how electoral reform has progressed.

Northern Ireland (1999)

- **System**. Single Transferable Vote (STV).

- **Operation.** Multi-member constituencies in elections for the Northern Ireland Assembly and in local government. There are several seats in each constituency (normally four). Parties may put up any number of candidates up to the number of seats available. Voters may vote for all candidates, from any party, in any order of preference. First preferences count more, but all preferences may be relevant. An electoral 'quota' is calculated which is the minimum votes a candidate needs to be elected. The quota is roughly the number of votes cast divided by seats available, but not exactly. The first four (if that is the number of seats) to achieve the quota are elected. First preference votes are counted first and a candidate achieving the quota is elected automatically. Very few can do this, so second and subsequent preference votes are progressively added until enough candidates have achieved the quota.

- **Effect.** This is a highly proportional system. Party representation is very close to the proportion of votes cast for each. Small parties do well and a number of independents have won seats. It also maximises voter choice, allowing them to show all their preferences and to discriminate between candidates of the *same* party.

- **Why used**. It was vital in a very divided society, as Northern Ireland is, to reflect the many different groups in the assembly. So a highly proportional system was needed. Fourteen different parties or independents were elected in a small assembly.

Scottish Parliament (1999), Welsh Assembly (1999), Greater London Assembly (2000)

- **System.** Additional member system (AMS).

- **Operation.** A mixed or hybrid system. About two-thirds of the seats are elected by the first-past-the-post system.   However, each voter has a second vote. This is for a party. About one-third of the seats (known as 'top-up seats'), are elected from a list of candidates put up by the parties. These seats are awarded according to the proportion of these second votes won by each party. However this proportion is adjusted. Parties which do well on the constituency votes will have their list proportion adjusted downwards. Conversely, those who do poorly in constituencies will win more than the normal proportion of seats on their list. In this way small parties receive a boost from the top-up list system.

- **Effect.** The system has meant that Labour still dominates. However, in all three places where it has been used, no party has won an overall majority. In Scotland and Wales, Labour has had to go into coalition with the Liberal Democrats. In the Greater London Assembly, no party dominates and there are signs of political inertia as a result. The Conservatives, who lost all their parliamentary seats in Scotland and Wales, won a fair proportion of seats in the elections to the devolved parliament and assembly. The Welsh and Scottish Nationalists did well from the system.

- **Why used.** Had first-past-the-post alone been used in these elections, Labour would probably have won decisive majorities at the first elections. This would have defeated part of the object of the exercise – to disperse power *away* from Westminster. By introducing an element of proportional representation, the Nationalists have received fair representation and the systems do appear truly democratic.

Elections to the European Parliament (1999)

- **System.** Regional list system (closed list).

- **Operation.** A very common system in Europe. The country is divided into large regions. In each region voters are presented with a list of candidates from each party. They vote for a list, not an individual candidate. Seats are awarded off each list in accordance with the proportion of votes cast for each party. Therefore it is strictly proportional. The system first used (there are proposals for change in the future) was a 'closed list'. This means that the party leaderships decide which individuals are elected off their lists. An open system would mean that the voters would choose not only a party list, but would be able to determine which individuals are elected off their chosen list.

- **Effect.** There are no constituencies, though members do represent a region in an indirect way. The result is fully proportional. Small parties do well and the Green (2 seats) and UK Independence (3 seats) parties won representation. It was roundly criticised because the closed list system means that voters have no say in which individuals are elected. This is in the hands of party leaderships.

- **Why used.** Something of an experiment in an election which was not considered of great importance at the time. It brought Britain more into line with most other European states. It also satisfied in some small way, demands for greater proportional representation. Constituencies were abandoned as this is not seen as particularly important in the context of the European Parliament.

The Jenkins Proposal (1998)

- **System.** AV plus. In full, alternative vote plus list top-up.

- **Operation.** This is the same as the additional member system described above. However the constituency MPs would be elected differently. This would be by the alternative vote system, which is used in Australia. Voters make a first and second choice on the ballot paper. If a candidate wins at least 50 per cent of the first choice votes (s)he is elected. If no candidate achieves this, the second choice votes (i.e. the alternative votes) are added to those who have come first or second. In this way, one of the two must have an overall majority of first plus second choice votes.

- **Effect.** Though never used, it was estimated that this system would most favour the third party – i.e. the Liberal Democrats. Very small parties would probably gain few or no seats. It would be difficult, but not impossible for a major party to win an overall majority. Voter choice would be greatly enhanced without electing too many small party candidates.

The future of electoral reform

One word can sum up the prospects for future reform. That word is 'uncertain'. The Labour leadership has gone cold on the issue as far as general elections are concerned. There are a number of reasons for this.

- New Labour in the mid-1990s assumed it would need the co-operation of the Liberal Democrats to be able to govern effectively. To secure their future collaboration the party had to be prepared to entertain electoral reform, the likely price for Liberal Democrat support. This turned out to be a correct assumption in the case of Scotland and Wales, but not at Westminster. So Labour duly delivered on electoral reform for the devolved governments, but has prevaricated in the case of general elections.
- Two enormous election victories in a row both exaggerated Labour's success by converting votes into seats generously. In 2001, for example, a 40.7 per cent share of the vote netted 62.6 per cent of the seats. The party was, therefore, unenthusiastic about changing a system which was now working to their advantage.
- Conversely, the first-past-the-post system, which used to favour the Conservatives, was now working against their interests. In the 2001 general election, the Conservatives' 31.7 per cent share of the voted yielded only 25.2 per cent of the seats. Furthermore, Conservative representation for Wales and Scotland at Westminster had been all but wiped out. The desire to defeat Conservatism in the long term runs deep in Labour mythology, so these figures strengthen the resolve not to change the system which is helping to keep them out.
- Above all, perhaps, the leadership of the party is largely opposed to reform. No matter how many MPs want to see change, without the support of the majority of the leadership, especially Tony Blair, their hopes are in vain.

The best hope for reformers is that local government will be next in line for a new system. The very low turnouts in local elections are causing concern and some form of proportional representation might go some way to reviving public interest. Many local authorities are already controlled by two party coalitions, so a change to PR would not cause major disruption but would give voters more choice.

FREEDOM OF INFORMATION

The lack of any citizens' right to obtain publicly held information was one of the features of the British constitution which lagged behind the European and American experience in the 1990s. The Labour party, supported by the Liberal Democrats made a firm commitment to introduce such a measure. In 1997, however, the legislation, when it appeared, proved to be a disappointment to civil rights campaigners.

There are two strands to freedom of information. The first gives the right to citizens to see information which is held about them by public bodies. These include government, schools, medical bodies and other institutions of the welfare state. This has been relatively uncontroversial. Indeed, the right to view records held on computer files had long been established already under the Data Protection Act. The main disappointment here was that the right would not come into existence until 2005.

The second strand has caused more problems. This concerns the right to see documents and reports which are held by government and its agencies. In other words there was to be a public right to see inside the very workings of government. The ability to suppress information would be limited, while the media and parliament would have much greater access to information. In theory this represents a major move towards more open government. If implemented in full, freedom of information would have virtually ended the British culture of secrecy in government.

As with electoral reform, the new Labour government proved to be less enthusiastic about reform once it was in *office* than when it had been in *opposition*. The legislation which appeared in 2000 was very much a watered down version of similar measures in operation elsewhere in Europe. The security services were completely exempt while the rest of government was given a key concession. The 'normal' situation is that governments have to justify any reason for suppressing information. The British version, however, gives government the right to conceal information if it feels it might prejudice the activities of government. In other words, the onus is on the 'outsider' to prove that a document or other information should be released.

Civil rights groups see the new Act as virtually useless. It will not be possible to reveal more information than before in any field which the government considers critical. Hopes that there might be a dramatic shift in power over information towards citizens and the media had been dashed.

LONDON GOVERNMENT

The abolition of the Greater London Council (GLC) in 1986 by Margaret Thatcher's government was a bitter experience for the Labour party and it left a lasting scar. The GLC had been seen as something of a socialist experiment, especially when it had been controlled by its left-wing leader, Ken Livingstone. Its programmes of subsidised education, transport, employment schemes and housing were designed to counterbalance much of the social deprivation which, it was believed, was largely the result of Thatcherite policies.

When Labour saw the prospect of returning to power, therefore, the restoration of London government stood high on its political agenda. There was, however, no prospect of re-creating such a powerful body as the GLC again. A powerful lesson had been learned – that it was dangerous to create a political institution which could rival central government power in its own heartland. Devolution was all very well, but autonomous government in London was too radical for New Labour. Instead the Labour party proposed a limited form of government in the capital.

The most prominent proposal – to elect a mayor for London – was a unique measure. No part of the British political system had ever seen, throughout its history, a single *elected* figure. True, all local authorities had had mayors as figureheads for centuries, but these were not elected, but appointed by the rest of the council. The ancient institution of *Lord Mayor of London*, was also an appointment, in this case of the traditional livery companies which control the small 'City' of London. The idea of an elected mayor was imported from the USA and France and represented a complete break with the past.

The people of London took to the idea with enthusiasm and a 1999 referendum endorsed the measure decisively. Thereafter, however, matters began to take an unpleasant turn for the Labour government. Firstly, the party's own candidate, Frank Dobson, was thoroughly beaten by Ken Livingstone, who had left the party to stand as a radical independent candidate. Secondly, the Greater London Assembly (GLA) of 25 elected members, was not, as the party had hoped, dominated by Labour candidates. In fact, the Conservatives secured as many seats as Labour – 9 each – so Labour's influence in London was extremely weak.

The Labour government had never intended that independent London government should be strong, but Labour's setbacks at the first elections ensured that it should remain weak, however much Ken Livingstone might try to raise its profile. In effect the GLA has some control over public transport and traffic management, together with powers to veto major building developments. It started with a small budget – £4 billion – and little power to raise any of its own funds. It is not allowed to raise local taxes, for example. Furthermore there is an almost permanent deadlock between the mayor and the assembly, which has power to veto many of his proposals.

Thus autonomous London government has proved to be largely cosmetic. The battle over how the London Underground is to be funded was won decisively by central government. Their plan to involve the private sector in a partnership with the state prevailed over Livingstone's desire to see the service totally state funded. This demonstrated the inherent weakness of the elected mayor. So the city has its figurehead, but even a charismatic figure such as Ken Livingstone cannot overcome the built-in limitations to his role.

LOCAL GOVERNMENT

As with London, the government's enthusiasm for reform of local government in general withered very quickly after Labour was elected to office in 1997. Cities, towns and districts have been given the opportunity to elect mayors following a local referendum. However, in the first few years, very few had held referendums and fewer still had voted in favour of an elected mayor. Furthermore, if the new mayors suffer the same fate as Livingstone in London, it will prove to be an ineffective reform.

Similarly, local authorities have been given the option of changing to a 'cabinet' system of government. This involves the creation of a central cabinet of leading councillors from the dominant party or from a coalition who may take over central control of the council's work, making key decisions and setting general policy. This replaces the former system where the work of the council was divided between a number of functional committees.

As with elected mayors, the take-up for the new cabinet system has been patchy. Moreover, it is generally acknowledged that this kind of internal change does not tackle the real problems of local government. These are seen as threefold:

1 lack of autonomy from central government;
2 lack of accountability to local electorates;
3 largely as a result of the first two problems, very low public interest in local government and politics.

The Labour government elected in 2001 does promise progress on these fronts. However, reform of local government remains low on the list of priorities and it seems unlikely that any radical change will be forthcoming for some time to come.

AN ASSESSMENT OF CONSTITUTIONAL REFORM AFTER 2001

The position with regard to constitutional reform in Britain at the start of the twenty-first century is certainly paradoxical. On the one hand, the years after 1997 have seen the greatest constitutional changes in Britain probably since 1832 and, some have suggested, even since parliament became effectively sovereign in 1688. On the other hand, New Labour's reforms have disappointed many, inside and outside the party.

The Liberal Democrats and constitutional pressure groups such as Charter 88 and Liberty see reform as only half completed. They point to the following gaps in the programme needed to make Britain a truly modern democracy.

- The new largely appointed House of Lords falls well short of being properly accountable, authoritative and representative. Only a fully elected second chamber, they argue, is acceptable.

- The House of Commons remains ineffective and inefficient. Lack of government accountability is seen as a fundamental problem and only a reformed, revitalised House of Commons can provide this.

- The Human Rights Act, though a vital development, has not been given the political status it needs. The fact that the European Convention cannot overrule Acts of Parliament, means that rights can still be trampled on by powerful governments. The anti-terrorism measures which were enacted after the 11 September terrorist attacks on the USA were seen as a case in point.

- The Freedom of Information Act is too weak and allows government to remain over-secretive.

- Perhaps most importantly, Labour has failed to deliver electoral reform for parliamentary or local elections. It is this measure which is most often seen as the way in which the political system can be fundamentally changed for the better.

Whether future Labour governments will listen to these criticisms and act upon them remains to be seen.

SAMPLE QUESTIONS

1 Why did the Labour government institute a programme of constitutional reform after 1997?

2 What arguments have been advanced in favour of, and against, electoral reform on the UK?

3 Why has parliamentary reform been so difficult to implement?

4 In what ways have the rights of citizens become more safeguarded since 1997?

Devolution

12

➤ Review of the background to devolution

➤ Past attempts to introduce devolution

➤ Analysis of the reasons why devolution was introduced after 1997

➤ How devolution was implemented in various parts of the UK

➤ Analysis of different political attitudes towards devolution

➤ Speculation as to how successful the implementation of devolution has been

BACKGROUND

Movements which were dedicated to the introduction of greater self-government for Britain's national regions can be traced back as far as the nineteenth century. There has been a Scottish Nationalist movement for over a century although the Scottish National Party (SNP) did not come into existence until 1928. Welsh nationalism is a younger phenomenon, but Plaid Cymru – the Welsh Nationalist party – does date back to 1925. Both these movements were certainly influenced by the fact that Ireland had been granted virtually full **independence** in 1921.

The situation in Northern Ireland has been, quite clearly, very different. The full circumstances of nationalist movements are described in a separate chapter of this book. It should, however, be emphasised that Northern Ireland was granted devolved government in 1921 and enjoyed a large measure of independence until 1972 when direct rule from London was established. Since 1972, the idea of devolution receded in Northern Ireland. The republican or nationalist communities wanted to see re-unification with the Irish Republic. The Loyalists or Unionists were more concerned with resisting nationalism than with re-establishing devolved government.

> **independence**
> If one of the countries of the UK became independent it would become a separate sovereign state, with full sovereign powers and a separate independent seat in EU institutions and the United Nations. It would also cease to recognise the authority of the crown.

The origins of devolution

Much of the background to the **devolution** movement refers specifically to Scotland and Wales for reasons described above. Despite the long history of nationalism, the modern devolution story really begins in the 1970s. In that decade there was a distinct rise in nationalist feeling. The most obvious symptom was an increase in voting for nationalist parties at elections. The SNP had 1 seat at Westminster up to 1970. By the October 1974 election, however, the party had 11 seats as a result of winning over 30 per cent of the vote in Scotland.

> **devolution**
> The transfer of powers to regional assemblies and executives, but not sovereignty, i.e. powers can be taken back by the central authority.

Plaid Cymru secured 11.5 per cent of the vote in Wales in 1970 but no seats. However, by October 1974 it had 3 seats and had established itself in Welsh politics.

The reasons why there was an upsurge in nationalist voting in Britain in the 1970s are complex, but a number of key strands can be identified.

1 The poor performance of the British economy in comparison with most of Europe and the United States was blamed on inadequate government in London. In Scotland and Wales there was a feeling that locally based government could do a better job. It can be noted that there was a simultaneous rise in voting for the third party – the Liberals – in the 1970s. This was a further indication of disillusionment with the performance of the two main parties.

2 More specifically, the decline in traditional industries was under way by the late 1960s. These industries, including iron and steel, shipbuilding, coal and engineering were heavily concentrated in Wales and Scotland. The decline caused a great deal of resentment against English government. This was exacerbated by the fact that the south-east was becoming noticeably more prosperous than the rest of the kingdom. So the gap in economic well-being between England (especially the south) and Wales and Scotland was widening.

3 During the second half of the 1960s there was a widespread movement, largely among the young, who had become dissatisfied with political authority in general. There were demonstrations and riots throughout Europe and the United States, often led by a coalition of students and workers. Although most of this revolutionary youth movement demanded such reforms as women's rights, racial equality, greater democracy and extensions of civil rights, it also had the effect of creating new recruits for nationalist movements.

4 The discovery of huge deposits of oil in the North Sea gave an enormous boost specifically to Scottish nationalism. The oil had two effects. Firstly, it suggested that Scotland could become a viable independent country if it enjoyed use of this hugely valuable national resource. Secondly, it was claimed

by Scots that the tax revenues from the oil (in the form of petroleum revenue tax) were mainly being used to the benefit of England, though most of the oil was geographically in Scottish waters.

Why devolution?

The nationalists were, on the whole, interested in full independence. In the 1970s this was an impossible aspiration. The union of the United Kingdom was strong and the people of Scotland and Wales would certainly not have voted for it. Neither of the main parties could have survived politically had they advocated independence. But the challenge of nationalism had to be met. Compromise was, therefore, in the air.

Federalism had to be considered. This would have involved the transfer of large degrees of actual sovereignty to regional bodies. There were plenty of models to choose from, including the USA and Germany. But again this looked to be too close to independence for most Westminster politicians to stomach. Granting powers to Scottish and Welsh Parliaments which could not be ultimately controlled or taken back by Westminster was simply too radical to succeed.

> **federalism**
> The transfer of sovereignty to regional government. These powers could not be restored, i.e. the new arrangement would be entrenched.

The solution was to propose something similar to the Northern Ireland form of government which had existed before direct rule was imposed in 1972. This became known as 'devolution'. A Royal Commission – the Kilbrandon Commission – had developed the idea for Scotland in 1973. The word 'devolution' was a new one in British politics. It reflected the idea that power could be transferred

> **subsidiarity**
> A principle of the European Union established at Maastricht in 1992. It requires that government should be carried out at the lowest level possible. It implies that many powers should be developed to regional and local bodies.

to a region, without ceding actual sovereignty. In other words, the national governments would be semi-independent, but would always be subject to oversight from London. Devolution was, therefore, adopted as the compromise. It was hoped that it would satisfy moderate nationalist opinion, but also be acceptable to MPs at Westminster.

The failure of devolution in the 1970s

The Labour government which was elected in October 1974 enjoyed a very narrow parliamentary majority. It was therefore clear that it would need to rely on the support of smaller parties to survive for long. The small parties in question were the Liberals, the SNP and Plaid Cymru. All three were pressing the government for some transfer of powers to Scotland and Wales. The

Labour party itself was split on the issue. The Scottish and Welsh Labour MPs were mostly in favour (with the notable exception of Tam Dalyell, the West Lothian MP who remained implacably opposed for many years to come and was to play a key part in the devolution story in the 1990s). These MPs saw and feared the rise of nationalist sentiment. Their seats were, after all, in danger from the new movement. Most English Labour MPs were less enthusiastic but many recognised that support for devolution might be essential.

The new Labour government had shown a lukewarm commitment to devolution and this was reflected in a series of abortive attempts to push legislation through the House of Commons. By 1976 the position of the government had become critical. It had lost its majority altogether as a result of by-election defeats and was hanging on to a shaky alliance with the Liberals – the so-called Lib–Lab pact. It was time to press for devolution more decisively.

The Scotland and Wales Bills, which appeared in 1977, revealed a limited set of proposals for the transfer of power to elected bodies in the two countries. However, the Liberals were reasonably satisfied and agreed to support the government. This would secure a majority for the government in favour of the measure. At this point, however, a group of dissident Labour MPs (including Tam Dalyell) entered an alliance with the Conservatives which was to deal the devolution movement a mortal blow.

In January 1978 an amendment was passed to the Scotland and Wales Bills concerning the referendums which were required to approve devolution. The original legislation required only a simple majority vote. The amendment, however, required that approval would be needed from at least 40 per cent of the *total electorate*. Given that it was expected that up to one-third of the electorate would not vote, this was a difficult threshold to meet. In March 1979 the Welsh voted decisively against devolution in any case, but the Scots produced a 'yes' vote. But only 33 per cent of the Scottish electorate had approved, so the Conservative amendment had its desired effect.

The political fallout was dramatic. Apart from the subsequent events, political commentators pointed out how unusual the events of 1978 had been. The House of Commons had defeated the government on a major piece of its legislative programme. This was something which had not been seen since World War II. The government was clearly doomed. Shortly afterwards a vote of no confidence was passed and prime minister Jim Callaghan resigned. The election which followed ushered in eighteen years of continuous Conservative government.

Apart from a failed experiment with devolution in Northern Ireland during 1982–84, devolution was put on the political back burner. Nationalist sentiment declined markedly as prosperity began to rise in the second half of the 1980s. We can identify three main reasons for the failure of devolution in 1978–79:

1 In the end there was simply insufficient enthusiasm for devolution, especially in Wales.

2 In London there was not sufficient political will within the Labour party to force the measure through. The small number of MPs who defied the whips and supported the Conservative referendum amendment in 1978 were in fact representative of wider opposition in the party.

3 Devolution was an idea whose day was coming, but 1979 was too early. It would take a more worldwide movement for nationalism in the 1990s to see Scotland and Wales swept along to partial self-government.

As we shall see, by the second half of the 1990s the conditions described above had been reversed so the whole devolution picture was transformed.

THE DEMAND FOR DEVOLUTION IN THE 1990S

As we have seen, there was a lull in interest in devolution for most of the 1980s. The prosperity of the mid-1980s helped to head off nationalism temporarily, but it re-emerged after the 1987 general election. The reasons for this were very different to the circumstances of the 1970s. Among them were:

- Under Margaret Thatcher's three administrations the Scots and Welsh began to resent the fact that, however dominant the Conservatives might be in England, their mandate in the two countries was weak. In Scotland, where there were 72 parliamentary seats, the Conservatives won only 22, 21, 11 and 10 seats respectively in the elections of 1979, 1983, 1987 and 1992. In Wales's 38 seats, the Conservative showing declined from 14 in 1983 to only 6 in 1992. So, as Conservative support in the two countries declined, demands for self-government grew.

- The Labour party in Scotland and Wales felt threatened by a new growth in nationalist voting. They feared they may suffer the same fate as the Conservatives. The Scottish Labour party in particular changed its attitude markedly during the late 1980s.

- In Scotland there was huge resentment at the fact that the unpopular poll tax had been introduced there one year earlier than in England and Wales. Many Scots felt they were being used as mere guinea-pigs, a trial run for the wider introduction of the tax. It was a hated measure in Scotland and resulted in the collapse of support for the Conservatives.

- The Scottish Constitutional Convention of 1988, which was led by the Labour party, but also contained a wide range of Scottish political opinion, came out firmly in favour of devolution as a solution to Scotland's problems.

- In 1993 the Welsh language gained official recognition. Signs and documents were to be in two languages, Welsh was to be offered in all schools and individuals could opt to speak Welsh in court cases. This created a fresh impetus for Welsh nationalism.

- On a global level, the end of the Cold War saw a huge upsurge in national feelings all over the world. This new spirit of nationalism and the desire for popular self-determination spread to Wales and Scotland.

- John Smith, who took over the Labour leadership in 1992, was a convinced devolutionist.

- As we see in this book's chapter on constitutional reform (11), the Labour party in the 1990s believed it would probably need the co-operation of the Liberal Democrats to secure and retain power. Devolution was a key policy for the Liberal Democrats so it made pragmatic sense for Labour to adopt it as a firm proposal.

Devolution, therefore, was made a priority by the incoming Labour administration of 1997. It wasted little time in bringing forward the legislation.

HOW DEVOLUTION CAME ABOUT

Principles

The Scottish Constitutional Convention which had reported in 1988 provided the blueprint for a devolution settlement. However, when Labour was constructing its election manifesto in 1997 it adopted three key principles.

Firstly, it differentiated between Scotland and Wales. In Scotland, where it was expected that the people would embrace devolution enthusiastically, there was to be a parliament with extensive legislative powers. The Scots were also to be offered some control over taxation. In Wales, where approval was not ensured, it was decided that legislative power could not be devolved and there was to be much less financial flexibility there. This proved to be a wise device. Nothing less than a Scottish Parliament would do for the nationalists there, but the Welsh might certainly be frightened off if too much power were offered.

The second principle was the intention to use a form of proportional representation – the additional member system – when electing the Scottish Parliament and Welsh Assembly. It was essential that devolution was not seen as an attempt to tighten Labour's grip in the two countries. Under first-past-the-post Labour would probably have won outright majorities, just as it had done in Westminster elections. This would have defeated the object of devolution, which was to disperse power and not centralise it. Much as the Labour party might have liked to control the new governments, it had to be pragmatic in relinquishing full power. It was part of the price of making devolution acceptable. Furthermore, it was vital that the nationalist parties be given their fair share of the seats. The additional member system was the ideal way of achieving this.

Thirdly, there were to be referendums on the devolution proposals. This was needed for a number of important reasons:

- New Labour accepted the general principle that *any* major constitutional change would require popular approval.
- A positive referendum result would head off opposition from UK unionists and Conservatives.
- It was vital to secure popular consent for the measures in Scotland and Wales. Without it the new institutions might not command respect.
- Referendums would help to 'entrench' the changes. In other words it would make it very difficult for any future government to unravel devolution, at least without a further referendum.

The programme

The progress towards devolution proved to be relatively smooth. The steps were as follows. In some ways they can be seen as a model of how constitutional change can be effected in a parliamentary democracy such as Britain's.

1 Labour, of course, had to win the general election with devolution as a clear part of its manifesto. This would provide a mandate for change. It was important for Labour to win decisively to prevent any questioning of its authority to carry through radical changes. This was achieved comfortably.

2 It was not just important for Labour to win. It also needed to win well in Scotland and Wales. A resurgence of Conservative voting there would call the devolution idea into question. If, on the other hand, the nationalists were to make significant gains, it would suggest that the proposals were not radical enough. In the event, the Conservatives failed to win a single seat in Scotland and Wales in 1997. The nationalist parties, meanwhile, made little progress. Labour support held up well, suggesting that it had got its devolution plans about right.

3 Before the legislation was to be considered, referendums were held. These took place in 1997, soon after the general election. Two factors were important in these referendums. Firstly, there needed to be a good turnout. In the event just over 60 per cent of Scots voted – just enough to give the result authority. In Wales, however, the turnout was only just over 50 per cent and this has certainly had the result of reducing the effectiveness of Welsh

self-government. Secondly, of course, a 'yes' vote was needed. There were no problems in Scotland: 74.3 per cent voted in favour of devolution and 63.5 per cent voted separately for the tax-varying powers which had been hotly contested in the general election campaign. In Wales, however, the 'yes' majority was only 50.3 per cent. Nevertheless, the government decided to approve Welsh as well as Scottish devolution.

4 The legislation had to be passed. With a huge parliamentary majority, this was unlikely to be a problem and so it proved. The only major stumbling block was the proposal to allow the Scottish parliament to vary UK income tax in their own country by 3 per cent up or down. The Conservatives had dubbed this a 'tartan tax' – a means of raising taxes by stealth (so-called 'stealth taxes' had formed a major element in the Conservatives' 1997 election campaign). The new government, however, was not to be diverted and the legislation – the Scotland and Wales Acts – survived largely intact. The Acts were passed in 1998.

THE ARGUMENTS FOR AND AGAINST DEVOLUTION

For

- There has been a growing popular demand for more self-government in the national regions.
- The national regions have different needs to England which should be reflected in stronger regional government.
- By conceding devolution the demands for fuller independence will be headed off, thus preventing the break-up of the United Kingdom.
- It is more democratic because government will be brought closer to the people.
- It will reduce the workload of the British parliament and government.
- It recognises the new idea of a 'Europe of the regions' rather than separate states.

Against

- Conservatives in particular believe it may lead to the break-up of the United Kingdom because demands for independence will be fuelled by devolution.
- It was argued that demand for devolution was over-exaggerated, especially in Wales, so it was unnecessary.
- It creates an extra layer of government which will increase costs to the taxpayer.
- In Scotland it was feared that taxes there would inevitably rise because Scotland is less prosperous than the United Kingdom as a whole.
- It will lead to confusion because there is an additional layer of bureaucracy.
- Nationalists have argued that devolution does not go far enough. British government has retained all the important powers for itself.
- Nationalists also argue they should have a separate voice in Europe but devolution does not give them this.

5 The final hurdles were the actual elections to the Scottish Parliament and Welsh Assembly. Would enough people turn out to vote? Would the results be such that it was possible to form viable governments. As with the referendums, support in Wales was lukewarm, with a turnout of 46 per cent. In Scotland, there was a better result – 58 per cent – but there was still some concern that too few people were interested in the devolution project. The results by party, however, were more encouraging. Though Labour dominated both elections, the party failed narrowly to win overall majorities in both countries.

So it was that, in 1999, the Scottish Parliament and Welsh Assembly came into existence. The Scottish Executive was formed from a coalition between Labour and the Liberal Democrats. Donald Dewar, the Labour leader in Scotland (who had died by 2001) became the country's first minister. In Wales, Labour formed a minority executive under Alun Michael. Michael was replaced by Rhodri Morgan in 2001 following a kind of coup d'etat by Labour assembly members. In the same year Labour gave up trying to govern with a minority and formed a coalition with the Liberal Democrats. In both countries the main opposition duties are shared between the Conservatives and the Nationalists.

DEVOLUTION IN SCOTLAND

The Scottish Parliament

This came into existence, after a gap of 292 years, in 1999. There are 129 seats; 73 of the seats are elected by normal, first-past-the-post constituency elections. The other 56 seats are the result of voting for party lists, where each party is awarded seats from its list according to a combination of what proportion of the votes were won by them in both the constituency and the party list elections. In other words each Scottish voter has two votes – one for a constituency MSP (Member of the Scottish Parliament), the other for a party. The electoral system is known as the additional member system (AMS). The parliament sits in Edinburgh. It has fixed electoral terms. Elections take place every four years. Following the first elections to the Scottish Parliament in 1999, the strength of the parties was as shown in table 12.1.

Table 12.1   Allocation of seats in the Scottish Parliament after 1999

Party	Seats won
Labour	56
Scottish Nationalist	35
Conservative	18
Liberal Democrat	17
Others (Green and Independent)	3

We can see that no party won an overall majority in the Parliament. As the largest party, Labour were asked (by the British government) to form an executive. They did so, but decided they would have to form a coalition with the Liberal Democrats. The coalition's joint tally of 73 seats gave them a comfortable overall majority.

The powers and functions of the parliament

It is important to note that the Scottish Parliament was granted the power to make **primary legislation** in selected areas. The term primary legislation essentially means two things. Firstly, it refers to the laws as we understand them: what is prohibited, how organisations must behave, what responsibilities citizens are expected to carry out. Secondly, it grants powers to other bodies to make regulations and rules which are as binding as other laws. We call this **enabling legislation**. Thus, for example local authorities, members of the executive and other public bodies will be given powers to make **secondary legislation**. Secondary legislation involves orders which do not need to be passed through the same process as primary legislation. They are simply announced and become law if there is no successful objection to them in parliament.

The decision to grant powers of primary legislation was crucial to Scottish devolution. It meant that the Scots were given the opportunity to make themselves and their society distinctive. It should also be remembered that Scotland has always had its own laws, especially criminal and civil law, but that after 1707 these laws were made by the British Parliament in Westminster. In

---

Functions of Scottish Parliament

1 To pass primary legislation in those areas of policy making which have been devolved to Scotland.
2 The main policy areas devolved are: criminal law; civil law; education; social services; local government; building and planning regulations; agriculture; fisheries; health; transport; emergency services.
3 To determine the level of income tax to within 3 per cent higher or lower than the general British rate set in Westminster.
4 To approve the overall Scottish budget.
5 To call the executive to account for its actions and policies.
6 To elect a first minister to form the executive (i.e. government).
7 To form committees to scrutinise legislation and the work of Scottish executive departments.
8 To oversee and scrutinise secondary legislation produced by Scottish ministers, local authorities and other public bodies.

other words the final say on Scottish law rested with the British government. With its own primary legislating powers after devolution, however, Scotland was granted a significant amount of autonomy. As we shall see below, the Welsh Assembly was not granted the power to make primary legislation and so has to consider itself very much an inferior body.

Constraints on Scottish Parliament

1 It can only pass legislation in areas allowed under devolution legislation.
2 It cannot pass legislation which conflicts with British law.
3 It cannot pass legislation which conflicts with European Union law.
4 Its legislation must conform to the European Convention on Human Rights.
5 It cannot raise its own national taxes, other than a 3 per cent variation in income tax levels.
6 It cannot amend the devolution legislation, i.e. it cannot change the system of government in Scotland.

The Scottish Executive

The term 'executive' is used in the devolved systems to replace 'government'. This is to avoid confusion with British government in London.

The Scottish Executive is headed by a first minister, who is effectively the Prime Minister of Scotland, without being given that title. The first minister is effectively chosen by being leader of the largest party in the parliament. However, he or she must be elected to office by the whole parliament.

The rest of the executive is formed by the heads of the various departments which make up Scottish government. The role of the executive is as follows:
1 To formulate policy for Scotland and draft appropriate legislation to be presented in parliament.
2 To negotiate with the British government for funds.
3 To implement policies which have been developed within the executive and approved by the Scottish Parliament.
4 To make decisions under powers delegated to it by either the British or the Scottish Parliament.
5 Liaison with the British government where there are overlapping functions such as law enforcement, environmental and industrial policies
6 To negotiate with institutions of the European Union (though Scotland has no seat at the Council of Ministers) for regional funds and favourable policies.
7 To organise and oversee the provision of services by executive departments (i.e. the Scottish Civil Service), local authorities and other public bodies.

DEVOLUTION IN WALES

The Welsh Assembly

In Wales, the representative body is known as an assembly rather than a parliament. This reflects the fact that it has considerably fewer powers than its Scottish counterpart. In particular, it has no powers to make any primary legislation. This is a key difference. It means that the British parliament and government still rules Wales.

The assembly was elected at the same time as the Scottish Parliament, using the same AMS electoral system. There are 60 seats in all. They were allocated as shown in table 12.2.

Table 12.2   Seats in the Welsh Assembly after 1999

Party	Seats won
Labour	28
Plaid Cymru (Welsh Nationalist)	17
Conservative	9
Liberal Democrat	6

As in Scotland, Labour failed to win an overall majority but was the largest party. However, unlike in Scotland the party decided to try to govern alone, without a coalition party. Within two years this proved to be impractical and so they formed a coalition, again with the Liberal Democrats.

The assembly meets in Cardiff and, as with Scotland, has a fixed term of four years.

The powers and functions of the Welsh Assembly

The following list indicates the main policy areas devolved to Wales:
 • education;
 • social services;
 • local government;
 • building and planning regulations;
 • agriculture;
 • fisheries;
 • health;
 • transport;
 • emergency services.

The most important element of Welsh devolution is that the assembly (note that it is not called a Parliament) does not have the power to make primary legislation. This means it has to rely on Westminster for all its legislation. This is a considerable limitation. What is left to the Welsh Assembly, therefore, is as follows:

Functions of Welsh Assembly

1 It calls the Welsh Executive to account by questioning department heads both in committee and through the full assembly.
2 It elects the head of the Welsh Executive. It can also dismiss him/her.
3 It discusses Welsh affairs and makes resolutions which they hope will be influential on London and on Cardiff.
4 It discusses the implementation of policy on Welsh affairs.
5 It attempts to direct the Welsh Executive in its implementation of policy and allocation of funds to various uses.
6 It debates and requests changes to the Welsh budget.

Constraints on Welsh Assembly

1 It cannot pass primary legislation.
2 It cannot grant powers to members of the Welsh Executive.
3 It cannot call London government to account directly.
4 It cannot raise any special taxes in Wales.

The Welsh Executive

This is, to a large extent the government of Wales. However, because relatively few powers were devolved it must share this function with London, the Welsh Office in particular. The head of the executive is elected by the assembly and he/she appoints the heads of the Welsh departments. These department heads are accountable to the assembly, which can, effectively remove them. As we have seen above, the first Welsh Executive was a Labour minority government, but has since become a Labour/Liberal Democrat coalition.

The functions of the executive are as follows:
- to allocate funds, which are provided by the British government, among competing needs such as health, education, transport and industrial development;
- to negotiate with the Welsh Office in London for those funds;
- to negotiate appropriate legislation for Wales with the Welsh Office;
- to organise the implementation of devolved policy areas in Wales;
- to represent the interests of Wales at various institutions of the European Union, even though Wales is not separately represented in the Council of Ministers.

AN EARLY EVALUATION OF DEVOLUTION IN WALES AND SCOTLAND

Before attempting to assess how well devolution is working it is useful to consider what pieces of evidence we should look for. If we are to judge devolution a 'success' what are the signs to look for. Here are some suggestions:

1 High turnout at elections.
2 Public opinion surveys indicating high levels of satisfaction with devolved government.
3 A rise in the sense of 'national identity' in the two countries. This may be assessed by surveys, but is generally difficult to judge and the evidence is likely to be uncertain.
4 Have Scotland and Wales developed significantly different policies from those which apply in England? Let us remind ourselves of why devolution was introduced: because it was felt that Scotland and Wales may have different needs and demands to England. If this assumption is true, it must follow that there will be differing policies. In this respect, it is clear that Scotland, with powers of legislation, is bound to have become more independent.
5 Arguably, we could consider whether demands for federalism or full independence have subsided. If they have, devolution could be said to have achieved one of its objectives – to satisfy demands for more self-government. If not, it could be argued that devolution has failed in its primary objective.

At the time of writing, devolution is only a few years old and it is too soon to make a valid assessment. However, the early signs are interesting. Overall indications certainly suggest that devolution has been more successful in Scotland than in Wales.

Wales

There are signs of general dissatisfaction with Welsh devolution. The experiment got off to a bad start when the first chief executive, Alun Michael, was seen as merely a puppet of Labour party headquarters in London. It was suspected that he had been put there in order to prevent any radical policies emerging from Wales. He was replaced by the more popular Rhodri Morgan who has proved to be much more acceptable to the people of Wales.

During the foot-and-mouth epidemic, the Welsh Executive was heavily criticised (Wales is more agriculturally based than England) for failing to take Wales's different interests into account. Indeed there has been a general feeling among Welsh farmers that devolution has not fulfilled its promise.

At the same time, surveys indicate low levels of interest in or support for Welsh government. It seems to have made little difference – a reflection of its limited powers. Part of the low public esteem of the assembly has been the high degree of adversary politics and party 'in-fighting' which has been seen.

Having said this, there is no sign of growing Welsh demands for full independence. This suggests a successful outcome. The head of the executive – Rhodri Morgan – has proved to be personally popular and has given Wales some sense of independence.

Scotland

The picture here looks brighter for devolution. The first indication is that Scottish government has made a difference in some areas. Four examples are interesting:

1 The foot-and-mouth crisis was handled more successfully in Scotland and it escaped the worst effects.
2 The Scottish Parliament forced through a measure to make all care of the elderly in special homes free on demand (only medical care is free in England and Wales).
3 The extra tuition fees for Scottish higher education students was abolished. It was retained in England and Wales.
4 While the British House of Commons was locked in an exercise of mutual frustration with the Lords over foxhunting, the unicameral (single chamber) Scottish parliament had little difficulty in responding to public demands for its abolition.

While these legislative innovation were taking place, the feared rises in Scottish taxation have not emerged. Surveys indicate reasonable levels of satisfaction with the operation of the Scottish Parliament and executive. As in Wales, there are also few signs that demands for full independence are rising. The Scottish National Party made no progress in the general election of 2001 – a sure sign that nationalism remains quite weak.

On the other hand, there is little evidence of a stronger sense of Scottish identity emerging. There has always been a strong sense of Scottish cultural identity, but there is little evidence that this is turning into patriotism, which involves pride in one's political institutions.

NORTHERN IRELAND

Devolution in Northern Ireland has to be seen in the context of the Good Friday Agreement of 1998, which is described in the chapter on Northern Ireland (10). However, we can identify a number of reasons why devolution in Northern Ireland had to be very different in character from the constitutional developments in Wales and Scotland.

There is a deep sectarian divide in Northern Ireland. This is more fundamental in character than the division between those English people who favour a close union within the United Kingdom (largely Conservatives) and those who wish for more independence in Scotland and Wales, mostly nationalists and liberals. The Northern Ireland devolution arrangements had to take into account the fact that, in many policy areas, it would be difficult to find any consensus.

The normal, 'British' model of parliamentary government tends to ensure that a clear *majority* government emerges. Both the electoral system of first-past-the-post and the practice of forming executives from one single party, or at least *dominated* by one party, have ensured one-party government. In Wales and Scotland, Labour is the dominant party in the new executives and is likely to remain so for some time, even though it has a junior coalition party. In Northern Ireland the domination of all political life by the Protestant Unionists from 1921 to 1972 was the main source of discontent. A new system which simply restored majority Unionists rule would be unacceptable. Devolution, therefore, had to break the Unionist hegemony.

The electoral system had to reflect the diversity of the political community in the province. It is too simplistic to think of it as a duopoly of Unionists and Nationalists. The two communities have their own internal divisions, largely along the lines of moderates and extremists. There is also a large part of the political spectrum which does not hold dominant views on the relationship with the UK. They are interested in such issues as economic development, relations with Europe, agriculture and fisheries or women's rights. They have, in the past, been swamped by the Unionist–Nationalist split. So it was essential to develop a *pluralist* political system where all groups could participate.

It was clear that a power-sharing system was needed, for reasons described above. This meant that there would have to be a great deal of *innovation*. Devising ways of ensuring that political decisions are only made with a *consensus* of support is not easy and requires original thinking. This is especially true when there is a very fundamental division within the community. The Scottish and Welsh settlements were something of a combination of the British parliamentary system and coalition systems which are common on mainland Europe. Such a compromise was not appropriate in Northern Ireland. A unique settlement was therefore forged, not like any seen in the more stable political systems of Europe.

For these reasons devolution in Northern Ireland is very different from the rest of Britain. Having said that, the actual powers which were devolved to the

Northern Ireland Assembly and executive are not dissimilar from those transferred to Scotland. The main powers are:

- primary legislation;
- education;
- health;
- social security;
- social services;
- transport;
- agriculture and fisheries;
- local government;
- environment;
- housing and planning;
- regional industrial development.

This is an extensive list, but the most important functions of the state remain in the hands of the British government, the Northern Ireland Office in particular. These include:

- defence and foreign policy;
- relations with the Irish republic;
- security and policing;
- economic policy;
- taxation.

The governmental system has three main features designed to achieve the objectives described above. They are:

The electoral system

This is the **single transferable vote (STV)**, as used in the Republic of Ireland. It is a complex system whose essential features are as follows:

- There are multi-member constituencies, normally four.
- Each party can put up as many candidates as there are seats.
- Voters can vote for all candidates, placing them in order of preference.
- The result is based on counting, not just of first preferences, but also subsequent choices, right down to near the end of the list.
- The complex counting system ensures that some of the elected candidates are those who have the support of a wide range of the community, not simply their own party supporters.
- The system also ensures that those from small parties and independents have a chance of winning seats.

The result of the first election (table 12.3) demonstrates that STV achieved its objectives – to reflect the diversity of the community and to prevent any party winning an overall majority.

Table 12.3   Northern Ireland election result, 1999

Party	Seats won
Ulster Unionist	28
Social Democratic Labour party	24
Democratic Unionist	20
Sinn Fein	18
Alliance party	6
Northern Ireland Unionist	3
United Unionist	3
Women's Coalition	2
Progressive Unionist	2
UK Unionist	1
Independent Unionist	1

The result is highly proportional, reflecting very closely the division of political support for parties and candidates. Even the additional member system, as used in Wales and Scotland, does not produce such a proportional result.

Legislation

The legislative procedure of the Northern Ireland assembly is relatively simple. However, it must be emphasised that the make-up the assembly, which prevents an overall majority by one side of the community, means that a broad consensus must be found. Furthermore, the standing committees of the assembly which consider amendments are also constructed so there is no single party majority.

As in Scotland, all legislation must conform both the European Convention on Human Rights and to any European Union legislation which is binding on the UK, Naturally, the assembly can only make laws concerning powers granted to it by the devolution settlement.

The executive

It is perhaps the method for the formation of the executive that is most unusual in Northern Ireland. As with all the other arrangements the main objective has been to ensure consensus and prevent single party domination. The main features are:

- The first minister must be approved by both sides of the sectarian divide in the assembly. However, it is accepted that the first minister will be the leader of the largest party. David Trimble, Ulster Unionist leader, was therefore the clear choice in the first executive.
- The deputy first minister comes from the other community from the first minister. This creates a balance in the senior positions. Thus the first deputy first minister was Seamus Mallon from the Nationalist SDLP.

- The rest of the 12-strong executive is drawn from the various parties according to the number of seats won in the assembly (by a method known as *d'Hondt*). This ensures that some of the smaller parties may achieve some representation in the executive. The parties are free to nominate whom they wish (provided they are assembly members) to fill their allocation. Controversially, this system meant that Sinn Fein were able to choose two members. One of them, Martin McGuinness, was an acknowledged former IRA terrorist. This resulted in the extraordinary situation that a Republican extremist sat in the same executive as the moderate Unionists, their former avowed enemies. The more extreme Unionists, Iain Paisley's Democratic Unionists, were unable to face sitting down with Sinn Fein and decided not to take up their two seats.

So, despite teething problems, this innovative system achieved the apparent impossibility of creating an executive in which bitter political enemies from the past could coexist. It remains an uneasy set-up, but it survived into 2002 despite a number of crises and suspensions.

The real test, of course, remains whether the executive can achieve meaningful change in Northern Ireland. Certainly progress has been made in the restructuring of agriculture, improving higher education, in supporting the important fishing industry and in securing funds for industrial development. There has also been a good deal of innovation in urban re-development and support for the arts. In under-18 education, a key area given the trouble background of the province, attempts are under way (led by controversial education minister Martin McGuinness) to create more non-sectarian schooling. Little has yet been done, but at least the issue is on the political agenda.

Above all, however, the main success of Northern Ireland devolution is that it has survived (four years at the time of writing). Violence has not disappeared but has abated and most terrorists have been marginalised. It is believed that the longer the new institutions survive, the greater the hope for a lasting peace.

THE FUTURE OF DEVOLUTION

Three years after its introduction, devolution appears to be reasonably well established. The Conservative party has dropped its opposition and has committed itself to leaving the new system in place. At the same time they vehemently oppose the transfer of any more powers. As long as there is no major decline in support for the institutions, devolution may be here for many years to come. Of course, the Northern Ireland settlement is more fragile for its own special reasons, but there is greater permanence already established in Wales and Scotland.

The key question is whether there will be any further extensions in decentralisation. The possible options are:

1 There may be devolution to English regions, perhaps along the lines of the Welsh arrangements. Labour was committed to this in 1997, but seems to have dropped the idea. There is some administrative devolution through regional development agencies, and twelve Civil Service offices, but there is no sign of elected assemblies.

2 The Welsh Assembly might be granted powers to make primary legislation. As devolution has not established itself well there, this remains a distant prospect.

3 Greater tax raising powers may be given to Scotland and Northern Ireland. This may hold back demands for greater independence of a more fundamental nature.

4 There may be demands for federal system, as favoured by the Liberal Democrats. This would not necessarily involve the transfer of any new powers and functions, but would make the transfer of power more permanent, preventing Westminster taking its powers back in the future. In short it would mean the transfer of sovereignty rather than mere power.

5 Full independence might follow in due course. Certainly if a future Scottish Parliament and referendum were to vote for it there would be a major constitutional problem. Could the British Parliament resist Scottish calls for independence? Wales and Northern Ireland are a long way from such a development. Indeed in the case of Northern Ireland, reunification with the rest of Ireland is as likely as independence.

SAMPLE QUESTIONS

1 Why was devolution introduced in the UK at the end of the twentieth century?

2 For what reasons was devolution opposed?

3 Why did devolution vary in Scotland, Wales and Northern Ireland?

4 In what senses has devolution been a success?

5 Will devolution lead to the break-up of the United Kingdom?

The development
of European integration

13

> Review of the progress towards greater integration in Europe since the 1950s

> An identification of the key stages in integration

> Explanations of the different forms of integration which have emerged

> The main issues concerning integration

> Speculation concerning the future course of integration

POST-WAR EUROPE

After two world wars, both of which devastated European industry and threatened permanently to sour relations between its states, Europe woke up to the belief that a lasting solution to continental conflict had to be found. The inter-war League of Nations had failed and the United Nations was to be a world-wide organisation which would not solve Europe's problems. Therefore an entirely new kind of arrangement had to be found.

It soon became apparent that there were two rival plans for European integration. One was essentially a cultural, legal and political union. This was promoted by Britain, in particular by Winston Churchill, who had been prime minister from 1940 to 1945. The other was based on the concept of an economic union which would serve a dual purpose in making the states of Europe more interdependent, while at the same time speeding the economic recovery of the continent. This was essentially a French plan, led by one of its most prominent civil servants, Jean Monnet.

These two proposals had the same objective – to remove the fundamental conditions for conflict – but suggested completely different ways of achieving them. Political integration, underpinned by cultural convergence and a unified legal system, would provide institutions within which future disputes could be settled. The cultural dimension would also go some way to preventing extremist movements, notably fascism and communism, from emerging again in western Europe. The economic plan, on the other hand, would result in the great European powers having such a strong vested interest in peace, that war would become unthinkable. Put another way, once there was economic inter-dependence, the benefits of peace would always outweigh gains to be made through war.

The debates over Europe's future have to be seen in the light also of the geopolitics of the time. Firstly, there was an overwhelming desire to prevent a resurgence of German power. Furthermore, any future arrangements would need to ensure that Germany, which was likely to become the strongest economic power after it had recovered from the immediate devastation of war, should not be able to dominate the new Europe. Secondly, the important continental European states – notably France, Germany and Italy – were extremely wary of any British attempt to dominate a future settlement. Thirdly, it was clear that Europe would have to rely on American aid for many years to come. A new European community could not be allowed to threaten United States' interests in the region. Therefore, the idea of a military alliance in Europe which did not include the United States was unthinkable.

It is also worth considering at this stage some of the reasons why Britain became detached from the European 'project' even at its early stages. The distancing of Britain from Europe was to affect continental relations to the end of the twentieth century.

One issue was undoubtedly Britain's 'special relationship' with the United States. Certainly, Winston Churchill saw this as an opportunity for Britain to play a pivotal role in the post-war world. If she was able to position herself as a bridgehead between America and Europe, with close institutional links with both, she would be able to dominate the future of Europe. Interestingly, this same idea seems to have occurred to Tony Blair after 1997. However, the large European states were suspicious of British motives and were not prepared to consider any plans which would result in excessive American influence.

A second important factor in the estrangement of Britain and Europe was the strong influence of socialism on the early project. Many of the 'pioneers' of a European community were socialists or social democrats. They saw integration as a means to introduce greater equality and social justice throughout the continent. Although Britain had a quasi-socialist Labour government from 1945 to 1951, it was Conservative led by the time a more integrated Europe began to emerge in the 1950s. Naturally enough, the Conservative party was less than enthusiastic in supporting what they saw as a socialist enterprise.

Finally, we should remind ourselves that Britain was still an imperial power. Apart from the difficulties of reconciling Britain's special relationship with her colonies with membership of a European economic union, this led the other

Europeans to be suspicious of her motives. Could Britain be a truly European partner while its attention lay firmly in the wider world outside Europe? As we have seen above, this feeling also applied to the UK–United States axis.

For these reasons western Europe in the period after World War II was very much prepared to 'go it alone' at least in the economic sense. They were ready to accept American aid for reconstruction (the 'Marshall Plan') and to join NATO for collective security after the onset of the Cold War, but the economic situation was different. There was to be no permanent economic union with the United States as the latter would be too dominant. If an integrated political union was proposed they feared it would be British dominated.

So the development of a European Community was, therefore, very much a west European affair, with Britain and the United States kept at arm's length. Nevertheless, it is useful to consider the less successful of the two plans – the Council of Europe.

THE COUNCIL OF EUROPE

In 1948 Winston Churchill, then leader of the Opposition in Britain, delivered a speech to European leaders at the Hague in the Netherlands. When one considers how Euro-sceptic the bulk of the Conservative party had become by the end of the 1990s, this speech was breathtaking in its radical tone. Churchill not only proposed a new pan-European organisation, but also suggested that each state should be prepared to give up some of its national sovereignty.

Most of the states of Europe has recently fought two wars in order to preserve or regain their status as independent nation states. The concept, therefore, that they should be prepared to surrender some of that independence was optimistic to say the least. In the event, it was indeed unrealistic. Inevitably, the full plan was rejected. In its place, a watered-down version of the Churchill plan was adopted. The Council of Europe came formally into existence in 1949 with an initial sixteen member states.

The general idea of the Council was to create a new 'European culture'. It was to emphasise what Europeans have in common and so eliminate its differences. This common culture included such features as:
- emphasis on the importance of the arts and 'high culture';
- a respect for fundamental human rights;
- an attachment to democracy and the rule of law;
- stress on the importance of education.

In the event, the Council has proved to be a great disappointment to those who have hoped for cultural integration. The Assembly of the Council, which contains delegates nominated from member states, does little more than discuss matters of mutual interest. No decisions are binding and no controversial issues are ever adopted by members.

That said, the Council did enjoy one major success. This was the development of the European Convention on Human Rights and the Court which adjudicates on disputes under the Convention. The Convention, which was signed in 1950, has had a profound impact on the status of rights in Europe. Virtually all the members have adopted the Convention, either in its entirety, or as part of their own rights legislation. The last significant member to resist adopting the Convention was Britain. It was not until 1999 that the terms of the Convention were included in the Human Rights Act.

The European Court of Human Rights (which is *not* an institution of the European Union) hears appeals from European citizens who believe their rights have been abused. Britain has been especially affected by the powers of the court, having lost over fifty cases since the 1960s. These have included issues such as the treatment of prisoners in Northern Ireland, press censorship, the method of trial for juveniles and night flights over Heathrow which deprive residents of sleep.

Apart from the important activities of the Convention and the Court, the council has had a limited role. It does arrange cultural exchanges, organises educational programmes to improve European understanding and discusses such concerns as crime, drugs, terrorism and the media, but these are of little political significance. The narrowness of the Council's role demonstrates that, as an experiment in political integration, it is a failure.

THE DEVELOPMENT OF THE EUROPEAN UNION

While the Council of Europe was proving a disappointment to its supporters, the alternative institution – an essentially economic union – moved from one level of integration to the next with relative ease. Most of its members shared a common goal and enjoyed a great degree of unity in achieving it.

Two Frenchmen – Jean Monnet and Robert Schuman – believed that the most effective way of creating an integrated Europe was to pursue an economic union. There is no doubt that they both foresaw a wider political union in the future, but understood that a single economic market would be the first step towards such an objective. The first stage was a relatively modest arrangement and can be seen as something of a prototype for the European Community which was to follow.

The European Coal and Steel Community (ECSC)

In 1951 the Treaty of Paris brought together six countries – France, West Germany, Italy, Belgium, the Netherlands and Luxembourg (the last three named known collectively as *Benelux*) in a single industrial enterprise.

In itself the ECSC was a limited system. It provided for a single market in coal and steel among the member countries. Fair trade was established between them and a common external tariff established against these goods coming in from abroad. In this way it was hoped that the industries would flourish, encouraged by free competition within the community and some protection from the outside. The Paris Treaty also provided for a central body to regulate production among the member states.

At first sight this innovation – known as the Schuman Plan – seemed to be a modest one. With the benefit of hindsight, however, we can see how revolutionary it was. The radical measures which brought about the ECSC included the following vital principles.

Each member state was prepared to give up some of its national sovereignty to the Community. This idea, of 'pooled' or 'shared' sovereignty in specific functional areas was the first of its kind in the world. It set the tone for all future developments towards the creation of the European Union. All previous supranational bodies (such as the Council of Europe or the League of Nations) had allowed member states to retain their national sovereignty. This meant that they could choose whether to adopt any agreed measures or to ignore them. The ECSC, on the other hand, insisted that, to be a member, all states had to agree to conform to all decisions. It was this insistence on shared functional sovereignty that kept Britain out of the community. The Labour government of the day, which had recently nationalised both industries (coal and steel), was not willing to give up one ounce of British independence. This was to set a pattern for the British attitude to Europe for nearly two decades to come.

The three branches of national governments – the legislature, the executive and the judiciary – were to be replicated, in an amended form, within the new set-up. Thus there was created the following bodies:

- *The High Authority:* a kind of senior Civil Service which was to develop policy and organise the implementation of decisions.

- *The Council of Ministers:* ministerial representatives from the member countries which would make all important decisions.

- *The Assembly:* nominated members from the six states which were to give general advice to the High Authority and the Council of Ministers.

● *The Court of Justice:* to deal with disputes between member states. The judges were nominated from the different states and were to be independent.

The economic integration which was established in the ECSC was, it was clearly stated, to be the prelude to an even closer political union in the future.

Although the structure of the ECSC was essentially experimental – nothing like this had been attempted before – it proved to be so acceptable that, when the more ambitious successors of the ECSC, leading to the European Union itself, were formed, they followed much the same blueprint.

The 'Common Market' (EEC)

Encouraged by the success of the ECSC, and determined to take integration further, negotiations began among the six members to extend the scope of the market. During 1956 the creation of the 'Common Market' (European Economic Community: EEC) was discussed and the following year, 1957, the **Treaty of Rome** was signed. This was effectively the founding document of European integration. An additional treaty, for the pooling of nuclear energy resources was also signed. This was known as Euratom.

Britain did not take part in these early discussions. Both prime ministers of the period – Anthony Eden (who resigned in 1957) and Harold Macmillan (who took over from Eden) – made it clear that political and trade links with the Empire and Commonwealth were more important to Britain than a European system. It was also true that, following the humiliation of the failed Suez episode in 1956, Britain was licking her wounds and certainly not in a position to take part in the great experiment. The other potential members around the fringes of the central six were also less than enthusiastic. Spain and Portugal were still ruled by fascist dictators (Franco and Salazar respectively) and their intense nationalism did not allow them to consider integration. The Scandinavian countries, with their tradition of neutrality were also far from interested. So it was to be a small exclusive club. The Treaty of Rome contained five main agreements.

Treaty of Rome: main agreements

- to abolish tariffs among member countries;
- to establish a common external tariff – i.e. all members would charge the same tariffs on goods and services imported from outside the Common Market;
- the removal of all barriers to free competition among all members states;
- the intention to create the free movement of all goods, services, capital (i.e. finance) and labour between member states by 1970;
- a more general intention to establish a Common Agricultural Policy. This was part of France's price for joining.

The Treaty of Rome also established the institutions of the Common Market, very much along the lines of what we see today and modelled on the set-up of the ECSC. The functions of these bodies is described and discussed below. Put simply at this stage, however, they were:

Institutions of the Common Market

- **The Commission:** an unelected bureaucracy to develop policies designed to implement the Treaty of Rome.
- **The Council of Minister:** elected ministers from the member states who would effectively ratify the laws and regulations of the Common Market and discuss future policy.
- **The Assembly or Parliament:** to advise the Commission and council on policy, but unable to make or amend European law.
- **The Court of Justice:** to handle disputes between members and to deliver interpretations of European law.

We can see how similar this arrangement was to that of the ECSC.

So, in 1957 the great European project was under way. Only six original members had signed up and success was far from assured. By 2002 it had grown to fifteen members with several others queuing up to join. A single market had been established and twelve of the members were using a single currency. At first sight this seems an impressive achievement in a relatively short time, and so it was in many ways. However, a glimpse at the institutions which were established in Rome tells us that the economic development of Europe has not been matched by political progress.

Towards the European Community (EC)

By 1962 plans for the Common Agricultural Policy (CAP) were complete. The CAP is a complex system described more fully later in this book.

CAP: basic principles

- All agricultural products were to be traded freely within the community. There were to be no tariffs and any regulations, such as health or content standards, would be common to all members.
- There would be protection from outside competition in the form of tariffs and subsidies for producers within the community who found it difficult to compete with the outside world.
- Producers of a wide range of goods would receive guaranteed minimum prices.
- A system was established whereby the Community would buy up surpluses of goods in order to keep prices up. These surpluses could be used if there were serious shortages in the future, but could be destroyed if necessary.

The CAP was more than merely a free-trade system. It was also a device for protecting key industries and reaping the benefits of specialisation. As such it represented an important step in the further integration of Europe.

The Common Fisheries Policy (CFP), which had similar aims to the CAP and was also designed to preserve fish stocks, was signed much later, in 1983. It proved as controversial as the CAP, not least because the issue of territorial waters is one where national interest tends to clash with European integration. In some ways, therefore, its establishment was an even greater achievement.

The first phase of integration – the establishment of a tariff and regulation-free zone with free movement of goods, labour and finance – had been effectively established by 1968, ahead of schedule. Three years earlier, in 1965, the three European institutions, Euratom, the ECSC and the Common Market had been joined by the Merger Treaty. It was therefore time to consider the next phase of development.

In the meantime the Community was expanding at last. Three countries joined in 1973. These were Britain, Ireland and Denmark.

The Single European Act 1985–87

By 1985 the Community was ready to take a further step forward. This was movement towards the creation of a single market. This involved three main provisions:

1 There was to be completely free movement of goods, capital and people between member states. There was already such a provision *in theory*. However, in practice there were still various forms of restriction. For example members were still preventing some people from moving from one country to another. This inhibited the idea of a free labour market. There were still various forms of restrictions and concessions on the movement of goods through borders. Duty free concessions were an example, as were variable health and safety regulations. Banking practices also varied so that there was not a truly free capital market.

2 Each member state was to incorporate the Single European Act into their own laws. This meant that it would be *illegal* in terms of each country's own *domestic laws* to discriminate against any goods, labour or capital being exchanged within the EC. Each member was thus fully committed to the single market and would no longer be able to obstruct progress.

3 A target date of 1992 was set for the final completion of the single market.

The Single European Act (SEA) was finalised in 1985, ratified at the Council of Ministers in 1986 and had been incorporated into the law of every member state by 1987. It is, of course, an irony that the SEA was fully supported by

Britain's Prime Minister of the day, Margaret Thatcher. Possibly the most important step in the development of European integration (perhaps with the exception of the single currency) was therefore backed by the leader who was later to become one of the most implacable opponents of the extension of the European union.

The SEA also gave the European Parliament some additional powers, notably to veto the introduction of new members. More importantly, however, the SEA extended the scope of qualified majority voting. At this stage it may be useful to discuss the issue of qualified voting.

Qualified majority voting (QMV)

When European integration began, and especially when there were only six members, it was assumed that all decisions would require the agreement of *all* the members. This effectively meant that each member would have a veto over all decisions. The importance of this principle cannot be over-emphasised.

If a member state can veto decisions it means that it has not sacrificed its own national sovereignty to Europe. It also means that each state had an equal status since everyone's veto was worth the same. Little Luxembourg could obstruct a decision as easily as Germany, the biggest member. This is all very well in terms of sovereignty. However, it makes decision-making extremely difficult. In order to make progress, therefore, the Community had to introduce majority voting.

A straight forward majority vote system, as applies in domestic parliaments is not, however, desirable. This would take away the power of states to an unacceptable extent. Conversely, it would mean that an alliance of the smaller states could thwart the will of the larger members. For example, when there were six members, the four smallest states would have been able to outvote France and Germany together! Clearly a compromise was needed. A system was required which would take account of the differing size of member states, but would also protect the small states from being 'bullied' by the larger ones. The answer was qualified majority voting. Each state is given a differential voting power, according to size. With 15 members the voting powers were as shown in table 13.1.

It needs a total of 62 votes to pass any measure through the Council of Ministers. Thus a small group of countries, say UK, Italy, Belgium and Luxembourg, who total 27 votes, can prevent a measure being adopted. Conversely, even the four biggest members together cannot force a measure through as they only have 40 votes.

Table 13.1   EU members' voting strengths
before 2004 enlargement

Country	Votes
Germany	10
France	10
Italy	10
UK	10
Spain	8
Belgium	5
Holland	5
Greece	5
Portugal	5
Austria	4
Sweden	4
Ireland	3
Denmark	3
Finland	3
Luxembourg	2
Total	87
Qualified majority	62

The QMV system has steadily been extended, both at Maastricht (1992) and Nice (2000). So more and more sovereignty has been given up by members. But the unanimous vote remains for crucial issues.

Jacques Delors, 1985–94

Jacques Delors, a French socialist, became President of the Commission and thus the most senior permanent policy maker in 1985, the year the Single European Act was developed. His election (by the Council of Ministers) marked a new direction for Europe. He wanted to see progress in two areas.

Firstly, Delors recognised that there would eventually have to be monetary union if Europe were to move towards a genuinely single market. His idea was a four-part plan:

1 Prospective members of a single currency system would be required to adhere strictly to the Exchange Rate Mechanism (ERM) which already existed. He understood that this system of fixed exchange rates to bring the economies of Europe closer together had to be supported.

2 The economies of member states would have to 'converge'. Convergence meant that key economic variables such as inflation, interest rates, government borrowing and unemployment would have to become similar in all the member states. This would reduce the potentially disruptive effects of adopting a single currency.

3 There would be an interim phase during which the currencies would be absolutely fixed against one another and interest rates would be set for all members by the European Central Bank. This would prevent disturbances in the finance markets of Europe. It would also enable countries to adopt the single currency smoothly in a short period.

4 There would be a rapid changeover to the single currency by all member countries at the same time.

In the event the Delors plan was adopted and came to fruition on 1 January 2002.

Secondly, Delors wanted to see progress towards closer political union. It was this intention which infuriated Margaret Thatcher. During the negotiations for the Single European Act she had accepted what was seen as an inevitable development. After the SEA, however, Delors wanted to see further progress as quickly as possible. His determination led to Thatcher's speech at a European conference in Bruges in 1988 in which she repudiated the idea of a closer union. This marked a clear watershed in Britain's relationship with Europe. The Conservative party moved decisively towards a Euro-sceptic position. Even so Britain did join the Exchange Rate Mechanism (a decision which Thatcher agreed to with great reluctance). In theory, therefore, Britain could have entered the single currency system up to the point when she was forced out of the ERM in September 1992.

Delors was undaunted by Thatcher's opposition and moved steadily towards the ratification of his plan. He was finally successful at Maastricht in 1992.

Maastricht Treaty 1992

Formally known as the **Treaty of European Union**, Maastricht marked a significant step forward. The name of the organisation changed to the European Union. This change was more than cosmetic. The term 'Union' suggested that members intended to form a closer, more permanent institution.

Maastricht had a number of facets, making it not only one of the biggest steps forward, but also one of the most extensive. Its main provisions were as follows:

- The future *political* development of the Union was to be based on the principle of **subsidiarity**. This established that government institutions should be as de-centralised as possible. The concept of subsidiarity is discussed in more detail below.
- The Single European Act was incorporated into the Treaty of Rome. In effect this gave the European Union a 'constitution' for the first time.
- A number of further decision-making areas were to become the subject of qualified majority voting rather than unanimity. The significance of this

has been described above. By removing national vetoes over a number of functions, national sovereignty was further eroded. It was this measure which caused the British Prime Minister, John Major, so many problems with his own party.

- A commitment was made to establish in the future a European Defence force and to move towards a common set of foreign policies.
- There was a final commitment to move towards a single European currency. The year 2002 was agreed as the target date. Three countries, including the UK were allowed to opt out of this aspect of the Treaty.
- In order to facilitate and maintain the single currency, the principle of **convergence** was developed. It was recognised that it was essential, if the Euro was to work, for all members of the system to adopt economic policies which would prevent major disruption of monetary union. Thus, for example, it was recognised that member countries would have to keep control over inflation, public borrowing and unemployment according to fixed targets. In this way a single interest rate, set by the European Central Bank, could be applicable to all the European economies.
- It was agreed that there would be movement towards the idea of 'European citizenship'. This implied completely free movement of people between member countries (a process which had already begun as a result of the **Schengen Agreement of 1985**), equal citizenship rights throughout the Union and some progress towards common policing for international crimes. In the longer term there was an intention to create a 'European Bill of Rights' which would be binding on all members.
- An attempt was made to reduce the democratic deficit in the Union's political institutions. In particular, the Parliament was given greater powers of legislative amendment and veto. There were also increased powers given to the Court of Auditors which would better enable them to investigate cases of corruption.
- The **Social Chapter** was negotiated. This established a wide range of rights for workers such as the 'working hour directive' to prevent excessively long hours of work and short holidays, rights for women workers with or without children, equal treatment for part-time workers and stronger safeguards against unjustified job losses. As with the single currency issue, Britain negotiated an opt-out from the Social Chapter based on demands from the Conservative party. It was felt that the protections offered would make the labour market considerably less flexible and make Britain uncompetitive. In the event, the Labour party made a commitment to sign the Social Chapter and did so as one of its first acts when it won power in 1997.

The first four clauses of article B of the treaty is worth reproducing in full as it summarises clearly the direction the Union is to take:

TREATY OF EUROPEAN UNION, 1992

Article B

The Union shall set itself the following objectives:
- To promote economic and social progress which is balanced and sustainable in particular through the creation of an area without internal frontiers, through the strengthening of economic and social cohesion and through the establishment of economic and monetary union, ultimately including a single currency in accordance with the provisions of this Treaty.
- To assert its identity on the international scene, in particular through the implementation of a common foreign and security policy including the eventual framing of a common defence policy, which might in time lead to a common defence.
- To strengthen the protection of the rights and interests of the nationals of its member states through the introduction of a citizenship of the Union.
- To develop close co-operation on justice and home affairs.

So the European Union became wider and deeper. Maastricht was very much the creation of Commission President Jacques Delors and proved to be his greatest achievement. This is not to say that it was an unqualified success for the supporters of European integration. We can assess the significance of the Treaty by comparing its successes and failures.

Successes

- At least twelve of the members did commit themselves to closer union. Indeed the outcome of Maastricht was entitled 'Ever Closer Union'.
- All signatories to the single currency accepted that they would have to accept economic disciplines in order to maintain stability under the convergence criteria.
- The Social Chapter represented a major step forward for the rights of workers and for establishing a genuinely open labour market throughout the continent.
- The single currency issue was resolved and, as we now know, the timetable towards union proved to be realistic and achievable.
- By insisting on the concept of subsidiarity the European Union made some progress towards allaying fears that it was becoming little more than a centralised bureaucracy.

Partial failures

- The treaty failed to establish a firm principle of citizenship. Although there was an intention to move towards common rights and responsibilities, no specific measures were taken.

- Despite committing themselves to the idea of common defence and foreign policies there was little progress in determining how this might be achieved.
- Schengen had begun the process of establishing free movement but Maastricht failed to persuade all members, notably the UK, that they should abandon border restrictions.

Failures

- Clearly the fact that the UK remained determined to opt out of key elements – mainly the single currency and Social Chapter – can be seen as a failure to persuade John Major to stand up to the rebels in his own party. In the event this proved to be a disaster for the Conservatives. Britain's uncertain position at Maastricht split the Conservative party and contributed to its heavy defeat in the 1997 election.
- Attempts the democratise the political institutions were feeble and did little to reduce claims that the Union was not really interested in democracy.

So we can see that Maastricht enjoyed limited success. It is likely that the movement towards a single currency will prove in the future to have been its principal achievement.

Amsterdam Agreement 1997

Negotiated between 1995 and 1997, the Treaty came into force in 1999. If Maastricht had been a series of intentions, Amsterdam was a confirmation of those policies, converting them into commitments. It was also designed to establish and modernise many of the Union's institutions. This was for three purposes. Firstly, the various bodies needed the necessary powers to carry forward the plans which had been agreed at Maastricht. Secondly, the changes were intended to make the institutions more democratic. Finally, the agreement anticipated the enlargement of the EU.

The areas covered were:
- The establishment of common rights for all, completely free movement of people, common policies on asylum and immigration. This to include a common system of freedom of information for all citizens.
- Common standards in the fields of the environment, consumer protection and public health standards.
- There was a more precise commitment to common defence and foreign policies. A 'High Representative' to express common foreign policy and represent the Union as a whole was to be appointed (in the event Javier Solana was the first holder of this post).

- The voting allocations in the Council were agreed to take account of the next group of new members.
- A series of proposals to democratise the institutions of the Union before they were to be enlarged by the addition of new members.

It was especially recognised that future new members might have extremely variable standards of human rights, treatment of immigrants, health and consumer protection arrangements. By establishing these standards new members would be left in no doubt as to what was expected of them.

Potentially, however, it was the institutional changes which are likely to have the most profound results. These are described in more detail in the 'Institutions' chapter of this book (14).

THEORIES OF INTEGRATION

Now that we have reviewed the various stages by which European Union has evolved and integration has matured, we can examine the various theories of integration which have guided the process and which are likely to inform the debate about future developments.

International co-operation

This is the weakest form of integration. It means that groups of nations may meet regularly to discuss matters of mutual concern. However, if they are unwilling to give up national sovereignty, action can only be taken if they succeed in reaching agreement among themselves. Countries may be legally bound by the resulting agreement if a treaty is signed, but nobody needs to feel coerced.

In such a scenario, each issue must be negotiated in its own right. There is a general commitment by countries to try to reach agreement, but this may not prove possible. If there is no supra-national body to which they have given up sovereignty, the organisation need not be threatened if agreement cannot be reached. The North Atlantic Treaty Organisation (NATO) has always operated largely on the basis of such co-operation. Members sacrificed no national sovereignty to NATO, but have agreed from time to time to engage in mutual action, sometimes even committing their own troops to military action under 'foreign' commanders. But in every case the member countries have been free to withdraw co-operation without losing their membership of NATO. The British Commonwealth is a further example of this kind of organisation. It only acts if members can agree (for example to adopt sanctions against the apartheid regime in South Africa in the 1970s and 1980s). The Commonwealth, like NATO, has never been able to act independently of its own membership.

Had the European Community adopted this form of integration, there can be little doubt that it would have made little progress towards a single market and may not, indeed, have survived at all. The steps needed to create a single market and monetary union were so radical, that they required members to accept that they had to cede some sovereignty to the Community.

Neo-functionalism

When the European Coal and Steel Community was created there began a process by which European countries began to transfer national sovereignty to a supra-national body. In these early stages it was clear that the way forward was for various government *functions* to be given over by member states. At first it was control over the trade in coal, iron and steel. When the European Community itself was formed, controls over trade in general were transferred. As we have seen in the review which is described above, more and more functions have moved over to Brussels. Policy and law on agriculture, fisheries, environmental control, consumer issues, working conditions and many others followed trade as functions which member governments were willing to give up.

This approach to integration can be described as neo-functionalism. It is a gradualist approach which is attractive to those of a more conservative disposition. Countries do not have to give up control over a function if they do not wish to. The European Community has always allowed members a veto over any change in functional responsibility. Thus Britain was able to negotiate opt-outs from the single currency and the Social Chapter when Conservative governments felt they were a step too far, functions which they were not willing to give up. By the same token, functionalism means that a consensus is always needed if further integration is to take place.

The alternative to functionalism is to transfer political sovereignty to the supranational body and then allow that body to decide which functions it wishes to take over. The end result may appear similar, but the *process* of transference in functionalism is more cautious and remains in the control of individual members. It is this latter principle which has always governed the way in which European integration has proceeded.

Pooled sovereignty

Opponents of European integration have always stressed the fact that national sovereignty has to be sacrificed if progress is to be made. In other words the transfer of sovereignty is seen as a *negative* development. In some ways this is a valid argument. It is undeniably true that members of the European Union have had to give up some of the independent functions of their national governments.

A less sceptical view can, however, be considered. This suggests that members are not giving up sovereignty, but simply sharing it with others or 'pooling' it. The losses of national sovereignty are, in this way, compensated for by *gains* in sovereignty over *other* states in the Union. Thus, for example, when Britain finally signed the Social Chapter in 1997 it lost some national sovereignty over the regulations concerning conditions in the work place. On the other hand, any future developments in this field have to be negotiated and Britain will have some say in future working conditions in Germany, Greece, Spain and every other member state.

There are also functions which are, by their very nature, supranational. This certainly applies to environmental protection (pollution, for example, does not recognise national borders). Similarly, as an increasing proportion of output is accounted for by multi-national companies, national governments become unable to control their operations. Policy on competition (i.e. opposing monopoly power) must, therefore, be carried out at supra-national level. In such cases sovereignty has to be pooled.

This notion of pooled sovereignty will not do for its opponents They have argued that national sovereignty is of a much higher order than shared sovereignty. The domestic government has much more interest in managing its own affairs – after all national governments are elected primarily to do that – than in interfering in the affairs of others.

Federalism

This model of integration has been a common way in which groups of sovereign states have come together to form a larger union. Perhaps the most celebrated example of a federal settlement was the creation of the United States of America in 1787. Germany is another prominent example, as are Nigeria, Russia and India.

Federalism is the consequence of a tension which exists between two opposing forces. One is an overwhelming desire to create a new state. The Americans felt that they could not survive in a hostile world as thirteen separate countries. In Germany the driving force for union was partly economic, partly cultural, a need to unite the Germanic peoples and restore national pride. The other is the determination of the states which are to be absorbed by the new union to retain some of their own sovereignty.

The result of such a conflict is a federal settlement. All the uniting states agree to give up sovereignty over certain government responsibilities. Furthermore, their decision is permanent. They do not expect ever to repossess these sovereign powers. At the same time the participants identify which powers they wish to retain for themselves. Here it is understood that the central, or federal, authority will never be able to take over these 'reserved' sovereign powers without the permission of the separate states.

At first sight, federalism seems an attractive blueprint for the constitutional future of the European Union. Member countries would retain their own sovereignty and there would be no way that Brussels would be able to get its hands on them in the future. But there remain problems, the main examples of which are shown in the box.

Problems with federalism

- A European federal state would be a new state which would stand *above* the member states. In other words, national governments would be downgraded and seen as inferior. This is certainly the experience of other federal states.
- Federalism also implies permanence. Under existing arrangements member states feel they have the opportunity to change their relationship with the centre through negotiation. This is not the case with a federal settlement which would be 'entrenched'.
- There is a fear that there would be a tendency for the federal authority to gather more and more powers to itself. Until President Reagan began to reverse the process in the 1980s, it was certainly true that the federal government of the United States gained power over the individual states.
- In all other federal arrangements, the most important powers have been given to the centre. These include economic and monetary control, defence, foreign affairs and internal security. The individual states have, by contrast, been confined to less fundamental activities such as social policy, transport and planning.

Nevertheless federalism is seen by some as the way forward for Europe.

European government

Opponents of complete political integration tend to refer to this vision as the European *super-state*. Supporters see such a development as possibly inevitable and certainly desirable. The latter view is both radical and genuinely internationalist. It is based on the proposition that the independent nation-state has had its day. They believe that its survival will hinder progress and argue further that the nation-state has been a historical phenomenon which is not appropriate in the modern age of globalisation and interdependence.

Ironically, it was a great Conservative politician, Winston Churchill, who was one of the first post-war statesman to dare to suggest the idea of a European government. He suggested that a single sovereign government for Europe would be the only way to prevent conflict between the nations of the continent. To those who feared that such a government would destroy cultural diversity, Churchilll replied that culture was a European phenomenon in itself, more important than national cultures.

In the event Churchill's ideas were far too radical for most British politicians. Meanwhile, on continental Europe, they were rejected as an attempt to sponsor British domination. There remain a few supporters to this day, but the idea of sacrificing all national sovereignty to a European state is unlikely to find widespread favour in the foreseeable future.

Subsidiarity

This principle was adopted for the European Union at Maastricht in 1992. It is fundamentally a liberal idea, but has also been shared by many socialists and even some conservatives throughout the continent.

To understand it we should be aware that government in Europe can be carried out at four different levels. These are: supranational (Europe), national, regional, local.

We can now consider what functions of government can and should be carried out at each level. Clearly there are some functions which should be divided between two or more levels, but the principle of subsidiarity suggests that there is normally a rational division of powers. The box demonstrates a likely scheme of subsidiarity.

A scheme of subsidiarity

- *Supranational.* International trade; environmental protection; defence; foreign affairs; long-distance transport; finance; some indirect taxation; energy planning; competition control; consumer protection; workers' protection; agriculture and fishing.
- *National.* Health care; criminal law; direct taxation; micro-economic development; arts and culture; personal taxation; national transport; welfare benefits; environment; higher education.
- *Regional.* Regional transport; environment; urban planning and regeneration; rural affairs; economic development; some indirect taxation.
- *Local.* Education; personal social services; local planning; local transport; local environment; crime prevention and detection; provision for the aged; mental health provision; local taxation.

There are two striking features of such a scheme. The first is that a large number of key functions are shown at supranational level. This may appear alarming to defenders of national interests. However, it should be pointed out these are issues which do not impact on the everyday lives of citizens so that

European government may not bear down on citizens quite as heavily as may be feared.

The second feature is that most functions in this scheme are *not* placed at national level. To some extent this is a natural process. It is becoming increasingly impractical for nation-states to be able to control many issues. Some examples can illustrate this second point.

- *Defence.* Traditional wars of invasion and defence are over. Conflicts are increasingly international, highly technical and can only be dealt with through international action. Problems in the Balkans, the Gulf and with terrorism after 2001 are clear examples.

- *Foreign policy.* Individual countries have insufficient influence to be able to shape international events. As Europe becomes a single economic bloc, issues concerning trade and economic issues must be conducted collectively.

- *Environment.* Environmental problems such as global warming, emissions control, energy depletion, conservation issues do not recognise national boundaries.

- *Competition.* Since most large corporations are now multinational, control of monopoly power must also be carried out on a supra-national basis.

At the same time the process of European integration itself has taken functions away from nation-states. Again some examples are shown below:

- *Monetary union.* Control over finance, interest rates and money supply is now European based.

- *Single labour market.* Uniform regulations concerning working conditions etc. needed.

- *Single product markets.* Consumer protection and trade regulations are controlled in Europe.

SAMPLE QUESTIONS

1 In what ways and to what extent has European integration eroded the sovereignty of nation-states in Europe?

2 Why was the Maastricht Treaty considered a major step towards European integration?

3 Identify, describe and analyse the key stages in European integration since 1957.

4 Is Europe destined to become a new 'super-state'?

Institutions
of the European Union

14

➤ Introductory information concerning the study of institutions

➤ Analysis of the concepts used to assess the nature and operation of the institutions

➤ Descriptions of the role, composition and operation of the main institutions: the Commission, Parliament, Council of Ministers and Court of Justice

➤ Analysis of some of the problems and issues concerning the institutions

➤ Brief descriptions of the role of other, less central institutions of the EU

PROBLEMS FOR STUDY

One of the errors which is often made in studying the institutions of the European Union is to attempt a comparison with *national* political systems. This carries a number of difficulties. The EU is *not* like a national state (though it may be ever closer to becoming one). There are crucial distinctions which must be borne in mind. These include the following.

The EU remains an organisation of nations rather than a full-scale *supranational* body. The members are not yet prepared to abandon national interests completely. Instead, they have shown a willingness to reach a series of agreements with other states. This may involve compromises, deals and accommodations to the interests of others, but it does not mean that national distinctions can be put aside. This affects very deeply the nature of the EU's institutions. They have to have different functions and methods of operation to national governments. The latter do not have the problem of attempting to reconcile national differences (though divergent regional interests are often a problem). This is not the case with the EU.

Partly because of its international nature, and partly because of the great variations between member states, the EU lacks political *coherence*. This means it is difficult to find common purposes in the way that individual states do. Britain in the years following 1997, for example, has had a clear need and desire the improve public services. Germany has had to overcome the problems of reunification since 1991. Poorer countries like Portugal, Ireland and Greece have naturally been concerned with the need for economic development. France worries about the future of its agricultural base. The EU has had one overwhelming goal – to achieve the single market and monetary union – but thereafter its purposes are less clear. Also less coherent are the main political *issues* and *conflicts*.   This is what makes the party system meaningful and gives the electorate a clear picture of what government is doing and how it is performing. Conflicts within the EU tend to be national in nature, rather than about political issues. We tend to think about political institutions in terms of parties, policies, manifestos and mandates. This does not work so well with the EU.

Each member state has its own distinctive political system. Furthermore, political control of each country may change at any time. As we have seen above, the EU is very much about negotiation between member states, so problems are bound to arise when the political situations within member states are liable to change at any time. For example, when the issues surrounding the single currency and the Social Chapter were being resolved, Britain was governed by a party which was both fundamentally split on these concerns and eventually decided to opt out. After 1997, however, the British position changed, particularly in the case of the Social Chapter. Thus the landscape of discussion has altered. Similarly, we may consider the practice of Denmark and Ireland to put important constitutional changes to a referendum. Thus Denmark voted against the Maastricht Treaty (on deeper economic and monetary union) and Ireland against the Nice Agreement (on enlargement). Both events caused consternation and delay within the EU. The European Union does not operate in a vacuum. Its institutions, therefore, must take account of the fact that it is at the mercy of political currents within member states. After enlargement this problem is likely to grow more serious.

We must also be careful, when considering the institutions, not to assume that they carry out the same functions as their apparent 'counterparts' in national governments. The European Parliament, for example, cannot be described accurately as a 'legislature', even though that is its title. Its functions are certainly different in most respects from that of Westminster. Similarly, we may think of the Council of Ministers and the Commission as the Union's government and bureaucracy respectively. This would be a mistake. The Commission, as we shall see, carries out some functions normally assigned to government. The Council, meanwhile, is, to a large extent, the main legislative body. The Court of Justice does interpret law as national judiciaries do, but the main judicial role is played by national courts.

Useful approaches for study

If it is dangerous to think of institutions purely in terms of functions and processes, how can we usefully study them? An answer may be to apply a variety of political *concepts* to them. In this way we can judge how well they perform and where there are weaknesses which need to be addressed. Some examples of this approach are shown below:

Democracy

If we use the term democracy in its broadest sense, i.e. government being open to the influence of popular opinion and ensuring its decisions are based on popular will, every institution can be usefully interrogated. Does the European Union respond meaningfully to European opinion? Is it possible to have influence over the institutions? Do decision makers take opinion into account? Do parties and pressure groups reflect opinion effectively through the institutions? These are all important questions about European democracy.

Representation

Political institutions have a primary duty to represent the people and the various groups which make up civil society. All the EU institutions seek to do this. They have a special difficulty in that they must be nationally representative as well as seeking to reflect the many political ideas and interests which flourish throughout Europe. All the four main institutions – Parliament, Commission, Council and Court of Justice – have arrangements to try to make them representative. How well these arrangements serve the people, however, is another matter which we will consider below.

Accountability

This is a special problem in so large a political community as the EU. It is also difficult as only one body – Parliament – is directly elected. The ministers who meet regularly to make key decisions are accountable to their *own* people and parliaments, but not to the people of Europe as a whole. If you are a British citizen, some decisions which will affect you are made by ministers from Italy, Belgium, Portugal and the rest. But these ministers cannot be made responsible to that British citizen.

Authority and legitimacy

Political power should only be exercised in a democracy where there is proper authority for that power. Only with such authority can an institution be said to be legitimate. European Union institutions draw their authority from less secure sources than do national bodies. Parliament is elected, of course, which helps a great deal. However, turnouts to these elections vary and it is rarely clear how well or otherwise an MEP (member of the European Parliament) has performed his or her duties. They also represent huge electorates who cannot be expected to know where they satand on many issues. The leading Commissioners are appointed by the European Council, which gives them a high form of authority, but we are used to members of the government needing a more direct form of authority. The Council of Ministers carry the authority *as individuals* of their own governments. However, as a collective body they have much weaker authority, especially as we may not know how individual ministers have reached their own decisions.

Limited government

It is a basic principle of liberal democracy that government should have strict legal limitations placed on its powers. There should also be instruments in place to ensure that it does not overstep these limits. We may usefully ask, therefore, whether strong enough safeguards do exist and, if so, how well they are enforced.

Students of European government and politics may well consider other democratic concepts in the same way. For example such issues as human rights, the separation of powers, the rule of law and open government may be treated in the same way.

The European Commission

Role

It is difficult to sum up the role of the Commission in one single word. In some ways it is like a cabinet which discusses policy and sets agendas, it is a bureaucracy which administers the operation of the EU and it is also a policy-making machine. The term **executive** is possibly the best single term if we are to insist on one, but even this is not wholly satisfactory. One thing the Commission is certainly *not* is a decision-making body. It has no democratic legitimacy and no popular mandate to be able to do so.

The main thrust of the Commission has been to drive forward the strategic development of the Union. In particular this has involved the creation of the single market and, since 1992, the achievement of monetary union. The Commission has developed the timetable and procedures for such change and has recommended the measures needed to realise the aims of greater union. At each stage towards closer union the Commission has produced initiatives which provide the Council of Ministers (which is the union's regular decision-making body) and the European Council (which makes strategic decisions) with the framework for progress. In effect the Commission therefore produces draft treaties and amendments to existing ones or draft legislation and regulations for discussion by the Council of Ministers or European Council.

It also administers the existing systems of the European Union, such as the Common Agriculture and Fisheries Policy, environmental protection, regional policy, transport projects, competition policy and the Social Chapter. Working with member governments the Commission is occupied with the task of ensuring that all these programmes operate effectively. In cases where it feels that a country may be in breach of laws and regulations it will report the matter to the European Court of Justice for possible legal enforcement. Part of this wider task is to produce an annual budget for the Union. This means setting the level of contributions from member states (according to agreed formulas) and determining how the finances should be distributed through the programmes referred to above. The budget must be approved by the European Parliament so there may be a period of prolonged negotiation before it is settled.

Particularly after 2000, the Commission has a special role to play in the enlargement of the Union. It must make the plans for the admission of new members. This may involve special transitional arrangements, adjustments to existing policies and major reform of budgetary arrangements. As new applicants have emerged, the Commission have conducted negotiations and research into the prospective member's suitability.

The European Union, as a single political entity, must deal with other states and organisations. This may involve trade disputes and agreements, transport arrangements, environmental protection, diplomatic problems, issues of international crime and the like. Though the heads of government may often capture the headlines at international conferences, it is the Commission which deals with day-to-day international relations.

We may now summarise the Commission's functions as follows:
- developing policies to realise full economic and monetary union;
- managing existing European Union programmes;
- developing the Union's annual budget;
- making the necessary arrangements for enlargement;
- managing the union's external relations.

Structure

The Commission is headed by its **President**. He or she is the most visible symbol of European unity and can therefore be seen at the outset as a figurehead. As we shall see, the Commission is divided into nineteen functional sections, but the President is able to represent the Commission *as a whole.* It is the President who represents the strategic policies coming out of the Commission. He or she has the authority to deal with members' most senior ministers up to head of government level, and can also deal personally with other states and international organisations outside the Union. The best-known President was, arguably, Jacques Delors (1985–94) whose vision and drive led to the development of full economic and monetary union. His successor, Jacques Santer (1994–99) was charged with the realisation of monetary union. Romano Prodi (1999–) has been very much concerned with issues surrounding enlargement and a common defence and foreign policy.

The President is nominated by the European Council on the retirement of the existing holder. This nomination must be approved by the European Parliament. Naturally, it is a crucial decision and the subject of extensive political activity. Three main issues arise: the nationality of the candidate, their political stance in domestic politics and their more general position on the future of Europe.

A word of caution is needed at this stage. The term 'President', like so many in the Union, may be misleading. Normally a political President is a country's head of state. He or she becomes the representative of a whole people who takes the lead in international affairs, crises and emergencies. Presidents also involve themselves in the business of government formation, often nominating heads of government and other ministers for parliamentary approval. This does not describe the EU President. There is no European state (yet!) so there can be no head of state. He does not have the legitimacy of national presidents because he is not elected by the people and so has no popular mandate. There is also no European 'government' in the normal sense of the word so he has no role in that direction. The use of the word 'President' simply refers to the fact that he is head of the Commission.

European Commission

Presidency	Development and Humanitarian Aid
Vice Presidency (Administrative Reform)	Enlargement
Vice Presidency (Transport and Energy)	External Relations
Agriculture	Trade
Competition Policy	Health and Consumer Protection
Internal Market	Regional policy
Research	Education and Culture
Enterprise and Information	Budget
Economic and Monetary Affairs	Environment
Employment and Social Affairs	Justice and Home Affairs

The rest of the Commission is divided into nineteen sections, each one headed by a Commissioner.

This list also demonstrates the range of activities which are the current concerns of the European Union.

Commissioners are appointed by the relevant Council of Ministers. Their nomination must be approved by the European Parliament and they can be removed by the Parliament. They are required to be politicians who have held a 'prominent' position in their own countries before entering the Commission. Some of Britain's commissioners illustrate this principle. Chris Patten was Conservative party Chairman, cabinet minister and the last British Governor of Hong Kong, Leon Brittan had been Home Secretary and Neil Kinnock was a former leader of the Labour party. Each operates with a small 'cabinet' (not to be confused with the British-style Cabinet) who are close advisers. Below them comes a small army of European civil servants, who make up the European Union bureaucracy. They number 15,000 approximately. This is, in fact, a very small figure. It would, for example, represent the same size as a single small government department in Britain. The limited size of the Commission reflects, firstly, the fact that its role is limited and, secondly, that much of the administrative work of Europe is carried out by member countries themselves.

Each Commissioner must work closely with their own Council of Ministers (see below). They must also forge close links with relevant ministers in all the member countries. Their role is, therefore, political in the sense that they must attempt to resolve conflicts and seek compromises or consensus. They are not, however, political in that they are expected to be politically neutral and not to favour any single member state.

As a group the Commissioners sit as the Court of Commissioners – the nearest the European has to a cabinet, though it does not finalise any decisions. They are presided over by the Commission President. The court co-ordinates the policies of all the sections and discusses and recommends future policy for the Union as a whole.

Operation and processes

Each section of the Commission is expected to formulate policies which will carry forward the aims of the Union in their own particular area of jurisdiction. These policy suggestions are known as **initiatives**. They are often confused by the media with decisions. Initiatives are not decisions. They are merely proposals for discussion by the Council of Ministers or the European Council.

In developing policy the Commission consults very widely. Apart from the governments and other politicians from member states, pressure groups centre a great deal of their activities on the Commission. Political groupings in the

Parliament may send delegations, as may parties from individual states. Much of the process also involves senior members of the bureaucracies of member states. Indeed each state has a permanent Civil Service establishment in Brussels whose role is to liaise with Commissioners.

Initiatives are sent both to the European Parliament and the Council. A number of outcomes may result. They may simply be rejected outright. They may be amended by Parliament or the Council and referred back to the Commission. The Commission may accept amendments, but, if there can be no agreement, they may insist that amended proposals are passed by a unanimous decision of the Council, rather than just a majority. In some cases the initiative will be accepted unaltered.

When a policy has been adopted the Commission is charged with the task of implementing the decision. As we have already said, this may involve making arrangements with member governments. In such cases they will oversee the operation of the policy. In some cases the Commission itself will implement the policy.

Commissioners must appear regularly before the European Parliament and its committees. On these occasions they must account for what their section is doing and may be asked to explain their policy initiatives. The budget which the Commission produces annually is also the subject of parliamentary scrutiny. Often the Commission is forced to reconsider the budget after it has been rejected by the Parliament. In extreme circumstances the Parliament can also dismiss the whole Commission or an individual commissioner. The best known example of such an event occurred in 1999 when the entire Commission was forced to resign amid charges of corruption and nepotism against some of its members. Since then the European Parliament has conducted much closer scrutiny over commissioners.

Problems and issues

Many of the arguments concerning the 'democratic deficit' in Europe have centred on the Commission. This is because it has not been accountable enough for its activities. However, its legitimacy can also be questioned as can its credentials as a representative body.

Before 1999 the Commission was usually seen as a law unto itself, exposing itself to the minimum of accountability. In its defence the Commission could always claim that it was not the decision-making body of the Union and control was therefore exercised by the Council of Ministers. This has certainly been true. However, its strategic position means that it has had a huge amount of influence over the development of the EU. As such, it has always needed to be accountable. Since 1999, when the whole Commission was forced to resign by parliamentary action, commissioners have been forced to report to

Parliament on a regular basis. Corruption of any kind can mean instant dismissal. Parliament also now reserves the right of veto over major appointments. So, to some extent, the problem has been addressed.

Representation is said to be assured by the fact that every member state shall have one of its nationals as a commissioner. The larger countries have more than one. This is largely a cosmetic device as commissioners are required to put aside any national leanings they may have. It should, therefore, not be necessary for them to be drawn from a representative sample of member countries. Despite this there remains a problem. As an unelected body the Commission cannot be said to be truly representative. It has no elective mandate and the peoples of member states have no say in their appointment. It may be that, in the future, there will be demands for at least the senior commissioners to be elected.

The Commission draws its authority, and therefore its legitimacy, from the Council of Ministers. This is a partially democratic process, but the appointment of commissioners remains shrouded in some mystery and may lie very much in the hands of the larger countries. A greater involvement for Parliament may improve the situation, but popular participation in the formation of the Commission, which would enhance its authority most effectively, looks to be impractical.

The final major issue for the Commission concerns enlargement. With more members it may be that there will have to be a larger Commission simply to ensure that each country is properly represented. On the other hand, increased size may have the beneficial effect of diluting the influence of larger countries in both appointments and policy making.

The European Parliament

Role

Despite its name and the fact that it is directly elected, the Parliament is not the legislative body of the European Union. It does not make law, nor legitimise it, nor does it act as the source of authority for the executive branch. It is not required that a proposal receives parliamentary approval to be enforceable. It is also not in a position to develop and propose legislation of its own. The government of the EU is shared between the Commission and the Council of Ministers or European Council. None of these bodies are drawn from the parliament. In other words the European Parliament does not perform three of the most important functions of most national parliaments.

Having established what it is not, we must ask what the European Parliament actually does. Its main role is a consultative one. It would be false to suggest that the Parliament has the power to veto a proposal outright. The role of the

Parliament in legislation is a complex one and it is not the intention here to describe it in full. To simplify the system, which was mostly established at Maastricht in 1992, we can identify a number of activities:

- It can attempt to reject a proposal. However, if the Commission and Council are determined enough, they can force most measures through. However, Parliament can insist that some proposals require the unanimous approval of the Council.

- It can suggest amendments. This is more powerful than the veto, but in most cases an amendment need not be accepted by the Council of Ministers.

- It can refer proposals back to the Commission and the Council for further consideration, i.e. a delaying power.

- It can approve proposals and so give them greater legitimacy.

As we have seen above, Parliament also has some of the functions we would expect of a representative assembly. It can:
- oversee and veto the appointment of senior commissioners;
- insist on the dismissal of commissioners who may be corrupt or incompetent;
- question commissioners on Union policy and administration;
- examine the annual budget, reject it and seek amendments to it;
- request the Commission to consider new policy initiatives;
- represent and publicise during debates the views of important interest groups in the Union;
- it has the right to approve or veto an application for membership from a new country.

Structure

The membership of the Parliament is very complex. It is divided on both national and political lines. This means that each member (MEP) represents a nation, a region within that nation and a political position. At different times and on different issues an MEP might adopt a variable stance. Green party representatives, for example, are likely to see environmental issues on a Europe-wide basis and therefore not consider national and regional interests. Typical Conservatives, on the other hand, will tend to be more interested in their own nation's interests. A Liberal might be European oriented on human rights issues, but protective of regional interests where economic development is concerned. Table 14.1 shows the representation of the parliament in terms of nations and of party groupings:

All these MEPs are elected directly and represent areas which are roughly similar in size. The party groupings are inevitably loose. However, they do

Table 14.1   National and party representation in the European Parliament

National representation		Party groups (1999)	
Germany	99	European Peoples[a]	233
France	87	Socialists	180
UK	87	Liberal Democrats	51
Italy	87	Greens and radicals	48
		Left-wing coalition	42
Spain	64	Nationalists	30
		Others	42
Holland	31		
Greece	25		
Belgium	25		
Portugal	25		
Sweden	22		
Austria	21		
Denmark	16		
Finland	16		
Ireland	15		
Luxembourg	6		
Total	626		

[a] Essentially conservative parties.

attempt to act in a unified way wherever possible and where a political issue is clear cut. However, this is often not possible because of the contrasting regional, national and political allegiances which MEPs have.

As with most representative assemblies a great deal of the work of the European Parliament is done by committees of MEPs. These are mainly **standing committees**, but there are also special committees convened to deal with special temporary circumstances. These approximately 'shadow' the main sections of the Commission. Indeed there has developed a growing relationship between commissioners and their cabinets and the relevant parliamentary committee. It is through committees also that the accountability of the Commission can be achieved. The committees also act as focus of attention for the many pressure and interest groups which now operate at the European level.

Operation and processes

Since the Maastricht Treaty was ratified in 1994 the main legislative work of the Parliament has been known as **codecision**. This suggests that, in a variety of policy areas, the Parliament has equal power with the Council of Ministers to approve new laws and developments. The following subjects are subject to codecision procedure:

- labour markets;
- research and technology;
- matters related to the single market;
- environment;
- consumer protection;
- education and culture;
- health issues.

This list may appear to be quite impressive, until one appreciates what is left off. Policy areas such as the common agricultural and fisheries policy, taxation, defence and foreign affairs, new treaties, and regional policy are not yet the subject of codecision. In other words, Parliament can only pass an opinion on such issues, a process known as **co-operation**.

For codecision procedures a proposal is normally considered by a senior committee member, known as a **rapporteur** who summarises the proposals and sets up the discussions. Committees consider proposals, taking evidence from commissioners and interested groups along the way. They then make recommendations for amendments or overall approval to the Parliament as a whole. This is not unlike the legislative system which operates in the Congress of the USA.

Parliament in plenary session (i.e. all members meeting), normally considers proposals in two readings. One reading considers amendments, the other looks at the complete proposal. The decision of Parliament is communicated to the Council of Ministers who may accept or reject the decisions of the Parliament. Where a dispute arises a special committee is formed to try to make compromises and reach a consensus. Where the Parliament only has co-operative powers, the decisions are also made known to the Council of Ministers, but the Council does not have to accept them.

In addition to its legislative powers the parliament, as a whole, or as individual members, may take up the grievances of groups of citizens or even individuals. This will involve calling commissioners to account for their decisions. A system of **petitions** exists whereby large groups from the Union can request special consideration from Parliament.

Special procedures exist for the other functions of Parliament, including the admission of new members, consideration of the annual budget, questioning of commissioners and disciplinary hearings.

Problems and issues

Alongside the Commission the European Parliament stands at the centre of the issue of the Union's democratic deficit. This is understandable. When considering any political system, it is natural to fix our attention on such matters as elections, representation, legislation and accountability. These issues always revolve around the legislature. The striking feature of the Parliament at first view is its weakness and this is the best place to begin a critique.

WHY IS THE EUROPEAN PARLIAMENT SO WEAK?

It is a very large, unwieldy body. Even before the post-2002 enlargements it contained 626 members who are divided, as we have seen, along political, national and regional lines. Parliaments need a degree of coherence to be able to act decisively. The European assembly lacks this. It may be in the form of a party majority, as normally occurs in the United Kingdom, or a logical coalition of parties, such as a Conservative group of the type which often dominates the French system. There is certainly no sense of 'government and opposition' which can reduce issues to clear alternatives.

The executive sections of the Union – the Council and Commission – are not drawn from the Parliament. Indeed the two branches of the political system are completely separated. This has two effects. On the one hand, it prevents the executive branch from dominating Parliament. There is no patronage system to keep MEPs in line, nor are their strong, unified party groupings. This prevents coherence of the type described above, from developing. On the other hand, the decision-makers in the Union do not rely on the support of the Parliament. Most important decisions can be forced through the Council if it is determined and united enough. Using the American model, therefore, the Parliament does not act as a 'check' or 'balance' to the power of the executive. They do not rely on each other so Parliament does not occupy a powerful central position.

MEPs have no clear political mandates. When they are elected it is on the basis of their *national* rather than *European* political allegiance. Most voters in Europe have limited knowledge of EU issues. This prevents them from granting any clear authority to those whom they elect. When it comes to European decisions, therefore, MEPs cannot claim to have the authority of their electorates. European ministers understand this and are not prepared to submit themselves to the weak authority of parliament. Indeed it can be argued that the popular authority of national ministers in the council is stronger than the uncertain authority of MEPs. This greater claim to authority is inevitably translated into political power. It is therefore more appropriate to think of Parliament as having influence, rather than power. As a representative body it can reflect the fluctuating interests and views of the European people, but its legitimacy actually to make laws is very shaky.

The power of legislatures is often based on their ability to call government to account. The European Parliament does have this power over the Commission and it has, indeed, been strengthened in recent years. However, **power in reality lies with the European Council and the Council of Ministers**. These bodies are not accountable to Parliament. In fact, individual national ministers are accountable only to their own parliaments.

Many EU decisions are extremely complex in two senses. Firstly, they are difficult to understand in terms of their consequences. Secondly, they are difficult to agree and implement because each decision must be applied to fifteen separate countries. Policies which tax the experience and expertise of full-time administrators in the Commission are often impenetrable for MEPs who are rarely experts in the field. The technicalities of the Common Agricultural Policy, the effects of environmental schemes or the implications for European labour markets of new regulations for part-time workers, for example, may be simply too complicated for MEPs to consider in a meaningful way. Where there are clear party groupings and political mandates, such issues may be reduced by leaders to their bare essentials. It is unusual for this to happen in the European Parliament.

Parliament has a President who presides over their deliberations, but in general it has no leaders of its own. Without leaders who can act as figure-heads and unifying forces the Parliament finds it difficult to deal *as a body* with external organisations. This has been especially noticeable in relations with the developing world. Many MEPs favour stronger European initiatives in the Third World but have difficulty in presenting a coherent case. With its own powerful leaders, this kind of parliamentary initiative might have a better chance of success.

HOW IS PARLIAMENT BECOMING STRONGER?

For supporters of parliamentary power the picture is not totally gloomy. After the Maastricht and Amsterdam Treaties the European Parliament became considerably more powerful. The codecision procedure gave it almost equal legislative powers with the Council of Ministers over an admittedly limited range of jurisdiction.

It is also true that the Commission and individual commissioners are more accountable to Parliament than before. The events of 1999 when the whole Commission was removed, demonstrated to parliamentarians the true extent of their potential. In future the nomination of new officials, not least the President of the Commission himself, will have to take careful account of parliamentary opinion.

The party groupings have, correspondingly, become more meaningful. The Socialist grouping, for example, has acted together very effectively in the field of workers' rights, while the Conservative Peoples' Parties grouping tends to take a special interest in agricultural affairs. As one would expect the Green alliance is extremely active in its own special field of interest.

The Commission has responded by strengthening its links with the Parliament. Their initiatives are now subjected to closer scrutiny by standing committees so they must take more account of how MEPs are likely to react.

With the d'Estaing Commission (see below) established in the spring of 2002, more reform is promised. It is widely assumed that the position of Parliament will form the centrepiece of any new proposals.

THE EUROPEAN COUNCIL

Although this body has a grand title and appears to be of great importance, given the fact that it is made up of heads of government, we need not spend too much time in discussing it. This is partly because it normally meets only twice a year and partly because it is largely only the confirmation of decisions which have been made elsewhere. Nevertheless, it is the EU body which received perhaps the most media attention. We must also be careful not to confuse it with the similarly named Council of Ministers, which is discussed below.

The European Council is the name given to the normally twice-yearly meeting of the heads of government of the member states. They meet under the 'presidency' of one of the members. Each country takes a turn at the presidency for six months. This means that a member will be President of the Council every seven and a half years (less often after enlargement, of course). Being President is largely symbolic and carries with it the now considerable expense of organising an international conference. The only other advantage of the presidency is that the holder may be able to add a few minor items on the meeting's agenda which are of special interest to that country.

The Council exists to ratify key strategic decisions. These proposals will have been negotiated by ministers and officials for months before the actual meetings. It is at the European Council where the principles of new treaties are agreed. It also maps out the immediate future of the Union. The heads of government have the opportunity to settle any final matters which are in dispute and to find out where each of their fellow members stand on important issues.

THE COUNCIL(S) OF MINISTERS

Membership

There is not one Council of Ministers, but several. In fact, the term refers to all meetings at ministerial level on every subject which comes under EU jurisdiction. Thus there are meetings of all ministers in charge of their own countries' financial affairs, agriculture, transport, trade, defence, foreign relations etc. There are normally over a hundred meetings of the various councils in a year.

When ministers meet it is to settle the remaining issues which need to be resolved. In other words they do not confront each new proposal from scratch. During the course of the year, a body known as the **Committee of Permanent Representatives (COREPER)** prepares the way for ministerial meetings. These bodies contain civil servants (i.e. not politicians) from member states who have the permanent role of representing their own countries in the consideration of policies. COREPER is, in many ways, one arm of the senior Civil Service of the European, the other being senior members of the Commission.

Role and procedure

Before considering the work of the Council itself, we should consider further the position of COREPER, the permanent form of the Councils. COREPER is effectively the point at which the interests of the EU as a whole, represented by the Commission, meets the interests of the various member states – represented by their permanent officials. It is here, from day to day, that the supranational nature of the EU is played out and confirmed. Some national interests have to be sacrificed for the sake of progress and agreement. Others cannot be given up and so create problems which may have to be referred to the full Council of Ministers. Few people outside politics are aware of the existence of COREPER, but in many ways it is one of the key institutions of Europe.

When the ministers themselves meet they form the sovereign body of the EU. Their approval is needed for any proposal to become European law. In some cases, as we have seen above, a codecision is needed with Parliament, but on the whole it is the Council which is the ultimate source of authority. The Council has a number of alternative course of action when faced by proposals and initiatives. It can:
- reject them outright;
- refer them back to the Commission for amendment;
- amend them on the spot and then accept the amended version;
- where there is a difference of opinion with the Parliament they may be referred to a special committee for a compromise to be reached;
- they may accept proposals as they stand.

These procedures are relatively formal as this is effectively a law-making exercise. The system of voting is described in chapter 13, on European integration. Most decisions, as described there, require a qualified majority, which means that a minority of states can be outvoted. Where a unanimous decision is needed – that is, in all key decision-making areas – each member of the Council has a veto.

Law making is not the only function of the Council. General debates on policy also take place and the Council may decide that an issue should be referred to the Commission for detailed policy to be established. They may also issue instructions to EU officials where negotiations with foreign powers and organisations are needed.

Problems and issues

The Councils remain one of the more democratic institutions of the EU. Ministers are certainly accountable to their own parliaments and share some of their powers with the elected Parliament. However there are still a number of key issues which have to be faced if there is to be future reform.

Meetings take place largely in secret. Since the Councils are effectively making law, this seems remarkably undemocratic. We now expect the proceedings of Parliament to be fully public; why not the Council? There remains at present the suspicion that deals and agreements are being reached by ministers without popular knowledge or approval.

Although the balance of power between the Councils and the Parliament has swung recently in the latter's favour, it can still be argued that the *unelected* Councils should not be superior to the *elected* Parliament. As things stand this is not the case. Democratic politics normally insists that the law-making body should be fully accountable to the people. The line of both authority and accountability between the Councils and the people is indirect.

Ministers attend the Council meetings without clear mandates. True, they are delegated from their national governments and must report back to them, but there is no *popular* mandate. It is difficult for electorates to judge how their representatives have performed when most decisions are not openly reached. Of course it is said, understandably, that it is impossible to mandate ministers strictly as it is expected that they make compromises and accommodations with their counterparts from other countries. Nevertheless, the freedom of action of ministers may be too great to satisfy democratic principles.

It remains controversial which decisions should be the subject of unanimous votes and which require only a qualified majority. This question begs another: what issues concern *vital* national interests and therefore need a national veto, and which could be the subject of compromise and so only need a majority?

THE COURT OF JUSTICE

Role and membership

Firstly, it is necessary to emphasise what the European Court of Justice (ECJ) does *not* do. It does not prosecute individuals who may have breached EU law. This is the task of the courts of member countries themselves. They may hear appeals, but not cases of 'first instance'. They perform in the following circumstances:

- Where there is a dispute over the meaning of one of the EU treaties.
- An individual or organisation (usually the latter) may appeal to the Court on the grounds that a Commission decision, or a decision by a member government may have breached Union law or may be contrary to natural justice.
- If there is any dispute concerning the meaning and operation of a Union regulation or directive.
- If an individual or organisation believes that an interpretation of Union law by a court within the member country was wrong, they may ask for a final judgment.
- States which are members of the Union may be brought before the Court for breaches of Union laws and regulations.
- Disputes *between* member states over the meaning of the laws and treaties may be brought to the Court.

The judges in the court number fifteen and are drawn from all member states. Each judge sits for six years. As with virtually all democratic states judges cannot be removed on the basis of the decisions which they reach. Judges will not normally sit in judgment in cases involving their own country of origin. They are all highly experienced lawyers who have specialised knowledge of European law.

A flavour of the Court's work can be gained by reviewing the most common subjects of cases. In 2000–1, for example, the following subjects accounted for the majority of the court's time:

- agriculture (the Common Agricultural Policy);
- fisheries (the Common Fisheries Policy);
- competititon policy;
- environment;
- freedom of business;
- freedom of movement of workers;
- social issues (e.g. pensions, working conditions);
- taxation.

It is also interesting to review the record of individual countries in the Court. If we look at cases brought against countries for not complying with Union law (brought either by other states or by the Commission), we can see who are the most common offenders:

- France: 25
- Italy: 22
- Greece: 18
- Germany: 12
- Holland: 12

It is interesting to consider that the UK, thought to be one of the more Euro-sceptic of members, recorded only 4 cases in that year! Only Sweden seemed to be more conformist.

Issues

The ECJ is perhaps the most respected of European Union institutions. It conforms to the key democratic principle – that the judiciary should be independent of government. The judges are placed under no political pressure and have no vested interest in favouring any single party. It is fully represen-tative in that judges are drawn from all over the Union. There can be no suggestion that the larger, richer countries might be favoured.

This is not to say, however, that the Court is uncontroversial. In some ways it is symbolic of the degree to which member countries have given up sover-eignty to the EU. Domestic courts can be overruled by the ECJ. Furthermore, laws which have been passed by the parliaments of member states may be set aside if the Court decides that it does not conform to EU law or one of the treaties. On the other hand many individuals and organisations have cause to be grateful to the Court for the establishment of their rights. In some of its most celebrated cases the Court has, thus, confirmed the right of professional footballers to move freely from one club to another when out of contract (the famous 'Bosman' ruling), equalising the pension rights of men and women, granting part-time workers the same protections as full-timers and forcing car-makers to treat consumers equally in all countries.

So the Court is seen as both restrictive to individual countries and as the guardian of equal rights for all within Europe. There are some who resent the fact that 'foreign' judges can interfere in domestic affairs, but there are others who value the role of the Court in preserving freedom and equality.

OTHER EU BODIES

The Committee of the Regions

In recent years the concept of a 'Europe of the regions' has grown in importance. This embraces the idea that, as nation-states become less important, regional identities will take over. As economic integration gathers pace, the significance of national borders will diminish. Rather, economic issues will affect regions. It is therefore natural that this body has become more prominent. Created under the Maastricht Treaty and meeting first in 1994 it has steadily gained in status.

Although its members (222 in number) are nominated from regional bodies within member states, its role can be seen as quasi-legislative and Britain has seen it as a potential second chamber for the parliament based on regionally elected representatives.

Its role is to ensure that regions are properly represented in decision-making processes. In this sense it further undermines the claim of the Parliament to be an effective body. The Commission, Parliament and Council of Ministers are now required to consult with the Committee in case there are regional implications of any new proposals. They are also charged with the task of ensuring that Union funds destined for regional projects are shared out fairly.

Above all, however, the Committee is taking a proactive role in promoting the interests of the poorer regions of Europe such as Greece, southern Italy, Northern Ireland, south-west England and parts of Spain. It fights for an increased share of the EU budget and presses for more regional programmes in such fields as the environment, transport infrastructure, urban regeneration, rural protection and local employment.

The Court of Auditors

This fifteen-member body, drawn from all members, has the task of protecting the interests of European taxpayers who finance the Union. They have two main functions, both of which were strengthened after major inefficiency and widespread corruption had been revealed in during the 1990s.

Firstly, it examines the efficiency of the work of the Commission and the other agencies of the EU. It highlights examples of waste and recommends action to put matters right. Secondly, it investigates possible corruption. This can occur within member states, in organisations which are in receipt of EU funding (such as farmers or local government bodies) or within the Commission itself. It is important particularly because the European Parliament is so weak in this field.

The Economic and Social Committee

This is a parallel organisation to the Committee of the Regions. It is the same size and its membership is also nominated from member states. If the Committee of the Regions represents regional interests, the Economic and Social Committee represents the great variety of interest groups which flourish in Europe.

The various decision-making bodies are obliged to consult the committee on issues such as consumer rights, workers' rights, welfare provisions, citizenship rights, free movement of labour and trade union law.

It does not have the same high status as the Committee of the Regions, since many member states see it as a threat to their independence. Its role appears to be to speed the process of integration in many new areas. The Committee on the Regions, on the other hand represents a decentralising force which can bring benefits directly to people. However, if the EU is to maintain any claim to be a pluralist body it needs to ensure that group interests are properly represented.

The European Ombudsman

This individual, who is backed by a large body of investigators, is an agent of the Parliament. It hears complaints from European citizens who believe they have been the victims of unfair treatment or maladministration by a Union body.

Although the department of the Ombudsman is busy, hearing several cases a year, it is largely a cosmetic exercise. Few cases are upheld and the more serious claims tend to appear in the Parliament or the Court of Justice. The European Union has an Ombudsman mainly because it has become an essential feature of any democratic organisation.

The European Central Bank

The European Central Bank (ECB) came into existence in 1998 and resides in Frankfurt, Germany's financial centre. It was needed during the preparations for the introduction of a single currency in 2002 and became a key body when the euro came into full use. Some basic economic principles must be understood in order to grasp why this body is so essential. Three ideas summarise the position:

1 With a single currency there must be control over the total money supply in the Union. This used to be the responsibility of each member country, but, with one currency, it must be done centrally. Control of total money supply is essential to maintain confidence in the currency and to prevent inflation.

2 A single currency means a single financial market. Banks and other financial institutions will have to operate in full competition with each other. As such, they must all operate within similar interest rate levels. It is therefore essential, in order to maintain stable financial markets, to set a single European interest rate.

3 The fiscal policies of each country are likely to affect the total supply of money. When governments borrow money to finance their expenditure, most of the borrowing is raised from the banking system. In order to finance government borrowing, banks are allowed to create new money. Thus, if one country decides to borrow significant amounts of finance, it will have the effect of increasing total money supply. Before the single currency this only affected the country in question. With a single currency, however, the actions of one country may affect the money supply of all. Therefore, countries must be subject to fiscal disciplines, i.e. to keep borrowing down to a reasonable level. This principle has been enshrined in the so-called 'stability pact' among member states. To demonstrate its importance, even Germany, the Union's biggest economy, received a warning over its high borrowing levels early in 2002.

The ECB is charged with the task of maintaining the three principles described above. It does this by controlling money supply, setting an interest rate for the euro-zone and by ensuring that members keep within set borrowing levels.

Although the Bank is non-political, its role can be politically controversial. Its problem is that the same interest rate does not necessarily suit all countries at the same time. Those who are suffering slow growth and unemployment want low interest rates to stimulate borrowing, investment, spending and therefore production levels. At the same time, countries enjoying a strong economy do not want low interest rates as this might over-stimulate their economy and lead to inflation. The ECB must, therefore, balance the contrasting interests of different countries when setting rates. Similarly, they may be forced to exercise control over borrowing when individual governments may feel they have very good reason to borrow heavily. They may argue that the expenditure is needed to stimulate employment and growth or to promote better public services. In such cases the bank is liable to find itself in conflict with some member governments.

In order to prevent any charges that it might be put under political pressure the ECB is an entirely independent body. However, the fact that its directors are not accountable to any democratic bodies has led to criticism that there is no adequate control over how it operates.

OVERVIEW

The institutions of the European Union have tended to grow and expand without any coherent plan. Extra bodies have been added as new issues and problems have emerged. The existing bodies have also evolved to meet new circumstances. Since the Treaty of Rome, however, no serious attempt at overall constitutional reform has been made. In 2002 this situation was about to change.

The prospects for further reform are considered below as one of the issues facing the European Union in the new era of economic and monetary union.

SAMPLE QUESTIONS

1 What problems have been associated with the role and performance of the Commission of the European Union?

2 What problems are associated with the role and operation of the European Parliament?

3 How are the main institutions of the European Union likely to be affected by future enlargement?

4 To what extent has the European Union become a 'supranational' body and to what extent is it still 'intergovernmental'? Illustrate your answer with reference to the main institutions of the Union.

5 How democratic is the European Union?

➤ Descriptions of the main issues facing the European Union

➤ Review of these issues

➤ Speculations as to the future course of the issues

THE DEMOCRATIC DEFICIT AND INSTITUTIONAL REFORM

The nature of the democratic deficit

The issues concerning individual institutions of the European Union are described in chapter 14, on EU Institutions. However, a number of general remarks can be made at this stage. The main concerns which politicians from member countries and commentators have include the following:

● It is generally felt that the institutions of the European Union are not accountable enough.

● There is too much secrecy in the EU and too much of its proceedings are carried out behind closed doors. This is connected with the lack of accountability, as it is clear that if the public and their elected representatives are not provided with information, they will be unable to make judgements about the performance of the institutions.

● Representation in much of the EU is indirect. The Parliament is elected, but no other bodies are (unless we accept that the Council of Ministers is indirectly elected).

● No decision-making bodies have a clear mandate. The public of Europe cannot, therefore, judge how well their political leaders are responding to their demands.

● There is no European constitution. The political system of the EU has been formed though the various treaties which have been negotiated since 1957. This means that the relationships between the institutions are not clear.

- There is a lack of a system of 'checks and balances' within the system. For example, the Parliament is a single chamber, without an upper house to check its power, Parliament itself has limited powers over the executive branch (i.e. the Commission and Council of Ministers combined). The European Court of Justice does provide some degree of control, but the absence of a constitution means they have little documentary evidence on which to base their decisions.

- Some member countries such as the UK and Denmark have argued that there cannot be any further political integration until the democratic deficit is addressed. Others, such as Germany and Italy, on the other hand, have suggested that, if Europe can move towards a federal system, many of these problems will be automatically resolved. Meanwhile the impending enlargement of the Union makes the need for democratic reforms more pressing. The new members will want their interests safeguarded and will be unwilling to accept the general lack of accountability. The democratic problem is particularly acute for those countries, such as Poland and the Czech Republic, who have quite recently escaped from the yoke of totalitarian communist regimes.

Some solutions

In recognition of these problems the European Union set up a Constitutional Convention in the spring of 2002 under the chairmanship of Valery Giscard d'Estaing, a former French President. With over a hundred delegates from both existing and prospective members, it has been given eighteen months to report back on political and constitutional reform. If the Convention fails, the future progress of the EU will be seriously impeded. Should it produce workable and effective proposals, the prospects for greater integration will be enhanced.

What kind of issues and possible solutions will the d'Estaing Convention consider?
- Reform of the Parliament to make it more representative, accountable and effective.
- Changing the nature of the Commission, probably making it more accountable, possibly making arrangements for more control over appointments by the Parliament. It may also recommend popular elections to the Commission. The way in which the Commission works may also be made more transparent.
- The relationships between the Commission, Council of Ministers and Parliament will be reviewed to make decision making clearer and more efficient.
- The problem of the lack of political leadership for the EU may be addressed. It is conceivable that there will be a proposal for an elected President for the Union.

- A British idea is that there should be a bicameral legislature. Some kind of second parliamentary chamber is certainly on the cards.
- There are proposals for a European 'Bill of Rights' which would, once and for all, establish the basis of citizenship and rights for all members of the EU, including its millions of new citizens to come.
- Students, academics, media people and politicians may now enjoy a year or two of speculation, but after d'Estaing reports, it will be up to the heads of government to make key decisions in this area.

THE COMMON AGRICULTURAL POLICY

The Common Agricultural Policy (CAP) was created in 1960, a time when there were only six members of the Community. Its founders can, therefore, be forgiven for not foreseeing the many problems which would arise when new members were admitted. It has to be said that it was France which was the prime mover in the CAP and it was seen as a price which had to paid for France's continued membership. It had a number of objectives:

1 To guarantee the incomes of farmers (and wine growers) even in markets which are extremely volatile.
2 To prevent agricultural prices from rising too much when there is an unexpected supply shortage. In this way consumers can be protected.
3 To ensure that European agriculture can survive in the face of world competition, system of price supports and subsidies provided protection.
4 Ultimately it was hoped that the Community could become self-sufficient in food. To some extent this was the result of memories of the post-World War II period, when there were severe food shortages. This aim had been achieved by 1973.

The ways in which these objectives have been pursued constitute a wide range of systems of intervention. The main measures are:

- *Subsidies* to try to ensure that some agricultural sectors can survive despite low market prices and to maintain high output levels.

- A *price support* and *levy system* to protect some sectors from external competition. If prices fall below a certain level which will not give farmers sufficient income, tariffs are placed on imports to hold up the price.

- *Quota systems* in those sectors where there is long-term over-production with the danger that prices will fall too low to sustain farm incomes. Each country, region and individual farm may be given a maximum quota or production limit. In this way the total production of the EU is controlled. Milk, for example, is produced under this system.

- *Stock intervention* is also used in some sectors. This is a scheme which prevents prices rising too much by releasing stockpiled goods onto the market and so keeping the price down. More often, however, it is a system of buying up stocks in order to hold up the price. This is the most controversial aspect of the CAP as it works against the interests of consumers by keeping prices artificially high. It has also resulted in huge wasteful stocks of goods building up and sometimes having to be destroyed. There have, in the past, been infamous 'wine lakes' and beef or butter 'mountains'.

- *Over-production* is a major problem in the CAP. In the 1990s, therefore, a system known as 'set-aside' was developed. This was a device where farmers were actually paid to take land out of production altogether.

Problems and reform

An attempt to reform the system in 1965 failed when France exercised its veto. The consequent deadlock was broken in 1966 by the so-called 'Luxembourg Compromise'. This plan meant that the Council of Ministers would retain control over the CAP and that each member would be able to retain a veto over key decisions. The EU was saved, but has been saddled ever since with the problem that reform of the CAP has been made difficult by the power of each country to block change.

Ever since then, the CAP has proved to be one of the most unpopular aspects of the EU and certainly the most difficult to reform. Indeed, the CAP illustrates one of the most important problems for the EU as a whole. National interests show themselves to be at their most powerful when agriculture is at stake. Member governments are reluctant to alienate their own agricultural interests and so fight tenaciously to protect them when agriculture meetings are held. The idea of a 'supranational' body controlling agriculture seems out of the question for many years to come.

The most frustrating aspect of the CAP for those who do not have an interest in agriculture, is this difficulty in instituting reform. Indeed, for most members of the European public, complete abolition of the CAP seems the best option. The CAP is unpopular for a number of reasons.

- It eats up a huge portion of the EU budget. It is the taxpayers who pick up this bill. In 2000 a total of 41.5 billion euros was spent on the CAP, nearly a half of the total EU budget.
- It is seen to be supporting farmers, irrespective of whether they deserve this support.
- It is a system of trade protection. This raises food prices in Europe and discriminates against Third World producers. Campaigners argue that the system keeps Third World farmers poor, while European farmers grow rich.

- The huge quantities of unused intervention stocks are viewed as obscene when large parts of the world are on or over the verge of starvation.
- Those countries which do not have large agricultural sectors, the UK being a prime example, resent the fact that it favours countries which do rely more on their own agricultural industries.

With the many problems which the CAP throws up, it is hardly surprising that frequent attempts at reform have been made. Two main stages of reform can be identified. The first was in 1992 when the set-aside system was introduced and began to slow-down over-production and so reduced the need for interventions in the market. Over-production of cereals and oils was partly tackled in this way. The second tranche of reforms came in 1999 when some subsidies, for example on cereals and beef, began to be progressively reduced (not least because the World Trade Organisation has been working towards a progressive reduction in protective tariffs and subsidies). To some extent countries were also allowed to apply to divert former subsidies into environmental projects. Britain is the most enthusiastic supporter of this new innovation and has a target of converting 20% of agricultural subsidies into environment schemes. This new system effectively pays farmers to reduce their output and become guardians of the environment instead.

Under the pressures of enlargement after 2004, the CAP will have to reform itself more radically. The main issues in this area are discussed in the next section. It may well be that the enlargement issue will become the fillip needed to break the influence of powerful farming interests in Western Europe.

ENLARGEMENT

The increases in the size of the EU up to the end of the twentieth century created relatively few problems (see table 15.1). The countries which joined late were already economically well developed and, by and large, had fully democratic political systems. There were, therefore, relatively few problems over their ability to make contributions and the demands which might have been placed on the Union budget. Fears that the membership of Greece and Portugal – the two poorest of the first fifteen members – might be disruptive, were largely unfounded. The post-2004 entries, however, were to be of a very different character.

Table 15.1   Stages of EU enlargement, 1957–95

Year	Entrants
1957	France, Germany, Italy, Belgium, Netherlands, Luxembourg
1973	UK, Ireland, Denmark
1981	Greece
1986	Spain, Portugal
1995	Sweden, Finland, Austria

Conditions of entry

States which wish to enter the EU must conform to a number of conditions according to the Treaty of Rome. These are:

1 They must accept all existing EU legislation.
2 They must be members of NATO (to avoid any conflict of interest over foreign and defence policy).
3 They must have adequate safeguards for human rights.
4 They must have democratic political systems.
5 Their economies should be basically capitalist. This does not prevent some public ownership of industry and public services, but, essentially, free markets must be allowed to operate. Otherwise, Europe would no longer be a truly single market.
6 They must be experiencing reasonable healthy rates of economic growth. This does not mean that they have to be particularly wealthy, but that at least they are moving forward economically.
7 Since the original conditions were set, it has also been added that new entrants have to adopt the euro as their currency (after a suitable transition period).

These conditions are mainly there to protect the interests of the existing members. However, they have also proved to be an incentive for the candidate countries. Many of the prospective entrants are former communist regimes who are desperately trying to restructure themselves economically and politically after the end of the Cold War and the collapse of the Soviet Union in 1990–91. The criteria for entry have encouraged them to introduce free markets, introduce democratic institutions and improve human rights. It will be for the Commission to make a judgement on these criteria, although the final decision on new members will be made in the European Council.

The way forward

The prospective members of the EU have been negotiating for some time, but the general plan for the admission of new states was agreed at Nice in 2000. The following scheme is in place:

- *First wave (2003–4?)*. Cyprus, Czech Republic, Poland, Slovenia, Hungary, Estonia.
- *Second wave (2007?)*. Bulgaria, Slovakia, Latvia, Lithuania, Romania, Malta.
- *Third wave (?)*. Turkey, Croatia, Bosnia.
- *Distant future*. Russia, Ukraine, Belarus.

Although the agreement of the Nice Treaty of 2000 to enlarge the EU on the lines shown above was held up when the Irish voted against it in a referendum (ratification of the Nice Treaty requires unanimous approval), it is confidently expected that these countries will enter close to the scheduled date.

The benefits of enlargement

Although there remain a number of fears about enlargement (shown below), there has been a considerable amount of enthusiasm for admitting new entrants. Indeed, it was Margaret Thatcher who pushed the agenda forward in the 1980s. Her motivation was a belief that a larger community would also be diluted. She feared closer political integration and believed that, the more members there were, the more difficult it would be to achieve it. In the 1980s in general, there was a broad debate between the idea of 'widening' and 'deepening'. In the end, the larger members such as France and Germany, came to the conclusion that both could be managed at the same time, much to the chagrin of a sceptical Conservative Party. Apart from Thatcher's hopes, there are a considerable number of other perceived benefits:

- Enlargement into eastern and central Europe will finally confirm the end of the Cold War divide. In other words Europe will feel more permanently secure as a result of integration.

- It will speed up the process of democratisation and improving human rights throughout Europe.

- The size of the market will grow considerably. This will widen the opportunities for European companies.

- As the European single economy grows, there will be new opportunities for greater specialisation and the benefits which that brings. Economists understand that the larger market, the more specialisation with free exchange, the growing size of industrial or commercial enterprises and increased competition will all promote growth and efficiency.

- The increased size of the euro-zone will create a bigger and more stable world currency – indeed it will become *the* dominant world currency, replacing the dollar in that position.

- In terms of geopolitics, Europe will become a major world power (provided it succeeds in being able to develop a common position of foreign policy). This may bring benefits in terms of trade and stability.

Potential problems

The effects of enlargement are not all one-sided. It is recognised that many problems will emerge. Most European politicians believe that the balance of evidence favours admitting new countries, but this does not mean that the perils can be ignored. Some of the expected difficulties are as follows:

There will be a huge strain on the Common Agricultural Policy. Many of the new entrants have strong agricultural sectors. Were they do enter on the same terms as existing members, it would mean huge amounts would have to be spent on price support systems and subsidies. There would also be a danger of even greater over-production – one of the CAP's main bugbears. The prospect of the EU having to buy up huge stocks of unsold cereals, dairy products, wine and meat simply to maintain high farm incomes, is not an attractive one. It follows that the whole of the CAP will have to be re-negotiated. Western European farmers will have to accept that the levels of support they currently enjoy cannot continue. Whatever the size of the agricultural 'cake' in the future, farmers are going to have to share it out more liberally.

Staying with agriculture, two more problems may well emerge from the creation of a much bigger single market. The first is the danger that farm units will become much bigger as levels of competition increase. The development of huge industrial farms, especially in Europe's so called central 'breadbasket' in Poland and Hungary would have serious adverse environmental effects (memories of the great American 'dustbowl', which was created in the 1930s, spring to mind). Secondly, an even more powerful agricultural bloc would damage further the interests of the Third World. If an enlarged European agricultural system were to continue with protective policies, there might be even less opportunities for poor farmers from the 'south' to penetrate the market.

The prospective members are considerably poorer than the current ones. This will place a strain on the regional development programme of the EU. It is recognised that subsidies for the poorer parts of Europe will have *long-term* benefits for all – larger markets, greater competition etc. - but in the *short* and *medium* terms, this will be a huge burden on the Community budget. It may be difficult to persuade taxpayers that some sacrifices now, which hit them hard, will lead to benefits later which will be much less tangible.

There are many, on both the political right and left, who fear the influx of huge numbers of economic refugees into Western Europe. In other words, admitting new members may open the floodgates to new immigrants. There are two aspects to this. Firstly – largely a right wing concern – it has a cultural element. With potentially huge movements of ethnic populations around Europe it is feared that there will be a major threat posed against traditional Western European cultures. Secondly – where trade unions are worried – there are economic concerns. Labour in the candidate countries is cheap. Some of this labour is likely to move into western Europe, attracted by higher wages and better conditions. This is likely to have the effect of depressing levels of pay. It is good news for consumers who may see prices fall, but bad news for existing workers who will see their wages and job security threatened.

Apart from these main potential problems, there is a collection of concerns which are more contentious. Some, for example, fear the import of organised crime from eastern Europe. Similarly there is a suspicion that the way will be more open for the infiltration of illegal drugs. Business groups have also expressed fears that they will find it difficult to deal with their counterparts in the new members as their normal practices are so different from those in western Europe.

Enlargement and the political institutions

One final set of problems can be treated separately. These concern the changes will be needed to the Union's political structure. The effects of enlargement will be far-reaching, but here we can introduce the three most pressing issues.

Parliament

With many new MEPs the Parliament would become simply too big. It therefore seems likely that existing representatives will have to cope with much larger constituencies. A British suggestion is that a second chamber will be needed in order to represent the regions of Europe as existing MEPs will find it difficult to do so. We have already alluded to the fragmentation of the Parliament in the chapter on institutions (14). With perhaps 25 or 30 members in the future, the range of national groupings increases again. Lessons may have to be learned from the experience of the USA, where the Senate return two members from each state, no matter its size, while the House of Representatives returns members from large constituencies and is expected to reflect their *regional* concerns.

The commission

As things stood in 2002 each member state was entitled to one of the twenty commissioner posts. The largest five were allowed two. The purpose of this device was to ensure that each state at least *felt* represented at senior level. With further enlargement, it will not be possible for every member to send a commissioner to Brussels. It is accepted, therefore, that some countries in the future ill not be able to have a commissioner. This is likely to prove a contentious issue in the future.

The Council of Ministers

Enlargement does not present a problem in terms of numbers. However, a much larger Council does create difficulties with decision making. On those issues where a unanimous decision is required it will become increasingly difficult to reach a conclusion. In order to get round this problem, it is expected that even more decisions will have to become subject to qualified majority voting. This is all very well and will make decision-making more effective. However, the larger states are likely to become concerned that they may be outvoted by a large coalition of smaller states. The new voting strengths in the Council, which were negotiated at Nice in 2000, go some way to prevent this, but it remains a future concern. It is in the fields of defence and foreign policy that this issue is likely to be most acute.

A common defence and foreign policy for Europe

When the Maastricht Treaty was negotiated in 1992, a general intention to forge a common system of foreign and defence policy was made. The impetus for this initiative came from the conflict which had broken out in the Balkans in the 1990s following the collapse of Yugoslavia.

The Balkans was the first major armed conflict to break out in Europe after World War II. It had the effect of alerting political leaders to the fact that Europe was going to have to take greater responsibility for its own internal security. External defence would continue to be provided by NATO, but NATO had proved to be an unwieldy organisation to deal with a complex issue like the Balkans war. Attempts to adopt a common European position in Bosnia had largely failed, so that a more permanent apparatus had to be found. There was an organisation in place to deal with such issues – the Organisation for Security and Co-operation in Europe (OSCE) – but it proved to be a toothless body, lacking the authority of the European Union or NATO. Progress has been slow, but this is likely to be an issue for many years to come. The conflicts on Kosovo and Macedonia which followed Bosnia have served as reminders to EU leaders that a long-term solution needs to be found.

Foreign policy

The Common Foreign and Security Policy (CFSP) was confirmed by the Amsterdam Treaty in 1997. Two years later a new post of **CFSP High Representative** was created and its first holder, Javier Solana, was appointed. This was an important first step , as it is vital for the EU to be able to negotiate with other states and organisations through a single individual, otherwise any messages are likely to become confused and lack authority. Solana has a planning unit to assist him, but the development of an extensive, permanent, *supranational* body in charge of foreign policy is slower in coming.

Foreign policy remains in the hands of *intergovernmental* bodies – the Council of Foreign Ministers and the European Council (of heads of government). This makes foreign policy making difficult. Key decisions require unanimous approval in these councils and every issue becomes an *ad hoc* negotiation, in other words each is treated separately. The requirement to reach agreement among foreign ministers and heads of governments presents a number of serious problems.

- Member states have existing alliances of their own which may cut across European Union interests. Britain, for example, has a close relationship with the USA and Israel and has loyalties to Commonwealth countries. Italy and France have close links with Arab countries in the middle east, while Germany has a special interest in Turkey and the Balkans.

- Some countries, such as Sweden, Ireland and Austria now have traditions of neutrality which may be compromised by a common European foreign policy.

- The simple fact that fifteen countries (more after enlargement) have to reach agreement on very sensitive subjects is a huge stumbling block to decisive policy making.

- When foreign policy requires military backing – or at least the threat of it – there may be no guarantee that member states will support their intentions with such a commitment.

- Some states are, quite simply, less committed to European integration than others. This phenomenon is likely to vary as governments change, which they inevitably do. The British and Danish governments have, for example, been traditionally 'stand-offish'.

- Although the European project is designed to end conflict, we have to accept that old rivalries die hard, making the reconciliation of foreign policy difficult. France – normally a fiercely nationalistic state – finds it hard to come to agreement with Germany and the UK, the Dutch are naturally suspicious of Germany, while Scandinavian countries have traditionally little interest in southern Europe.

Thus, until most of the members are willing to sacrifice this highly sensitive aspect of national sovereignty to supranational bodies, it is likely to remain a problematic subject.

Defence

The difficulties involved in a common defence policy for the EU are perhaps more acute than those involved in foreign policy. Yet, surprisingly, progress has been more impressive. At a series of meetings in St Malo, Cologne, Washington and Helsinki in 1998–99 the idea of how Europe could move towards an independent, integrated defence capability was thrashed out. The agreement of the USA was sought and obtained, with various conditions, mainly safeguarding the role of NATO.

It was Britain's Tony Blair who solved the inevitable misgivings which some members had. He proposed a small, highly flexible force of about 60,000 soldiers. This was far from being a 'European Army' which opponents, mainly Conservatives, had suspected. It was described instead as a 'rapid reaction force'. For larger operations it was agreed that the European force should be effectively the armed forces of the Western European Union (WEU) which is a section of NATO without the USA. By insisting that the WEU would be the major European force, the relationship with NATO was preserved and protected. The WEU cannot act without the wider agreement of NATO as a whole. In this way the USA retained an interest in European defence issues.

At Helsinki in 2000 a permanent defence establishment was created and represents a considerable amount of progress. The bodies which came into existence are:
 • the Political and Security Committee;
 • the European Military Committee;
 • the European Military Staff.

Despite the apparently successful outcome of the negotiations, there remain a number of problems with control of a European force.

● The command structure of the force is a major problem, despite the existence of the European Military Staff. It may be difficult for armed forces to accept the command of officers who are not of the same nationality. This may not be a problem in peacetime, but could be a major concern on the battlefield.

● Armed forces need political direction. Although the foreign policy establishment of the EU appears to have been developed in the form of the Political and Security Committee and the Western European Union, in practice a coherent political direction may be difficult to achieve.

● There may still be occasions when the interests of NATO clash with those of the European Union. One might speculate that middle east tensions, which spill over into Turkey or Cyprus and southern Europe may evoke a very varying response from the USA and the EU.

● A key aspect of defence (and foreign) policy concerns intelligence. It may be difficult for European powers to share intelligence, an area where there is a notorious amount of secrecy and national self-interest.

EU defence and foreign policy abbreviations and definitions

- **NATO:** North Atlantic Treaty Organisation. Responsible for the collective security of Europe and the Western World. Comprises most European states plus the USA and Canada.
- **WEU:** Western European Union. The section of NATO comprising only European states.
- **CFSP:** Common Foreign and Security Policy. The European Union's commitment to adopt agreed common foreign policies.
- **CESDP:** Common European Security and Defence Policy. The agreement to co-operate on internal defence matters.
- **PSC:** Political and Security Committee. A permanent body whose role is to provide political direction for any military actions.
- **EMC:** European Military Committee. A committee of officials who have the task of co-ordinating military policy.
- **EMS:** European Military Staff. Officers of European armed forces who co-ordinate military arrangements.

EUROPEAN RIGHTS AND CITIZENSHIP

Most European states have adopted the European Convention of Human Rights. However this does not mean that the principle of human rights has been fully established throughout Europe. Some states, including the UK, do not treat it as binding and it is not fully comprehensive.

Civil rights campaigners have, as two of their goals, the establishment of a European Bill of Rights and a universal concept of European citizenship. At Maastricht this idea was built into the objectives of the EU, although little progress has been made since. What does this mean in principle?

1 It implies that there will be a codified set of rights to which all citizens of the European Union will be entitled. These rights would include those contained in the European Convention plus the economic and social rights which are contained in the EU Social Chapter.
2 These rights would be binding on all EU members, so that all laws and executive actions would have to conform.
3 A European Court – presumably the existing Court of Justice – would have powers to enforce these rights.
4 All citizens of member countries would gain all the rights contained in the Bill of Rights.

5 The rules for citizenship, i.e. who is entitled to call themselves a citizen of the European Union, would be common to all member states.

6 There would have to be common rules of naturalization and other means of acquiring citizenship which would apply throughout Europe.

On the face of it, there might be little problem in codifying such a set of principles. Most countries already conform to most of the same rules and there would be little argument over those terms already contained in the European Convention and the Social Chapter. Nevertheless there are potential problems. Some of the main ones are:

- Those countries and politicians who are worried about the growing power of the EU and the loss of national identities would perhaps object to the concept of European citizenship. They would place national identity above a European identity, and would be concerned if Europe were placed above the nation in this matter.
- There are likely to be disagreements about the rules by which individuals could become citizens of Europe. What, for example, would be the future status of refugees and asylum seekers? Who would decide whether such people should be entitled to apply for citizenship? It has to be remembered that, if citizenship were granted, the person concerned would have the right to live and work in any part of the Union.
- There might not be total agreement about what rights should be granted to all citizens. Most would be agreed, but perhaps not all. This may be a particular problem for new members who do not have the same tradition of rights as the rest of western Europe.
- Some countries, notably the UK with its doctrine of parliamentary sovereignty, might be unwilling to accept that a European Court could overrule elements of its legislation or could overturn the actions of its government.

So the development of European rights and citizenship is likely to remain a contentious issue. It calls into question fundamental questions of sovereignty and implies that national governments would lose control over who would be admitted to their territory. It also brings closer the concept that individuals may be expected to owe a higher allegiance to Europe than to their nation of birth or adoption.

THE EFFECTS OF THE SINGLE CURRENCY

The development of the single currency has, of course, been of great importance to the European project. However, it is no longer a live political issue. The single currency is here to stay for the time being and its successful introduction in early 2002 confirms that there is little point in discussing its advantages and disadvantages. For the UK and the other two states who did not enter the system in 2002 it is still a contentious matter, but for the twelve existing members of the Euro-zone the discussions are over.

But the effects of the single currency will still be far-reaching. It is worth, at this stage, reminding ourselves what problems and difficulties are likely to arise.

- The role of the European Central Bank, which will control interest rates and, indirectly, the fiscal policies of member states, is likely to become controversial, especially as it is unelected and unaccountable.
- If there is an economic crisis or serious recession, there will be those who suggest that it is the single currency which is the culprit.
- Similarly, if any individual states run into economic difficulty and discover that the European Bank cannot help them, and that their own governments find their hands tied by centralised policies, their own public may become disenchanted with the single currency system.
- If the external value of the euro declines, resulting in European inflation, support for the euro may ebb away.
- As economic harmonisation increases while the currency has its effect, there may be a reaction against the uniformity and loss of national sovereignty which has arisen from the single currency.

Yet, despite all this, the problems of returning to fifteen or more individual currencies would seem to be now impractical, so discussion of such issues remains largely academic and speculative.

SAMPLE QUESTIONS

1 What is meant by the term 'democratic deficit'? What proposals have been made to correct it?

2 What are the main problems associated with the Common Agricultural Policy?

3 Why is enlargement such a problem for the European Union?

4 What are the main problems associated with the development of common foreign and defence policies for the European Union?

5 Is it possible to develop the concept of European citizenship?

Britain and the European Union **16**

➤ The background to British membership

➤ The main impacts of British membership

➤ The ways in which the party system has been affected by the EU

➤ Future prospects for British involvement

THE STORY OF BRITISH MEMBERSHIP

Britain stays out

When serious discussions began to establish a successor to the European Coal and Steel Community (ECSC) in 1956, Britain made it clear that it was not intending to join any new organisation. Prime Minister Harold Macmillan, a Conservative who valued Britain's links with its empire and commonwealth, was opposed to the kind of close, supranational arrangement which Monnet and Schuman were proposing.

Macmillan also understood that, if Britain were to join the new Common Market, it would have to give up the system of trade preferences and agreements which it had with its allies in the Commonwealth. It would be seen as a betrayal to them if Britain were to abandon them in pursuit of its own interests in Europe. It was therefore decided to stay out and instead form a separate body. The Treaty of Rome was signed in 1957 with just six members.

EFTA

The European Free Trade Association (EFTA) contained seven members: Britain, Portugal, Sweden, Denmark, Norway, Austria and Switzerland. It had no political organisation and was therefore no more than a group of countries which agreed to reduce tariffs between them and so increase trade. Britain's agreements with the Commonwealth countries were preserved.

EFTA reflected the large amount of trade which was carried out among the seven members, but it was never designed to be a rival to the Common Market. It was, in effect, an alternative economic system, joined by countries who opposed the idea of closer political union within a free trade area. It also recognised the fact that Britain's alliances should be maintained, while the traditional neutrality of Switzerland and the Scandinavian countries would no longer be compromised by a mere set of trade concessions.

Britain's first two applications

By 1961 Macmillan had come round to the idea that Britain's fortunes might improve as a member of the Common Market. The disbanding of the British Empire was now under way, so this represented less of a tie than before. Furthermore, Macmillan had become aware that Britain was not the world power it had once been. He managed to persuade a sceptical Conservative party that an application should be made. Negotiations began in 1961, only two years after EFTA had come into existence.

Three major obstacles existed which were likely to prevent British entry. They were:

1 French President Charles de Gaulle, a vehement nationalist, was determined that France should dominate the Community. If Britain were to join, he felt that it would be a powerful rival (West Germany, weakened by postwar division and the need for reconstruction, did not worry de Gaulle).

2 It was clear that Britain wished to preserve some of the Commonwealth preference agreements and so gain an advantage over the existing members. The existing members were certainly not willing to offer Britain a special deal.

3 In 1962 Macmillan concluded the Nassau agreement with the USA, whereby Britain would be able to stay in NATO, remain America's closest ally, but also retain an independent nuclear deterrent. Once again, France was suspicious of Britain's close relationship with the USA. Britain was not a serious European, they argued.

In consequence of this, France vetoed the British application for membership (to this day, applications for membership require a unanimous vote in the Council of Ministers). This action set back relations between France and Britain many years. The suspicion with which the two countries treat each other, has remained to this day. It also demonstrated Britain's attitude to Europe.

Macmillan's desire to preserve Britain's links with both the Commonwealth and the USA are seen by other countries as a lack of commitment to the European experiment. Like British–French tension, this has endured ever since. Margaret Thatcher's constant sniping at attempts to create a closer political union and her opting out of the Social Chapter and the single currency at Maastricht in 1992 have reminded Europeans that Britain remains suspicious of European integration. It was, therefore, no surprise that Britain's half-hearted attempts at entry were rejected.

In 1967 the British government, now led by Labour's Harold Wilson, renewed the application. Once again it was a less than enthusiastic attempt. There were a number reasons for this.

- A majority of Labour's membership was probably opposed to membership. It has to be remembered that Labour was further to the left of the political spectrum than it is today. The very large left wing of the party saw the European Community as a 'capitalist club', whose motives were to be suspected. The concept of free trade was seen as benefiting business at the expense of workers' pay and rights. Wilson, who stood in the middle of the party, could not be certain he could carry the day.

- There was a great deal of residual resentment at France, especially after the 1963 veto. De Gaulle was still in power and making negative noises about Britain.

- Britain was entering a major economic crisis. In particular the UK balance of trade was in a very poor state so that the country was, effectively, bankrupt. Loans were negotiated from the International Monetary Fund (IMF) and sterling was devalued by nearly 15 per cent. This was therefore hardly an auspicious time to be undertaking such a radical new project.

Wilson hoped that British membership might provide a long-term solution to its economic problems. By comparison, the members of the Community were doing extremely well, with faster growth rates than Britain, falling unemployment and a surge in trade. However, de Gaulle exercised his veto once again, so Britain was left almost alone to try to solve its problems.

Britain joins

By 1971 Britain was led by Edward Heath, a Conservative Prime Minister who was deeply committed to the European ideal. He was a more internationally minded prime minister than any in Britain since Churchill who had retired in 1955. At the same time de Gaulle had gone, ousted during a period of political unrest and violence in 1968–69.

The year 1971 also saw the deepening of a recession which affected the whole of Europe. This did not stop the determined Heath from joining, but it did have the effect of creating suspicion in the minds of both Conservative and Labour supporters that membership might not be the economic saviour it had promised to be. It was also felt that, in his haste and determination to join,

Heath and his negotiator, Geoffrey Rippon, had negotiated a bad deal. Britain had not, it was claimed, gained enough protection for the Commonwealth, were paying too much in contributions and was getting a poor return from the Common Agricultural Policy. Despite the misgivings. Britain joined and became a member of the EEC on 1 January 1973.

In the general election campaign of February 1974, Labour argued that Heath had made too many concessions. Wilson therefore promised that, if elected, he would consider leaving the Community.

The 1975 referendum

Having won both elections of 1974, Wilson was true to his word and began to prepare for withdrawal. However, he soon realised that leaving the community might be a worse option than staying in. He therefore decided to try to renegotiate British terms and persuade the British people that the change of policy was justified.

Changing policy had created huge problems for Wilson. The Labour party was hopelessly split over British membership, largely along left-wing–right-wing lines, with the former opposed. The referendum idea was therefore very attractive. If Wilson could secure a 'yes' vote for membership he could outflank his opponents.

New terms were negotiated by Chancellor of the Exchequer, Jim Callaghan. Slightly lower contributions were arranged and an improved deal for agriculture agreed. Wilson was able to present a better package to the electorate in the referendum campaign.

The 1975 referendum campaign was an unusual time in British political life for a number of reasons:

- It was the first time a fully national referendum had been held on a political issue.
- Because the cabinet itself was split on British membership, Wilson did a deal with the 'no' Lobby that collective responsibility would be suspended. Cabinet members were free to speak their minds on the issue without any constraints. This was on the understanding that both sides would accept the verdict of the people.
- Special rules were made which ensured that both sides in the campaign were only allowed the spend a limited amount. This was designed to ensure a balanced contest. It was the first time a political campaign had been controlled by law.

The result – a win for the 'yes' campaign by 66–34 per cent – was mercifully decisive and the controversy subsided. The government survived both the

U-turn in policy and the bitter internal divisions which had threatened its survival. It is an ironic fact that the issue which Labour survived in 1975 – Britain's relations with Europe – was the same one which was to tear the Conservatives apart in the 1990s and consign them to two enormous election defeats in 1997 and 2001.

BRITISH PARTIES AND THE EU

The events of 1974–75 and of 1992–97, when British involvement in Europe cut across party lines, threatened the political stability of the country in these two periods. Some basic principles need to be identified to explain why Europe has proved to be so divisive.

1 The left wing of British politics sees the EU as a free-trade area which operates to the benefit of producers and employees at the expense of workers and consumers. It is therefore deeply opposed to its principles.

2 The right wing of the political spectrum view Europe as a socialist experiment, designed to establish uniformity and bureaucracy which are opposed to the ideals of business and place the interests of workers above those of entrepreneurs.

3 Liberals have seen the EU as an opportunity to decentralise some powers in a 'Europe of the regions'. Conservatives, by contrast, believe that Europe means increasing centralisation in Brussels. This will therefore enhance democracy, they argue, whereas many Conservatives see the EU as anti-democratic.

4 Many Conservatives are strong British nationalists. They believe Europe threatens the sovereignty of the UK.

5 Campaigners who are interested in the environment and the economic plight of the third world see the European Union as part of a global multinational movement which places rising prosperity in the west above the interests of the world as a whole.

6 Supporters of the EU, who come from all parties and who are essentially pragmatists, believe that economic integration is inevitable, a part of the process of globalisation. They therefore see opposition to the EU as futile.

7 Nationalists in the UK, such as the SNP and Plaid Cymru are generally pro-European. They argue that the EU will give them a better deal than the United Kingdom has done. In other words they believe they can have a louder voice in Brussels than they have had in London.

This extensive set of attitudes demonstrates how fragmented political opinion is on European issues. Small wonder then, that it is a major issue both *between* the parties and *within* parties.

Labour

For most of the period following the Treaty of Rome in 1957, Labour had been opposed to British membership. Labour had always been something of an isolationist party, unwilling to become involved in world affairs. The disaster of the Suez expedition in 1956, which Labour had opposed and which humiliated the Eden government, confirmed their suspicion of an international role for Britain. In the 1960s the Wilson government had refused to become involved directly in the Vietnam war, was granting independence to many of the colonies and initiated the 'east of Suez' policy. This last principle stated that Britain should withdraw from any major involvement beyond the middle east.

It was therefore hardly surprising that there was little enthusiasm in the party for EEC membership. When Wilson applied for membership in 1966–67, he could not be sure of carrying his party with him, so the French veto came as something of a relief.

In the 1975 referendum campaign on membership, Labour was split and only stayed together through the clever device of consulting the people directly. At that time and ever since, Tony Benn, the venerated left-winger, led the section of the party which was opposed to European involvement. As we have seen above, his view and that of his allies was that it was a capitalist enterprise, with little in it for consumers and workers. During the 1980s, official policy was suspicious of Europe, but since the Conservatives were totally dominating the political scene at that time, Labour's attitude to Europe counted for little.

But as the New Labour movement emerged in the 1990s under John Smith and Tony Blair, the party's attitude to international affairs in general began to change. Blair in particular believed that Labour would have to give up its traditional isolationism and accept that the world was becoming increasingly interdependent. Europe was here to stay and any modern state had to adapt to the challenges of globalisation. Labour now looked in both directions in its new internationalist outlook. As the relationship with the USA warmed after Labour came to power, the party embraced the European Union. Opponents of closer integration became an increasingly marginalised and irrelevant minority.

Labour inherited the Maastricht opt-out from the single currency from John Major in 1997. The questions for them now were:
- when to join the single currency;
- how to prepare for entry;
- how to prepare public opinion for entry.

There were small differences in emphasis over timing between those who were cautious and those who wanted to rush in as soon as possible. However, the leadership was united in the belief that entry into the single currency was both desirable and inevitable. By 2002, therefore, the nation waited for the Labour government to announce the date of a referendum. In the meantime Gordon Brown and Tony Blair continued to spar over what constituted the 'right moment'. Both agreed that the conditions had to be favourable, but there remained the question of what were these 'conditions'?

Conservatives

Britain's involvement with Europe has proved a painful experience for the Conservative party producing a basic split in the party between two considerations.

- Pragmatists in the party have long since believed that, like it or not, Britain's long-term best interests lie in Europe. Despite the country's traditional links with the USA and the Commonwealth, Britain could not resist the inevitable closer integration of Europe. Among the leading members of this group have been Geoffrey Howe (cabinet minister in the 1980s) and Michael Heseltine (a leading member of the 'liberal' wing of the party).
- A significant minority have been Euro-enthusiasts. They see no contradictions in British involvement, are fundamentally pro-European and see the single currency as the logical conclusion of integration. Key figures here have been former prime ministers Ted Heath and John Major, and ex-Chancellor, Kenneth Clark.
- Perhaps the largest group have been euro-sceptics. Led famously by Margaret Thatcher (especially from 1989 onwards), this group supports continued membership up to the terms of the Maastricht reforms of 1992. However, they oppose any further political union which would lead to further losses of sovereignty. They also believe that it is unlikely that conditions will ever exist where Britain should join the single currency (though some do not rule it out altogether).
- A small group of Euro-phobes wish to see Britain withdraw from the European Union. Thatcher seemed to be joining this group after her retirement from politics in 1997. She allied herself with such figures as Bill Cash and John Redwood. It is suspected that Iain Duncan Smith, who became leader in 2001, may have been a part of this group, but, as leader, he cannot afford to admit to such an extreme view.

The complete failure of the Conservative party to heal its internal divisions and to find some kind of compromise position which could at least paper over the cracks, has placed it in danger of oblivion.

During the 1992–97 government of John Major the party tore itself apart over Europe. Cabinet collective responsibility broke down and the government tottered from one crisis to the next. Major could not rely on any solid support and was constantly undermined by the euro-sceptics and anti-

Europeans. Major negotiated opt-outs from the Social Chapter and the single currency at Maastricht in 1992, but this did not satisfy the sceptics. They took every opportunity to make life difficult for Major, even on non-European issues.

Labour's crushing defeat of the Conservatives in 1997 had a number of causes, but the split over Europe was of great importance. When the party continued its internal feuding over the next four years, a second defeat became inevitable. After 2001 Duncan Smith tried to move the party away from Europe, but the expected referendum on the single currency threatens to re-open the old wounds.

Liberal Democrats

The Liberal Democrats (and their predecessors the Liberal and Social Democrat Parties) have always been largely united in their support for the European Union and, more recently, British participation in the single currency. There are a number of reasons for this enthusiastic support:

• Liberals are attracted by the freedoms created by a single market.
• The European Union offers strong protection for consumers, workers, social security claimants and all those who wish to trade on fair terms. These are ideals which Liberals support.
• The European Union political system seems to offer greater power to regions. Liberals favour such decentralisation.
• European countries have a stronger tradition of human rights protection than Britain. They therefore hope that the rights culture will be imported into Britain with closer involvement.

There is something of a paradox in Liberal democrat support for the European project. The democratic deficit which is said to exist in European political institutions should put Liberals off. They are strong democrats and so ought to be suspicious of the centralised, rather unaccountable European bureaucracy. But this does not outweigh what they perceive to be great advantages. Furthermore, they believe that closer British involvement will be a strong democratic influence on the other members.

It may be that, in a future referendum campaign on the single currency, the Liberal democrats may tip the balance of power towards a 'yes' vote.

Nationalists

The Scottish and Welsh nationalists are strong supporters of closer political integration in Europe. The believe that the European Union represents a weakening of the nation-state. Since they wish to see transfers of power away from the British state to their own countries, Europe provides them with the hope of greater autonomy.

Those nationalists who aim for full independence also see the EU as a means by which they could become economically viable. On their own, Scotland and Wales might not be able to sustain full economic independence, but in Europe they would benefit fully from regional policies of the kind which have produced an economic renaissance in the Republic of Ireland. With their own voice in Europe, an independent Scotland or Wales would be able to negotiate advantageous terms, rather than rely on the British government and its ministers.

Both the SNP and Plaid Cymru, therefore have campaigned hard for closer political union and a single currency. The more integrated Britain is with Europe, they hope, the more likelihood there is that they will be granted greater independence.

Minor parties

Two small anti-European parties have made some impression in Britain. These are the Referendum Party and the UK Independence party (UKIP).

The Referendum party was formed and financed by the multi-millionaire James Goldsmith. He pumped an estimated £20 million into the 1997 election campaign. Although the main platform of the party was to hold a referendum on continued British membership, it was clear that its supporters were anti-European. The party won no seats in 1997 and failed to make a significant impact on the results. Goldsmith died shortly after the election and the party disappeared.

Of a more permanent nature is UKIP, which is openly anti-European. This party has a small, but determined membership and fought both the 1997 and 2001 elections. Like the Referendum party it did not affect the results significantly. Indeed, if anything it helped to split the anti-Europe vote with the Conservatives and so helped Labour and Liberal democrat candidates. Nevertheless, it has survived and may gather strength in the future.

FURTHER POLITICAL EFFECTS OF MEMBERSHIP

The constitution

Membership of the EU and the gradual transfer of powers to Brussels has had a dramatic effect on the British constitution. We can identify the following features.

1 A significant part of the constitution is now codified. Those elements which deal with Britain's relationship with the EU are contained in the Treaties and

agreements which have been agreed. Thus the Treaty of Rome, the Single European Act, and the Treaties of Maastricht, Amsterdam and Nice are now, effectively, part of the constitution. The terms of these agreements are binding on parliament and government.

2 Because the agreements identified above and owing to the principle that European law is superior to national laws, the sovereignty of parliament has been eroded. While it is true that Britain can retrieve its full sovereignty by leaving the EU, as long as we are a member, Europe can overrule parliament on any issue which requires only a majority vote in the Council of Ministers. A constitutional certainty which has existed for over three hundred years has, therefore, been diminished.

3 Rights in Britain have always been more vulnerable than in the rest of Europe. The power of government and the sovereignty of parliament have meant that it has been difficult to safeguard the rights of citizens. The European Union has introduced a wide range of rights for workers, consumers and recipients of welfare benefits. Enforced by the European Court of Justice, various European Acts are now effectively entrenched in British law.

4 British courts must now bow to the superior status of the European Court of Justice where European laws are concerned. The House of Lords is no longer the ultimate court of appeal in many cases. This role has now been transferred to Europe.

Parliament

Britain has made remarkably few changes to the structure and operation of parliament to accommodate membership of the European Union. Both the Commons and the Lords have select committees whose role is to examine proposals coming from the European Commission, but they have little influence over ministers and are seen as the minimum concession which could be made to membership.

Of course the great European issues are regularly debated in parliament. Indeed, some of the great parliamentary moments of the 1990s were provided by battles to approve of the Maastricht Treaty. In the future, conflict over the single currency are likely to provide more periods of high drama.

However, the more specialised policy areas of the EU, such as the Common Agricultural Policy, foreign policy, environmental protection and regional development do not receive a great deal of debating time in parliament. Discussion on these policies tends to take place within government other institutions.

Pressure groups

There are five main types of pressure group which have been most affected by the EU. These are:

- trade unions;
- environmental groups;
- producer groups;
- farming interests;
- fishing interests.

Trade unions have been cautiously supportive of British involvement. They have been encouraged especially by the beneficial influence the EU has had on workers' rights. Working hours, holiday entitlement, pension rights, health and safety, part-time workers' rights and women's equality are all examples of improvements to the conditions of workers which have emerged from the EU.

British unions have federated themselves with their European colleagues and play their part in pressing the Commission for more worker-sympathetic legislation. They are, of course, confronted by commercial and industrial interests, but the EU has shown itself to be most sympathetic to workers' rights.

Environmental problems do not usually recognise national borders, so the environmental lobby, led by Friends of the Earth and Greenpeace (backed by European Green parties) is anxious to place pressure of European institutions. By influencing European legislation, environmentalists can hope to see benefits throughout Europe, not just in a single member state.

The kind of issues where environmentalists have sought action are genetically modified foods, coastal waters and river quality, species conservation, emissions and nuclear safety. As with unions the main environmental pressure groups are now European (as well as global) in their organisations.

Business groups in Britain have been largely in favour of membership, greater integration and the single currency. The creation of the single market has created new opportunities and reduced costs in general. However, the European Union has also brought many new regulations over such features as employment, health regulations, safety, consumer protection and trade conditions. To some extent business groups (largely manufacturing and commercial federations) have been engaged in holding back the tide of regulation, though, realistically, they have tried to obtain concessions in these areas.

On the finance side, too, banking and other institutions have sought to place pressure on the European Central Bank and the finance sections of the Commission, again to reduce regulation and to open up markets.

Farmers have proved to be an especially powerful interest in the European Union. It has to be remembered that European farming is more extensive than in Britain, but British farmers have, in some areas, ridden on the back of their more powerful European partners. On occasions, however, British farming interests have come into conflict with the rest of Europe. When British beef exports were banned for example, following the BSE scare, the National Farmers Union worked as hard as the government in trying to have the ban lifted.

The Common Agricultural Policy remains the main target for the British farming lobby. The CAP distributes subsidies, price supports and quotas throughout the community. British farmers are in competition for these benefits with other European farming groups. This leads to intense activity in Brussels, especially when the Council of Agricultural Ministers is about to meet. However the National Farmers Union also keeps a permanent organisation in place to lobby the Commission.

Fishing interests are in a similar position to the farmers. They ally themselves with other European fisherman to gain favourable policies for the industry as a whole. These concern the conservation of fish stocks, subsidies for some sectors of the industry and a variety of regulations concerning the way the fish are caught. But they are also in competition with the fishing industries of other countries. Fish quotas have to be distributed and the British campaign in Brussels for their fair share.

In addition to these main organisations, there is also a large collection of lobby groups operating in Europe in the fields of consumer protection, transport, trade, welfare, rights, law and order and the like. The recognition that an increasingly large number of decisions are now being made in Brussels has forced British pressure groups to move their operations across the Channel and to co-operate with their counterparts in other member states.

The media

The schism in British politics over Europe is reflected in the tabloid press. While the *Sun* remains largely euro-sceptic, the *Mirror* is enthusiastic for both integration and the single currency. When the referendum of the single currency is held, it is clear that these and other tabloids will play a major role.

Not surprisingly the broadsheet newspapers take a more measured view. Traditional Conservative-supporting papers like the *Telegraph,* the *Daily Mail* and the *Express* have argued against further integration, while the others, such as the *Times, Independent* and *Guardian* have tended take a more detached view, printing both sides of the case and refusing to make a firm commitment either way. In the referendum to come, they will probably have to come off the fence. In 2002 it seemed likely that most of the broadsheets are likely to favour entry into the euro-zone.

The broadcast media are required by law to be neutral as this is a partly political issue. However, debate on Europe has become one of the most common subjects for current affairs programmes. They may not be allowed to lead public opinion, but they may prove to be the main source of information for the electorate.

THE ECONOMY AND THE SINGLE CURRENCY

The effects on economic policy making of British membership in an increasingly integrated Europe can be divided into three main aspects. These are: firstly, the ways in which the British government no longer has freedom of action because of the superiority of European laws; secondly, the need to meet the so-called 'convergence criteria' which will enable Britain to join the single currency system; finally, policy making must bear in mind the Labour government's five 'economic tests' which will determine the time when an application to join the euro-zone could be made.

Policy making

A number of options in economic management have been taken out of the hands of domestic governments, including Britain's.

- The ability to introduce import tariffs to protect one of our home industries. Britain must accept the fact that the EU is tariff free and that tariffs on goods coming from outside the EU are determined in Brussels.

- Similarly there are strict limits upon the amount of subsidies which can be given to certain industries. There are subsidies available from the EU, but the destination of these funds is determined in the EU itself. So regional economic policy is very much European controlled.

- Although member governments remain free to set their own levels of indirect taxation, such as VAT and excise duties, it has become clear that they cannot be allowed to vary greatly from levels which prevail in the rest of Europe. Because there is now completely free trade, high levels of indirect taxation in the UK compared to the rest of Europe would damage the sale of goods to visitors from abroad. The tourist industry would suffer excessively.

- Financial markets in Europe are now extremely free and open. Though the Bank of England can set its own interest rate and the government is free to manage credit controls, in practice the British financial markets must be kept reasonably in line with the rest of the EU.

● Similarly, levels of income and corporate taxes (on profits) are still in the hands of the national government. But, because both workers and businesses now have completely free movement within the EU, Britain could not afford to set higher than average tax levels. If we did we might experience a movement of workers and businesses away from the UK to countries where taxes are lower.

In summary, therefore, we can say that some aspects of independent economic policy making have been removed, while others have become heavily influenced by the realities of European integration.

Convergence

The countries which have wished to enter the single currency system have been required to meet a number of 'convergence criteria'. These 'rules' are designed to ensure that the economies of member countries are reasonably in step with each other. By being so 'converged' there is less disruption caused by adopting the same single currency.

Britain has a long-term intention to join, so the Labour government which came to power in 1997 decided to pursue the convergence criteria in readiness for joining. The criteria include maximum levels of inflation and public borrowing, low unemployment, low interest rates and reductions in the level of accumulated or 'national' debt.

For Britain the targets on inflation, unemployment and interest rates seemed to occur naturally as the economy recovered from recession and entered a period of steadily growing prosperity. The high levels of government borrowing, however, needed positive action. Faced with the need to increase spending on public services in 1997–2000, Chancellor Gordon Brown chose, nevertheless, to pay back large portions of the national debt and avoid any short-term borrowing. In some ways he sacrificed some short-term spending options, in order to meet the criteria on debt. In other words, he favoured long-term benefits at the expense of short-term gains.

By 2000, therefore, Britain had achieved the criteria with a good deal to spare. Since then it has been necessary to try to ensure that the economy did not stray from the rules. Up to 2002 at least, this proved relatively comfortable. It may not always be so.

The five economic tests

These are Britain's own criteria for entry into the single currency. They are:
1 Membership must be favourable to inward investment into the UK (i.e. foreign companies setting up in the UK).

2 It must not threaten Britain's leading role in financial markets.

3 Britain's natural economic cycle will have to be reasonably in line with that of the euro-zone. In other words the levels of growth, inflation, unemployment and interest rates will need to be close to those existing in the rest of Europe.

4 Will there be a reasonable amount of flexibility to allow Britain to join on favourable terms?

5 Will membership be of long-term benefit to the British economy, especially terms of employment, growth and economic stability?

Many of these conditions do not require specific policy making, so they may not influence economic management directly. However, they remain influential. It may be that, as membership of the single currency seems to be imminent, the government may attempt to manipulate the exchange value of sterling, the level of public borrowing and the level of growth, so that Britain joins at the most favourable moment, according to these membership conditions.

THE FUTURE OF BRITISH MEMBERSHIP

The single currency

If Britain joins in the future, it is likely to be permanent and will certainly have far-reaching effects. It is, therefore, certainly the most important decision in the foreseeable future.

The effects of membership include loss of control over the setting of interest rates, much less flexibility in taxation policy and government fiscal budgeting, little control over credit restrictions and a general harmonisation of economic policy making with Europe as a whole. In other words it would represent a major 'sacrifice' or 'pooling' (depending on one's point of view) of sovereignty for Britain. We would also have to accept that decisions made by the European Central Bank and the Council of Finance Ministers will affect the performance of the British economy.

On a more general level, membership of the euro-zone will be heavily symbolic. It will be a powerful signal that Britain has finally abandoned its suspicions of membership.

Political integration

The Blair government has made it clear that it will oppose any further political integration unless the problem of the democratic deficit is tackled. Indeed, by 2002 Britain led the section of the EU which opposes further moves towards federation.

Should the Conservative party regain power, the prospects for closer union will become even more remote. It will require a major shift in public opinion for any British government to support a deeper union. So, for the time being Britain wants the EU to remain an intergovernmental organisation, rather than a supranational one.

Having said that, the Labour government has played a leading role in promoting integration in foreign and defence policy and is broadly in favour of further steps to harmonise policies on law and order, rights and immigration. These have become especially pressing issues as enlargement is just around the corner. In summary, therefore, current thinking is in favour of more integration of policy, but much less so in terms of institutions.

One final issue should be clarified. Despite the persistence of a sizeable minority on the right of British politics who want the country to leave the EU, there is little prospect of departure. British membership appears to be here to stay.

SAMPLE QUESTIONS

1 What have been the main effects of British membership of the EU on the political system?

2 How does membership of the EU affect the conduct of economic policy making in Britain?

3 How has the issue of Europe influenced British party politics?

Additional reading and research

Students and teachers will benefit from articles appearing in two publications which are designed for A level and introductory Politics courses. They are:

1 *Talking Politics*
Published by The Politics Association, Old Hall Lane, Manchester M13 0XT, Tel: 0161 256 3906.
politic@enablis.co.uk

2 *Politics Review*
Published by Philip Allan Updates, Market Place, Deddington, Oxfordshire OX15 0SE, Tel: 01869 338652.
sales@philipallan.co.uk

In addition students and teachers should review the materials available from:

The Politics Association Resource Centre (PARC), address and email as for Politics Association above. There are *revision packs* on the EU and on British political issues. In addition the **Politics 2000** series includes works on: • Britain and the European Union • Devolved Great Britain • The Northern Ireland question

SPECIFIC MATERIALS ON THE EUROPEAN UNION

For teachers and lecturers and for the library

Developments in the European Union. Laura Cram (ed.), Palgrave, 1999.
The Economics of the European Union. Michael Artis, Oxford University Press, 2001.
From Rome to Maastricht. Alexander Noble, Time Warner Paperbacks, 1996.
Policy Making in the European Union. Helen Wallace (ed.), Oxford University Press, 2000.

For students

Britain in the European Union Today. Colin Pilkington, Manchester University Press, 2001.
The European Union: A Very Short Introduction. John Pinder, Oxford paperbacks, 1996.
Understanding the European Union. John McCormick, Palgrave, 2002.
British Politics and Europe. Alan Davies. Hodder and Stoughton, 1999.

SPECIFIC MATERIALS ON BRITISH ISSUES

For teachers and lecturers and for the library

Politics Under Thatcher. Seldon and Collings, Longman, 1999.
The Major Effect. Kavanagh and Seldon (eds.), Pan Books, 1994.
The Major Premiership. Peter Dorey (ed.), Palgrave, 1999.
The Blair Effect. Anthony Seldon (ed.), Little Brown, 2001.
New Labour: Politics After Thatcherism. Driver and Martell, Polity, 1998.
The State We're In. Will Hutton, Cape, 1995.
New Labour, New Welfare State? Mark Perryman, Lawrence and Wishart, 1998.
The Welfare State in Britain Since 1945. Rodney Lowe, Macmillan, 1999.
British Politics Since The War. Coxall and Robins, Macmillan, 1998.
Northern Ireland Since 1945. S. Wishart, Longman, 1999.
Law, Order and the Judiciary. P. Joyce, Hodder and Stoughton, 1999.

For students

Developments in British Politics. P. Dunleavey *et al.*, Macmillan, 2000.
Issues in British Politics. Colin Pilkington, Macmillan, 1998.
Political Issues in Britain. Bill. Jones (ed.), Manchester University Press, 1999.
Government and the Economy. S. Lyons, Hodder and Stoughton, 1998.

WEBSITES

Some useful websites for factual research are:
• European Union: europa.eu.int
• Links to all government departments: www.open.gov.uk
• Commission for Racial Equality: www.cre.gov.uk
• Equal Opportunities Commission: www.eoc.org.uk
• Northern Ireland: www.nio.gov.uk

Index

Abortion Act 1967 99
active citizenship 91
Adams, Gerry 147
Age Concern 74
Agenda 21 124–5
Alliance Party (N.I.) 135, 136
Amsterdam Treaty 1997 112, 204, 224
Anglo-Irish Agreement 1985 137

Baker, Kenneth 83
Bank of England 261
   Monetary Policy Committee 24–5, 28
Barber, Anthony 9
Benn, Tony 18
Bevan, Nye 38
Beveridge, William 34–5, 53, 66
Black Papers (education) 59
Black Wednesday 5
Blair, Tony 5, 19, 28, 36, 47, 61, 85–6,
   153, 254, 263
Blunkett, David 58, 62, 89
Boyle, Edward 56
British–Irish Council 143
British Medical Association (BMA) 50
British Telecom 12
Brittan, Leon 217
Brown, Gordon 22–3, 25–9, 30, 45, 46,
   62, 71, 74–5, 89, 124
BSE (mad cow disease) 126
Bush, George jr 124
Butler, Lord (Robin) 159
Butler, R.A. 53–4

Callaghan, James 39, 252
Carrington, Lord 9

Castle, Barbara 18
Charter 88 157
Child Poverty Action Group (CPAG) 71
Churchill, Winston 191–2, 208–9
citizenship (European) 246–7
Clarke, Kenneth 30, 43, 83
Clean Air Acts 122
Clinton, Bill 138–9, 147
codecision (EU) 221–2
Commission for Health Improvement
   (CHI) 48
Commission for Racial Equality (CRE)
   110–12
Committee of the Regions (EU) 230
Common Agricultural Policy (CAP) 126,
   127, 197–8, 215, 224, 228, 236–8,
   241, 250
Common Fisheries Policy (CFP) 127,
   198, 215, 228
Commonwealth (British) 205–6, 250
community policing 82
comprehensive education 56–8
Compulsory Competitive Tendering
   (CCT) 14
Concorde (aircraft) 3
Control of Pollution Act 1974 122
COREPER (Committee of Permanent
   Representatives – EU) 226
Council of Europe 193–4
Council of Ministers (EU) 198, 212, 213,
   214, 218, 219, 223, 226–7, 243,
   250
Court of Auditors (EU) 220
Crime and Disorder Act 2000 87
Crime and Public Protection Act 2001 88

Crime Sentences Act 1996 84
Criminal Justice Act 1982 80
Criminal Justice Act 1991 82
Criminal Justice and Police Act 2001 87
Criminal Justice and Public Order Act
    1994 83–4, 93
Crosland Anthony 57
Crowther Report 56

de Beauvoir, Simone 98
de Chastelaine, John 146
de Gaulle, Charles 250, 251
decommissioning (weapons) 145
DEFRA (Department for Environment,
    Food and Rural Affairs) 126
Delors, Jacques 200–1, 216
democratic deficit (EU) 234–6
Democratic Unionist Party (DUP) 135,
    142, 149
Denmark (referendum) 212
dependency culture 68–71
devolution (general) 155, 160, 171–90,
    184–5, 189–90
devolution (Northern Ireland) 140–2,
    185–9
devolution (Scotland) 179–81
devolution (Wales) 182–3
Dewar, Donald 179
Divorce Law Reform Act 1970 100
Downing Street Declaration 138
Duncan Smith, Iain 36, 256

Eccles, David 56
Economic and Social Committee (EU)
    230
Eden, Anthony 196
education 52–65
Education Act 1944 53
Education Reform Act 1988 58, 60–1
electoral reform 161–6
enlargement (of the EU) 238–43
environment 120–8
Environment Agency 123
Environment Protection Act 123

Equal Opportunities Commission 102
Equal Pay Act 1970 100
European Central Bank 28, 231–2,
    259
European Coal and Steel Community
    195–6
European Commission 213, 214–19,
    223, 235, 242–3
    president of 215–16, 217
European Convention on Human Rights
    194
European Council 215, 225
European Court of Human Rights 194
European Court of Justice 212, 213,
    228–9, 235
European defence policy 243–6
European Exchange Rate Mechanism
    (ERM) 5, 21–2, 201
European foreign policy 243–4
European Free Trade Association (EFTA)
    249–50
European Ombudsman 231
European Parliament 199, 212, 213,
    217, 219–25, 234–5, 242

Falklands War 9, 16
Faulkner, Brian 136
federalism 207–8
Firestone, Shulamith 98
Foot, Michael 18, 19
Fowler, Norman 41
Freedom of Information (Act) 166–7
Friedan, Betty 98
Friends of the Earth 122, 126, 259

G7 5
Giddens, Anthony 20
Giuliani, Rudi 86
globalisation 4–5
GM (genetically modified) food 126
Goldsmith, James 257
Good Friday Agreement 1998 139–43,
    144–9, 155, 185
Greater London Assembly (GLA) 168

Greater London Council (GLC) 167
Green (Ecology) Party 122, 127
Greenpeace 126, 259
Greer, Germaine 98
Griffiths, Roy 41–2
Gummer, John 123–4

H.M. Inspectorate of Pollution 123
Hague, William 156
Heath, Edward 8–9, 251–2
Help the Aged 74
House of Commons 158–9
House of Lords 155–8
Howard, Michael 83–5, 89, 94
Human Rights Act 102, 159–61, 170
Hume, John 147
Hurd, Douglas 83

immigration 106–8
Inner London Education Authority
    57–8
institutional racism 114
International Monetary Fund 5
Ireland (referendum) 212–13
Irish National Liberation Army (INLA)
    134–5
Irish Republican Army (IRA) 133, 135,
    138, 139, 145–6, 148

Jenkins, Roy 19
    Report 165
Johannesburg conference 124
Josephm Keith 9

Keynes, John Maynard 6–7
Keynesianism 6–8, 10
Kinnock, Neil 19–20, 153, 217
Kyoto Agreement 1997 124

Lamont, Norman 21
law and order 78–96
Lawson, Nigel 21
Livingstone, Ken 161–8
local government 169

Local Management of Schools (LMS)
    60
London Underground 168

Maastricht, Treaty of (Treaty of
    European Union) 200–4, 212, 221,
    224, 254
McGuiness, Martin 142, 189
Macmillan, Harold 2, 196, 249–50
Macpherson Report (Stephen Lawrence
    Inquiry) 113–15
Major, John 5, 16, 18, 28, 85, 138, 254,
    255
Mallon, Seamus 142
Mandelson, Peter 147
Mayhew, Patrick 147
Maze prison 134
Michael, Alun 125, 179
Milburn, Alan 47
Millet, Kate 98
miners' strike 16
minimum wage 28
Mitchell, George 138–9, 147
monetarism 9–10
Monnet, Jean 194
Morgan, Rhodri 179
Mountbatten, Lord Louis 134
Mowlem, Mo 138–9, 147
multiculturalism 116–17
Murdoch, Rupert 15

Nassau agreement 1962 250
National Curriculum 60–1
National Health Service 32–3, 38–51
National Institute of Clinical Excellence
    (NICE) 48
National Rivers Authority 123
Nationality Acts 108
NATO 205–6, 244, 245, 250
Neave, Airey 134
neo-functionalism 206
Newsom Report 56
Nice, Treaty of 200, 212
Northern Ireland 129–50

Norton Committee 158–9

Office of Fair Trading (OFT) 27
OFGAS 13
OFSTED 61
OFTEL 13
OFWAT 13
Orange Order (N.I.) 149
Organisation for Economic Co-operation
    and Development (OECD) 5
Ouseley Report 114–15
Owen, David 19

Paisley, Rev. Iain 135–6, 142
Paris, Treaty of 195
Parliament Acts 1911 and 1949 152
Patten, Chris 144, 217
pensions 74–5
    stakeholder 74–5
Plaid Cymru 172–3, 253, 256–7
Plant Commission 163
Police and Criminal Evidence Act (PACE)
    1984 80
Politics Association 159
Poll Tax 175
Portillo, Michael 25
positive discrimination 104, 109
poverty trap 72–4
Powell, Enoch 108
Prescott, John 126
Prevention of Terrorism Act 1974 134
Prior, James 137
privatisation 11–12
Prodi, Romano 216
Progressive Unionist Party 136
Public Order Act 1986 81
Pym, Francis 9

qualified majority voting (QMV)
    199–200

Race Equality Unit 117
Race Relations Act 1965 109–10
Race Relations Act 1968 110

Race Relations Act 1976 110–11
Race Relations Amendment Act 2000
    112–113
rapporteurs (EU) 222
Rayner, Lord 41–2
referendum (on Europe, 1975) 252
Referendum Party 257
Regional Development Agencies 27–8
rights (EU) 246–7
Rio Accord 1992 124
Rodgers, William 19
Rolling Devolution (N.I.) 137–8
Rome, Treaty of 196–7, 249
Royal College of Nursing 50
Royal College of Surgeons 50
Royal Ulster Constabulary 132–3, 138,
    144, 149

Salisbury Convention 152
Sands, Bobby 134
Santer, Jacques 216
Scargill, Arthur 16
Schengen Agreement 202
Schuman, Robert 194
Scotland Act 1998 178–9
Scottish Executive 181
Scottish National Party (SNP) 172, 253,
    256–7
Scottish Parliament 179–81
selective universality 73–4
Selsdon Park 8
Sex Discrimination Act 1975 100–2
Shah, Eddie 15
Short, Clare 102
Single European Act 28, 123, 198–9,
    201
single European currency 29, 247–8,
    261–3
Sinn Fein 135–7, 139, 146, 149
Smith, John 19, 36, 153, 254
Social Chapter (Maastricht) 202–3
Social Democratic Labour Party (SDLP)
    142, 149
Social Democrat Party (SDP) 19

social exclusion 75–6, 91
social security 66–77
Solana, Javier 204
stealth taxes 27
Straw, Jack 86–8, 94
subsidiarity 201, 209–10
Sunningdale Agreement 136–7
Supply Side Economics 10–11

taxation 11
Thatcher, Margaret 4, 7, 9–16, 18, 21,
    35, 39, 57, 80, 104, 156, 175, 199,
    201, 255
Third Way 29
trade unions 15–16
    legislation 16–17
Trimble, David 139, 147

UK Independence Party (UKIP) 257

UK Unionist Party 136
Ulster Unionist Party 135–6, 149
Ulster Volunteer Force (UVF) 133

Waddington, David 83
Wakeham, Lord 156–7
Wales Act 1998 178–9
Walker, Peter 9
Welsh Assembly 182–3
Welsh Executive 183
Western European Union 245–6
Whitelaw, William 134
Williams, Shirley 19
Wilson, Harold 3, 251–2
Women's Coalition (N.I.) 136
World Bank 5
World Trade Organisation 5

zero tolerance 86